The Equal Cl

How much thinking have you done about gender?

What does it feel like to be gay, trans or non-binary at school?

How unbiased, safe and inclusive are our teachers, our schools and our systems, and what can we do about it?

The time is ripe for a re-think, and the issues are pressing. Our pupils are grappling with challenges around gender and sexuality, and they need our well-informed support. Providing evidence, prompts and the space to explore the implications, restrictions and constructs of gender, this book is here to help every teacher reflect on issues around gender roles and expectations in their class.

In this challenging and potent book, experts, academics and campaigners join forces to contribute important perspectives to complement Rycroft-Smith's own accessible and often provocative explanations of many facets of gender and sexuality, including media, literature, toys, clothing, sexism, expectations, sexuality, gender roles, harassment and consent. Humour and anecdotes are thoughtfully intertwined with fascinating insights into biological and cultural perspectives and societal norms, highlighting why it's so vital to teach pupils about gender issues, as well as modelling consent, good-quality relationships and tolerance to children at all ages and stages of their school career.

Providing clear, practical policy recommendations in an accessible and engaging way, *The Equal Classroom* is an essential read for any teacher or education professional who wants to ensure their school is a place where all pupils feel truly welcome and able to flourish, comfortable and safe in their emerging identities.

Lucy Rycroft-Smith is an education researcher and writer working at Cambridge University. Lucy is co-editor of *Flip the System UK: A Teachers' Manifesto* (Routledge, 2017).

Graham Andre is a primary school teacher who was involved with the BBC2 BAFTA nominated documentary *No More Boys and Girls: Can Our Kids Go Gender Free?*

'*The Equal Classroom* shines a timely light on current behaviour and attitudes about gender – gender identities, gender roles, gender expectations. It is a thought-provoking text on the role of schools in exposing the limitations imposed by existing gender stereotypes, offering an intriguing and accessible mix of personal narrative, of statistics for the curious, of exercises for the diligent and of expert opinion for the help-seekers. With musings from teachers working on the front line, from academic researchers and education specialists, there are clear and practical recommendations on how to shine a challenging light on gendered practices and, importantly, how to change them'.

–Gina Rippon
Professor Emeritus of Cognitive NeuroImaging
Aston Brain Centre, Aston University, Birmingham, UK

The Equal Classroom

Life-Changing Thinking About Gender

Lucy Rycroft-Smith
with Graham Andre

Routledge
Taylor & Francis Group

LONDON AND NEW YORK

First published 2020
by Routledge
2 Park Square, Milton Park, Abingdon, Oxon, OX14 4RN

and by Routledge
52 Vanderbilt Avenue, New York, NY 10017

Routledge is an imprint of the Taylor & Francis Group, an informa business

British Library Cataloguing-in-Publication Data
A catalogue record for this book is available from the British Library

Library of Congress Cataloging-in-Publication Data
Names: Rycroft-Smith, Lucy, editor.
Title: The equal classroom : life-changing thinking about gender / [edited by] Lucy Rycroft-Smith, with Graham Andre.
Identifiers: LCCN 2019035198 (print) | LCCN 2019035199 (ebook) | ISBN 9781138491007 (hardback) | ISBN 9781138491021 (paperback) | ISBN 9781351033947 (ebook)
Subjects: LCSH: Sex discrimination in education. | Sex differences in education. | Educational equalization.
Classification: LCC LC212.8 .E63 2020 (print) | LCC LC212.8 (ebook) | DDC 370.81--dc23
LC record available at https://lccn.loc.gov/2019035198
LC ebook record available at https://lccn.loc.gov/2019035199

ISBN: 978-1-138-49100-7 (hbk)
ISBN: 978-1-138-49102-1 (pbk)
ISBN: 978-1-351-03394-7 (ebk)

Typeset in Galliard
by Cenveo® Publisher Services
Printed and bound by CPI Group (UK) Ltd, Croydon, CR0 4YY

This book is not about telling you how to run your classroom, nor even (as you shall see) all that grounded in the classroom. Much of it feels like a conversation to me – the type of conversation I have been lucky enough to have daily with a few wonderful people. Their thoughts and words flow through this book just as surely as mine do, although any fault is mine alone.

Two of those people are my incredible daughters, Annabelle and Amelia. Thank you for teaching me about feminism, and thank you for telling me that my hair is penis.

Two more are my partner Dan and my work and study buddy Darren. Thank you for not turning away from feminism when I blamed you, got angry with you and challenged you. Thank you for listening and for your endless patience. Thank you being on the sticky end of my feminism, for being part of the drama and the conflict as these theories played out in real life, often painfully. Thank you for stepping back to let me take up my space and admiring my strength and size when I did. Thank you for calling me out on my bullshit.

One more: my dear friend JL. Thank you for showing me such a blazing, powerful example of a caring male. You were (and are) the doggedly kind teacher who made such a difference for so many pupils and the friend who saved my sanity. Your absence during the writing of this book was keenly felt, especially as I had to make my own coffee.

Contents

Acknowledgements   ix
List of contributors   x

   Introduction   1

 1 Gender identities: social and cultural   13

 2 Expert view: teaching gender   27
   KATH TAYLER

 3 Gender identities: brains and biology   31

 4 Expert view: gender from an early age   53
   JAYNE OSGOOD

 5 Gendered expectations   61

 6 Toys   80

 7 Expert view: let toys be toys   94
   JESS DAY

 8 Sexism and sexual harassment   103

 9 Clothing and uniform   127

10 Expert view: gendered clothing   143
   FRANCESCA CAMBRIDGE MALLEN

11 Language and the media   150

Contents

12 Trans people, trans issues   168

13 Expert view: trans pupils and the early years   188
    DEBORAH PRICE

14 Sexuality and sexualities   191

15 Relationships and PSHE education   213

16 Sports and physical education   228

17 Sex, touch and consent   245

18 Books, games and literature   266

19 Expert view: gender in classroom texts   279
    ROUSSEL DE CARVALHO

20 Conclusion   285

Index   287

Acknowledgements

I give sincere thanks to all those who read and commented on drafts, who offered opinions and criticisms and particularly who told me straight (haha) when I was being an idiot. Particular thanks to several friends who have offered very personal perspectives but who wish to remain anonymous, and a special shout-out to Iesha Small for her invaluable advice and feedback.

List of contributors

Graham Andre is a primary school teacher working on the Isle of Wight. He has always worked in the education sector, starting as a nursery nurse, then as a teaching assistant and subsequently having various roles in schools (including road crossing patrol, cleaner and mid-day supervisor) before doing a part-time degree and completing his GTP seven years ago. Graham is currently working at Lanesend Primary School on the Isle of Wight, where he is a Year 4 teacher and phase leader. Graham is a keen Twitter user who helped to start and grow the #primaryrocks group. This group has now held four sold-out teaching events. Recently Graham was seen working with his class on the BBC2 BAFTA-nominated documentary *No More Boys and Girls: Can Our Kids Go Gender Free?* The documentary has been shown in several countries, and Germany filmed its own version. Through this documentary he has been invited to speak on national TV and at live events around the United Kingdom, to talk about its impact. Graham is a patron of the Gender Equality Charter, a not-for-profit organisation that hopes to promote gender equality in schools, homes and businesses.

Jess Day is one of a team of volunteers behind the Let Toys Be Toys campaign, which initially grew out of a thread on parenting website Mumsnet. Organised entirely online, the campaign has succeeded in persuading 15 retailers and 10 publishers to change their marketing practices, and it has turned up the dial on the conversation about gender and marketing to children. In her day job, Jess works for a digital agency and organises and facilitates events. The biggest difference she's noticed between her son and her daughter is the way other people treat them.

Roussel De Carvalho is the Acting Director of Learning and Teaching for the College of Professional Services at the University of East London and the MA in Education Programme Leader. He taught physics and science for over ten years before moving into higher education when he led the PGCE Physics and PGCE Science at London Metropolitan University and at UCL Institute of Education. He has also been involved in international education consultancy on teacher education and textbook development. Oh, and he's been to Antarctica on a 23-day expedition.

Francesca Cambridge Mallen is the founder of Let Clothes Be Clothes, a UK-based campaign group set up to challenge the use of harmful gender stereotypes in the design and marketing of children's clothes. Francesca is a former museum curator and purveyor of trailblazing unisex kidswear, and her work has been described as both hugely inspiring by Caroline Lucas MP and lunatic by the *New York Post*. Currently hiding out on a hill in Shropshire, Francesca is encouraged by her two daughters and doesn't have enough time on her hands.

Jayne Osgood is Professor of Early Childhood & Gender at Middlesex University. She was expert consultant on the BBC documentary series *No More Boys & Girls: Can Our Kids Go Gender Free?* Through her activism and published work, she seeks to extend understandings of gender in childhood, an interest that culminated in her latest book: Osgood, J., & Robinson, K. H. (2019). *Feminists Researching Gendered Childhoods: Generative Entanglements* (Bloomsbury).

Deborah Price has been working with children or people who work with children for about 40 years. During that time she has been a children's zoo worker, playworker, youth worker, pre-school worker (on a converted bus), primary school teacher, local authority and Ofsted inspector, further education lecturer and university senior lecturer. Now she has semi-retired and works for the Open University teaching children's literature. She also writes and lectures, most recently in Athens at a conference looking at gender. She has contributed to an Amnesty pack and co-authored four books, two with Kath Tayler and two with Cathy Ota, and authored one on her own. She refuses to write with anyone not called Cath.

Lucy Rycroft-Smith was a teacher for ten years across primary, secondary and tertiary education. She is an education researcher and writer working at Cambridge University, with particular interest in mathematics education, gender and LGBTQ+ issues and education policy. She is co-editor, with J. L. Dutaut, of *Flip the System UK: A Teachers' Manifesto*, a 'brave and disruptive book' which aims to re-examine teacher agency in an age and time of punitive hyperaccountability. Lucy speaks internationally and writes for national platforms on education, and she currently hosts a podcast for the Times Educational Supplement. She is an occasional stand-up comedian, an enthusiastic Lindy hopper, a playful mathematician, a tie-wearer and an eye-roller extraordinaire. She tweets @honeypisquared.

Kath Tayler started working with young children and their families over 40 years ago when she was trained as a nursery nurse. She has recently retired from her role as a senior lecturer in early childhood education and care at Brighton University. She has co-authored two books (with Deborah Price) on LGBT and gender inclusion and diversity in the early years and has worked on a project on children's rights for Amnesty International. Kath sees life as a web of threads woven together in endlessly possible ways, with children as the newest threads, adding their voices and ideas. This metaphor is borne out in Kath's love of crafting.

Introduction

I'm 13 years old. I'm on the bus. Outside, the rain needles against the windows. A man sits down next to me, smelling of wax overcoat. My dad wears a wax overcoat. I shift over, trying not to touch his leg with mine. I can feel him looking at me. His hand appears on my thigh, unmistakable as a snake. I can see it but not feel it, like I'm watching a film. It doesn't make sense, but then so much of life doesn't make sense. Time stops and I cannot breathe, cannot think, cannot speak. I am frozen.

I don't question his right to touch me, and I'm not angry. I'm afraid, and I'm worried that I will make him angry. I am shaking, but not with rage. I'm mute and meek and cowed and cold. I don't know the etiquette. No one, in my 13 years, has told me explicitly that my body is mine, that I am allowed to be angry or aggressive with anyone about anything, but especially about this. I don't know that this is *sexual harassment*.

My daughter is now 13.

It is only since I have started explicitly caring and asking and talking about equality that I have realised many people have not had these sorts of experiences in the unremarkable background to their adolescence. Some of those others, who happen to have been born male, have been baffled when I tell that story. 'But why didn't you stop him?' they ask, incredulous. 'Punch him? Scream?'

Because I didn't know I could.

Because I didn't know for sure that I'd be believed, that adults would support me, that I even had a right to fight back in any tiny way. I didn't know that my body was mine. Why should I? No one had ever told me it was, and so many things had told me it wasn't. I didn't know that being a 'girl' could entail more than just accepting passively the decisions of men around me to control me in various ways. I really wish I had known that.

I know it now. And it breaks my heart to think of anyone *not knowing* they can assert themselves and actually object to behaviour like that, in a world where we so often speak of equal rights and fairness and we talk the talk so very well. I've been a teacher for ten years and have spoken these words many times before. But what does equality actually mean, and how do we actually effect change in our system, in our school, in our classroom, in ourselves?

What does gender mean to you? How do you interact with your gender?

'Gender is a social construction. In most of Western society, children born male (sex) are expected to behave like boys and then men (gender), which means a lot of things from playing with certain toys to assuming certain roles as an adult .... This is simply not realistic for everyday life, and it never has been',[1] Nicholas Teich writes in their excellent book *Transgender 101*.

You know what else? That assumption is so, so boring and limiting and tired.

It feels to me as if feminism and our notions of equality are changing. The generation of young people currently in our schools are doing a pretty amazing job, on the whole, of speaking up and speaking out about sexism and discrimination on the basis of gender and sexuality (among other things). Boys, and girls, and many who don't feel their identity is expressed by either label, are telling the world in voices loud and clear that they want schools to be different for them. That they are being sexually harassed, tormented, bullied. That their sex education has not prepared them for negotiating relationships, boundaries and consent. That their bodies – and their minds – are often not safe.

The disparity between the sensible, thoughtful things I hear many young people say about gender and the inflexibility of the school structures we are caging them in often feels wrong. It feels like cruelty, like misunderstanding, sometimes like trauma. Schools are enormously good at talking and writing about abstractions such as 'values', but as we know, living them out in the culture of a school is much more difficult. Schools are very often not safe for those – including teachers – who are LGBTQ+ – that is, lesbian, gay, bisexual, trans, queer; and the plus is important. I would include characterizations like questioning, asexual, non-binary, polyamorous and pansexual in this, which we will get to later. (These initials and who is included in them can be confusing, and they often change, so for the sake of clarity, I am including everyone who self-identifies as a member of one of these categories.) So often, claiming simple identity markers around gender and sexuality is confused with sexual deviance, with being predatory, inappropriately sexual or sexually promiscuous. The bodies of people socialised as girls and women have become battlegrounds in our schools and in our society, often through laws and customs which (may) seek to 'protect' them but end up patronising and de-humanising them.

'Sexual harassment, sexist language and gender stereotyping are commonplace in school settings, yet teachers report feeling unsupported and ill-equipped to respond', began a recent report from the National Education Union.[2]

In the same report, we find that less than a quarter (22%) of female students at mixed-sex schools think their school takes sexism seriously enough; 78% of secondary school students are unsure or not aware of the existence of any policies and practices in their school related to preventing sexism. Over half (64%) of secondary school teachers are unsure or not aware of the existence of any policies and practices in their school related to preventing sexism. Just one in five (20%) secondary school teachers has received training in recognising and tackling sexism as part of their Initial Teacher Education, and only 22% of secondary school teachers have received CPD (Continuing Professional Development) training in recognising and tackling sexism.

What is going on?

When we ask students how they feel, comments like this emerge: 'Being LGBT+ in school can be an isolating experience ... I have experienced ignorant remarks from students and teachers alike'.[3] Among students who identify as sexual minorities, the likelihood of death by suicide has been estimated to be two to seven times greater than that among heterosexual youth.[4] The reasons for their struggles with mental health and self-harm include gender nonconformity, low (or lack of) family support and victimisation for being a sexual minority.[5] In other words, these struggles are often preventable. As a society and as members of institutions, our lack of acceptance, flexibility and knowledge of gender and sexualities is hurting our pupils.

This book, although called *The Equal Classroom*, is solely about gender and sexuality, although gender discrimination and gender issues certainly do not exist in a vacuum. According to seminal work by Crenshaw[6] and many more, identities are intersectional – that is, who we are may be made up of a number of factors like race, sexual preference, weight, neurotypicism, degree of 'disability' and many more – and these factors may act in a multiplicative rather than an additive way in terms of disadvantage or advantage.

As a (relatively) wealthy white woman, it is hard for me to think about sexism without thinking it is all about me. There is an attractive righteousness to being the victim, isn't there? I'm so angry about being subjected to sexism that sometimes I forget to think about a wider context, a bigger picture. This isn't a competition for who's been more oppressed (and I would certainly not win, if it were). Rather, it is about having the courtesy and consideration to think about intersecting identities and how they might combine in others to create different profiles of discrimination.

I've realised that thinking about gender is only part of the story. There are other factors that act alongside gender to create different experiences of oppression. Put simply, many students (and indeed teachers) are subject to double or triple or n-times disadvantage because discrimination may work as a multiplier rather than additively. Black girls with disability may face tougher challenges than black girls without disability overall. Lesbian, gay, bisexual or trans students of colour may face more bias than white heterosexual students. These judgements may feel uncomfortable and difficult. But the system we currently work in *is* uncomfortable and difficult, and not talking about it isn't going to change that.

One of the many paradoxes of thinking about intersecting identity characteristics like gender, race, class, sexuality, disability and religion is that we may feel we need to establish some sort of framework, a hierarchy of power oppression. Statistically speaking, for example, we would expect a student who is both trans and a student of colour to have experienced some difficulties and faced some discrimination – how much, we cannot say, but starting from a basic expectation that they have is a matter of probability. However, this is also meaningless at too fine a level – it is particularly hard to quantify for individuals – and leads to a common defensive argument that 'you can't judge someone based on these things, *that's* the real discrimination. You're doing the thing you're saying people shouldn't do'. I often have people who have had really challenging lives, but happen to be white or male or able-bodied, react with frustration and anger. 'You don't know me!'

How do we assimilate these perspectives?

When we welcome a new student into our class, we might form an impression of them (and refine that over time) and consider what needs they might have that we can address, both academically and pastorally. We might notice that they are fat (there is a growing feeling among the body positivity community that straightforwardly using the word 'fat' is better than using euphemisms or withholding the term as a descriptor)[7] or that they present as female. We might notice that they wear a hijab, or have a fiddle toy for Asperger syndrome. We make judgements all the time about how they might fit into our class and how other students (and staff) might respond to them in terms of bias and discrimination. We might be wrong, and we should allow for that. But the starting point – that these things, in the aggregate, might well be widely predictable – allows us to try and focus our support in useful ways. It is about being attentive to possibilities. Someone wiser than I once patiently explained to me how paying attention to data as individual items and yet part of an important collective (or indeed several) at the same time is how statistics experts are able to think, and to me, this feels like a similar challenge.

You might have a very small student who has yet to hit puberty (although many classmates have), who is also female-presenting and a student of colour. Now, it is perfectly possible that this student is very confident and articulate and that their classmates are good at listening to them. It is, however, more likely that this *isn't* the case, and that they get shouted over and interrupted more than others. The reality might be messy and conflicting, but the idea – that you should be quietly attentive to whether this is happening – is important. If it doesn't happen, great. If it does, you can start to address and reduce the oppression. It is about giving some careful thought to which characteristics the world currently sees through a deficit model and trying to make your classroom, your staffroom, your school a place which seeks to change these patterns of behaviour. If your school policies or mission statements have the word 'equal' or 'fair' in them (and I'd be surprised if they didn't), this is what you signed up for. If those words do not appear, set your own standards.

It is also about paying attention to your own biases.

If you wanted to reply, 'but I'm not biased!' – congratulations, you are entirely wrong but entirely normal. It stings, that one. I've had to work past so many feelings of self-righteousness, and I still mess up all the time.

You and your interactions with others are undeniably biased. To what extent, and according to which characteristics, varies somewhat with the individual, but it is fair to say that bias exists everywhere. Knowing it exists is the first important step to doing something about it. The second is actively combating it.

In classrooms all over the world, teachers routinely choose boys to answer questions more often, allow them to speak longer and praise them differently than they praise girls.[8] They also widely underestimate students of colour – and teacher expectation is a significant predictor of student success.

'[B]oth math and English teachers were more likely to perceive their class as too difficult for students of color compared to White students, even after controlling for standardized test scores, homework completion, and a host of other factors'.[9]

Race is a crucial question, and race in the classroom is particularly crucial, but you will forgive me, I hope, for deciding that it is beyond the scope of this book (as well as beyond the scope of my lived experience for the most part). If you would like to read more about race issues in education and beyond, I highly recommend the wonderful *Between the World and Me* by Ta Nehisi Coates,[10] *Natives: Race and Class in the Ruins of Empire* by Akala, *Slay in Your Lane: The Black Girl Bible* by Yomi Adegoke and Elizabeth Uviebinené[11] and *Intersectionality and Race in Education* edited by Khalwant Bopal.[12] There are many, many more, and I do hope you'll recommend them to me. I'm trying to listen and learn. It has been pointed out to me that as a wealthy white woman, I have the luxury of not having to deal with race, and this is an excellent point.

So this book is not exhaustive. I've also left out a thorough discussion of sexual abuse issues – crucial and pervasive as they are – because I am emphatically not an expert, and this topic requires a high level of both expertise and care, and dealing with it as superficially as I would have to here would not do it justice. I've also skimmed through research, anecdotes and ideas at quite the clip, at times – because no one wants to read a doorstop-sized volume, and there are so many interesting and varied issues to talk about on the topic. I've taken something of a pic 'n' mix approach. I've written about issues that I've experienced, that have resonated with me, that make me angry – but most certainly not all the issues, not nearly all. And I acknowledge that my own race, upbringing and class may be different from those of other women reading. I hope that by acknowledging some limitations, we can find a way to improve some of these issues for our students and for ourselves. If I've missed something you care about, please tweet me or message me and we can talk about it, if you like.

In Bessel van der Kolk's seminal book on trauma, *The Body Keeps the Score*,[13] they talk about unacknowledged truths being one of the hardest things for a human to bear, noting that in order to be seen and understood, we have to have permission to *know what we know* and to *feel what we feel.* For some people walking around our schools, our classrooms, our corridors, our playgrounds, our staffrooms and our kitchens, the truth of who they are causes severe and painful conflict with the truth of who others perceive them to be. They know, on some level, deep or less deep, that they are different in a way that society might not deem acceptable; that they are not the gender that they may appear to be (or any gender at all); that they experience sexual attraction that society thinks is 'weird'; that they have a family that doesn't fit with the rigid expectations of others; that they don't behave according to the gender roles ascribed to them by others. Holding that truth inside them, concealing it and feeling shame, is causing them daily and quite unnecessary trauma. Instead of love, care and acceptance, we are serving them a daily repast of conflict on a plate. For them, school means learning lessons about pain, over and over again, until they are drilled in like times tables. These individuals are becoming fluent in hurt. Besides English, French or German, they are learning the language of distress: silence.

If that is you, I am deeply, deeply sorry. I'm sorry we haven't yet learned how to do better. I'm sorry we haven't yet learned how to welcome you with delight and acceptance, to meet your needs and to make you feel at home. That is your right, and we have failed you.

An important paradox to note: one of the central themes in this book is about challenging the gender binary, and yet I often refer to groups of gendered people, such as boys, men, girls, women and make generalisations about them. It has, in my view, been necessary to do this in order to engage with some of the important arguments. This is part of the way that we often struggle to conceptualise fluidity of gender in a world built on binaries, and if you have felt excluded by it or if I have not articulated this well enough, I am sorry.

Most of the chapters in this book contain the same structure of sections: **Stats; The issues; What needs to change; The strongest**

**counterarguments – and why they're wrong; Graham says; Now/
later** and **Tl;dr.** (This stands for *Too long; didn't read,* a section which
gives you a summary of the chapter. I am grateful to Dr. Emily Nagoski
for this idea).

As a great woman (Chana Messinger) once said: we should be creating
steelmen, not strawmen, from our opponent's arguments. To take issues
seriously, we should address the strongest, the most robust forms of the
arguments against what we believe and think, staunchly resisting the urge
to belittle, to humiliate or to dismiss. Argue with your opponent's best
arguments, not with their worst. That is something I have attempted to
do here, and I advocate taking this approach wherever possible.

In order to engage with what I have called 'the strongest counterarguments', I have used all kinds of debate websites and trawled comments sections of articles and newspapers (ugh) and have read academic
papers and talked to lots and lots of people. Of course, this doesn't
guarantee that I haven't missed something important, and if you feel a
strong counterargument has been missed, I'm sorry. I would be interested to hear it.

This book is designed for everyone in every setting, from early years
to colleges and beyond, and although some parts are obviously more
pertinent than others, it contains ideas, stories and prompts for teachers
teaching pupils of all ages. Many of the sections are simply designed to
provoke thought in the (teacher-) reader and to record some illumina-
tions I have experienced in my classroom career and beyond, as I have
explored gender through research and through the experiences of people who talk to me. Much of it is pondering, as is so much of the
important work we do around gender. Don't underestimate your need
to ponder on this stuff; I often have. As you will see, this book is not a
guide for how to think, how to manage your classroom or how to write
school policies on gender. Sometimes it's not even focused on
education – and that is because gender issues often do not stop, start or
even transform that much as they pass through the school gates in
either direction. That, to me, is part of the problem. Most schools are
not yet the haven of safety and critical challenge that can effect powerful change. Better minds than I have said that most schools are still
masculinity-making and femininity-making places, releasing into the
world pupils with some expectations, stereotypes and assumptions
about gender that are harmful and have far-reaching consequences.
I think we can do better.

If there is one overarching message that I am trying to explore here, it is that gender doesn't matter as much as we, in education, seem to think it does. Even more than that, ideas about binary gender, the roles and needs of men and women and the stories that go with them – heteronormative love stories – are so pervasive and entrenched in us that sometimes we can't see how damaging they might be. In this book, I'm not trying to destroy these stories (boys and girls of course can be very different; men and women can and do love one another romantically) but to offer different stories as well, so we can present our pupils with a wider range of them. We need more scripts. For example, I believe you can have a fulfilling relationship without sex, or with more than one person; I believe men and men and women and women can love one another, and that people who identify as non-binary or trans are whole and valuable and important and equal. I believe that saying 'we are all equal in our school' in grand speeches to parents or on the walls or in the policy documents isn't enough. It's what we do and say on a teeny tiny human scale that really matters.

The thing I keep coming back to, as I write this book, is the assumption that *telling our students about things will make them do it*. If we inform them about gender fluidity, homosexuality, polyamory, sexual acts, radical feminism – if we infect them with these ideas – then these seeds will germinate and spread, and we will be responsible. We will be encouraging and condoning all these things. Well, in the case of most of them – yes. If you don't support pupils' right to be gay, or non-binary, or feminist, or polyamorous – at pretty much any age – then we need to talk, and discuss why. It is possible, however, to separate providing accurate information from *sexualising* children at a young age. These are not one and the same. A small subset of information (graphic details of sexual acts or crimes, for instance) is worth withholding from pupils until they are in secondary school. But menstrual periods, LGBTQ+ issues, asexuality, criticising the gender binary, to name but a few legitimate topics, are all things that it is incredibly useful to know about *before* you encounter them personally. Can you imagine how terrified my own daughter might have been if, at age 10, she had started bleeding painfully from the vagina and didn't know that she was experiencing a perfectly normal and healthy human process, never having seen and heard and smelled and discussed it with me for years beforehand? Can you imagine having to discover on your own that you've had a wet dream, with all its concomitant feelings, with no idea about what has happened or why? Can you imagine the powerful feelings of being in the 'wrong' gendered body from age 4 or 5, feelings that only got stronger as you approached puberty, without knowing that this is normal, widespread and something you can get support and help with? Information about sex, sexuality and gender is not dangerous or shameful. Being deprived of that information is much more hazardous.

It's something of a trope that English teachers (God love 'em) tell their pupils that literature is about 'life and love' until they're old enough to hear the replacement truth: 'sex and death'. That's a transition and a half, isn't it? Sex and death, and attraction and gender questioning and pain and suffering and unrequited love and sexual urges don't all conveniently reside on one side of a magical line we call 'adult' that we get to gaily step across on our sweet sixteenth. Sometimes we just pretend they do, because we're so frightened of them. This book is about thinking, hard, about why that is.

In 2014, Graham Andre's classroom hit the national news when he was featured in the BBC series *No More Boys and Girls* with Dr. Javid Abdelmoneim. The series was nominated for a BAFTA, and Graham's journey, guided by Javid, was compelling to watch. Javid began the programme with a powerful statement: 'These children have lived their entire lives in a world that says it wants men and women to be treated the same'.[14] But, he says, do our classroom practices fit with this view? Spoiler alert – they don't. Graham was the brave teacher who volunteered to examine his own sexism, to try and make changes to his practice to help his children have a deeper appreciation of equality, and his journey has been fascinating to watch. In this book, we have tried to replicate the types of conversational approach that we have found to be effective – so I have written, and Graham has responded, and we invite you to join that conversation too, including challenging us as much as we are challenging you. We are all learning.

What about you? You might work in a school or classroom where you care passionately about equality and have started making changes already, or you might be right at the beginning of your journey, considering the ways gendered thinking in education can change. You might be up against school policies that are old or unhelpful, or staff members or parents who feel uncomfortable about change for a variety of reasons. Wherever you are on that journey, you are welcome here, and thank you for engaging with the ideas in this book.

Graham says

Before being contacted by Outline Productions to take part in the documentary *No More Boys and Girls*, I had really never thought about gender stereotypes and the impact they have on our children. In my defence (or perhaps not) I had been trained as a nursery nurse in the late eighties and as a teacher eight years ago – and in neither of these courses did the providers think to talk to us about stereotypes. The language we use with children, and the messages that they receive from books, the media and the home environment, can have an adverse impact on them – not just in their early years but as they grow older. For me the six weeks spent looking at this with my class was one of the most eye-opening and frankly mind-blowing lessons I have ever learned. The process was a difficult one for me. I had to analyse my own practice and language, the way I interacted with my children and had done for several years – and totally change it. I changed it because I could see the negative impact in the messages that my class were receiving from me, and I could also see that if they were going to change their perceptions of themselves, then I had to change too. I didn't set out to do it, but I was doing it unconsciously, as I am sure many people up and down the country who are working with children, or have their own children, are doing.

I hope this book will help to raise awareness of the negative impact that stereotypical messages have on our children. And I want to underscore a positive message too: there are so many things we can do to help change negative stereotypes and help our children to have a future where they can be whatever they want to be.

References

1. Teich, N. M. (2012). *Transgender 101: A Simple Guide to a Complex Issue.* New York, NY: Columbia University Press.
2. National Education Union/Feminista. (2019). *Sexism in schools.* Retrieved April 13, 2019, from NEU website: https://neu.org.uk/advice/sexism-schools
3. Terrence Higgins Trust. (2016). *Shhh … No talking: LGBT-inclusive sex and relationships education in the UK.* Retrieved from www.tht.org.uk/endthesilence
4. Haas, A. P., Eliason, M., Mays, V. M., Mathy, R. M., Cochran, S. D., D'Augelli, A. R., … Clayton, P. J. (2011). Suicide and suicide risk in

lesbian, gay, bisexual, and transgender populations: Review and recommendations. *Journal of Homosexuality, 58*(1), 10–51.

5. Mustanski, B., & Liu, R. T. (2013). A longitudinal study of predictors of suicide attempts among lesbian, gay, bisexual, and transgender youth. *Archives of Sexual Behavior, 42*(3), 437–448.

6. Crenshaw, K. (1994). *Mapping the margins: Intersectionality, identity politics, and violence against women of color.* Retrieved from https://www.racialequitytools.org/resourcefiles/mapping-margins.pdf

7. Friend, Y. F. (2018, August 29). *Who's hurt by being called "fat"?* Retrieved April 13, 2019, from Your Fat Friend website: https://medium.com/@thefatshadow/whos-hurt-by-being-called-fat-551930bc6989

8. Sadker, D. M., Sadker, M., Zittleman, K. R., & Sadker, M. (2009). *Still Failing at Fairness: How Gender Bias Cheats Girls and Boys in School and What We Can Do About It* (Rev. and updated ed). New York, NY: Scribner.

9. *Teacher racial bias matters more for students of color* (n.d.). Retrieved April 13, 2019, from NYU Steinhardt at a Glance website: https://steinhardt.nyu.edu/site/ataglance/2017/05/teacher-racial-bias-matters-more-for-students-of-color.html

10. Coates, T.-N. (2015). *Between the World and Me.* Melbourne: Text.

11. Adegoke, Y., & Uviebinené, E. (2018). *Slay in Your Lane: The Black Girl Bible.* London: Fourth Estate.

12. Bhopal, K., & Preston, J. (2014). *Intersectionality and "Race" in Education.* New York, NY: Routledge.

13. Van der Kolk, B. A. (2015). *The Body Keeps the Score: Brain, Mind and Body in the Healing of Trauma.* New York, NY: Penguin.

14. *No More Boys and Girls.* (2017). Outline Productions/British Broadcasting Corporation. Broadcast August 2017, BBC 2.

Gender identities: social and cultural

Car and beer or car AND beer – penis-fencing – men behaving badly – slaying – rudely placed – get out of my garden – gender as a shell game – AC/DC – girls line up first – masculinity needs realigning – gender category maintenance – is it relevant? – gender-free nephews – wearing a 'man's' suit - turban and heels – vegans have a bad name – lightfooting around – heteroyawn – what's in their pants – they acted dumb

Stats

A quarter of all secondary school teachers say they witness gender stereotyping and discrimination in their school on a daily basis, and a further quarter say they witness it on a weekly basis.[1]

For their profiles, Facebook users at one time were able to choose from more than 50 terms for their gender, including transgender, cisgender, gender nonconforming, genderqueer and agender (there is now, at time of writing, a free text box available to suit the user).[2]

The issues

I'm in that most god-awful of places, the greeting card shop. I'm with my daughter, choosing a card for a male loved one. We look around. Our options are:

– Humour about boobs
– Sexist joke

- Picture of car or beer, or car AND beer
- Picture of golf or football

She turns to me, rolling her eyes. This male loved one is a board games enthusiast, a gentle lover of cats, a quick-witted humourist who wouldn't dream of making a cheap sexist joke. The only sports he follows are broadcast on Twitch streams. He doesn't fit the small range of boxes we have in front of us. In fact, that's one reason we like him. We grin at each other and go home to make a card of our own.

In Dr. Adam Rutherford's *The Book of Humans*, they talk about a tremendous variety of sexual behaviours seen in the male of various species in nature – male child-rearing while females swan about wearing flamboyant ornamentation (pipe-fish); penis-fencing to find out who will become the egg-bearer (flatworms); hermaphroditism, wherein, without a female, the male's testes shrink down and the organism grows ovaries (clownfish); vigorous fellatio between males (bears). They also describe the way that men of the Marind-Anim people in New Guinea enjoy anal copulation with other men, believing that semen has magical properties that increase their masculinity.[3] They conclude that, despite popular and narrow discourses, especially revolving around what is 'natural' and what decidedly isn't, there are many ways to 'be' male.

Grayson Perry, in their excellent book *The Descent of Man*, is worried that these stories we tell about being male are too boring, too narrow, too confining and that they are killing men, quite literally. They call masculinity 'the lumbering beast within me which I have had to suppress and negotiate with my whole life'. What we need, they say, are more examples of men doing more different things than just 'pulling' women (ugh), driving cars and climbing mountains (with perhaps the occasional round of golf for a rest).[4] I heartily agree. In nature, we see a tremendous range of behaviours, both 'good' and 'bad', displayed by males, and our tired contemporary stories about what men do and like as humans often just don't reflect reality. Plenty of people, when questioned, rely on an argument that suggests certain behaviours are 'natural' for males and females, which very much falls apart under scrutiny. Yuval Noah Harari explains it well: 'Culture tends to argue that it forbids only that which is unnatural. But from a biological perspective, nothing is unnatural .... No culture has ever bothered to forbid men to photosynthesise'.[5]

I remember as a teenager and young adult watching the sitcom *Men Behaving Badly* – a pastiche of lager-drinking, female-chasing, messy, lazy chaps having an incompetently fun time – and thinking 'is this all there is?' That, for me wasn't 'behaving badly'. It was exactly what I expected. I wanted to see men wearing outrageous evening gowns in the supermarket, learning to be experts at medieval tapestry, taking their children to see anti-religious musicals, splashing extravagant cash on luxury stair carpets, proclaiming the pointlessness of football through comic song, hand-rearing baby lambs ... *breaking the rules of masculinity.* (Now there's a sitcom I'd watch.) Had the series *RuPaul's Drag Race* been around when I was young, I would have eagerly lapped it up, because it expertly does this with humour and flair – considers and dismantles ideas about masculinity that restrict and harm men. The point is not just to be fabulous, but to be actively proud of the new identities you have created and owned, to *feel your oats*, to be *dusted*, to *let them have it the house down.* You *slay* – metaphorically scything through the rules and restrictions about identity that actively work against your happiness. You show people new ways to be. You change history to herstory as well. It's a show that has totally challenged my thinking on masculinity and femininity.

This is not just for men, of course. This is for everyone.

What does it mean to be male? What does it mean to be female?

Can you conceive of an identity that is both or neither?

'There is no real "'essence" of gender, rather, it is the various acts of gender which perpetuate the notion of gender: without the acts there would be no gender .... The categories "male"/"female" are illusory constructions'.[6]

You might be happy with the gender identity boundaries present in our society – seeing them as guidelines only – or they might happen to fit your preferences. Congratulations! I am happy for you and respect your choices. But what about those that 'fail' to fit?

Picture this: One morning, you wake up to a commotion. It's early. You're confused. People seem to be walking through your garden – hordes of people, wandering through, looking through your windows and throwing rubbish in your garden and picking raspberries off your bushes. They harvest your crops and pluck your flowers and picnic on your lawn. What has happened?

15

If you are someone who is challenging a boundary, you almost certainly are regarded as aggressive and confrontational. But what if your very existence is challenging that boundary and what if that boundary has been rudely placed right through your home? What would you do? Would you up and leave?

Of course not! You stay. You defend. You stand up and challenge. 'Please walk around my house, not through it', you say. You put up signs. You file lawsuits, prepare paperwork and keep going until something happens.

'That X is so angry', hisses everyone under their breath. 'Of course I am!' you think, indignantly.

Welcome to challenging gender boundaries 101.

'Gender is a shell game. What is a man? Whatever a woman isn't. What is a woman? Whatever a man isn't. Tap on it and it's hollow. Look under the shells: it's not there',[7] says Naomi Alderman in their dystopian feminist story *The Power*. Women are so often defined as not-men; more rarely, the reverse also happens.

In our world, gender is defined by alternative, complementary, yin and yang, AC/DC. We continue to see man/woman binaries all over the place, despite good evidence that they are not reflective of real life. How can we crack that misconception open so that tall or fat or strong or hairy women, and blonde or curvy or short or delicate men, feel okay too?

What's this got to do with schools?

'Schools are uniquely poised to open the minds of students of all ages about gender diversity. Instead of reinforcing accepted cultural training of gender, schools can teach children to think for themselves about gender'.[8] So schools and, of course, the people within them (because 'schools' are nothing but collections of people doing work together) have an important choice to make: be part of the solution or part of the problem.

Gender stereotyping in schools reinforces particular ideas about what is expected and acceptable behaviour from women and men, such as that women are weak and emotional, while men are strong and brave. 'A significant portion of teachers report that sexism is an everyday occurrence in the classroom, and that small, seemingly insignificant events together create an environment in which pupils of both sexes come to see each other as different'.[9]

In the BBC TV series *No More Boys and Girls* that featured teacher Graham Andre's classroom, Dr. Javid begins by stating, 'children as young as seven think that boys and girls are fundamentally different'. One of the pupils says, 'men are better at being in charge'; another says that 'men are more successful'. Girls are 'pretty'. The series follows a class of 7-year-olds through a project to make their class more gender-neutral, with the desired effect of supporting young people to become adults with more developed ideas about equality and the better opportunities that could bring them. In case you missed it, this isn't a small thing. 'Every child deserves the same opportunities in life', he says. 'But unless we stop treating our boys and girls differently, that isn't going to happen'.[10]

'Hasn't society got bigger problems?' some might ask at this point.

Examining masculinity can seem like a luxury problem, a pastime for the wealthy, well-educated, peaceful society, but I would argue the opposite: the poorer, the more undeveloped, the more uneducated a society is, the more masculinity needs realigning with the modern world, because masculinity is probably holding back that society. (Perry in *The Descent of Man*[11])

So where the heck do we start?

What needs to change

In schools, we do work of 'gender category maintenance'[12] from the very start. Ask children at various ages to count or spell, and they will reply with varying degrees of competence; ask them to classify their own gender, and they will most likely ace that test. The gender binary is so simple and straightforward that even a young child can understand it. That's its strength, right? Neat, easy, simple. I have seen a variety of practices in schools, from unthinking gender stereotyping about dressing up (boys, here are some lovely fireman's outfits; girls, we have fairy wings for you) to the almost daily practice of splitting up boys and girls into groups (the boys are being noisy today; girls line up first) to some deeply upsetting stories of female pupils and teachers being sexually harassed on a daily basis. We must start with a thorough audit; we must start from the truth. If we are imposing gender identities on students, we are not providing safety and opportunity for them to learn and grow. We also need to challenge the very idea of gender binary – of 'boy things' and 'girl things'.

The strongest counterarguments – and why they're wrong

- 'Gender binary thinking is simple, and young children need simplicity. Gender is an important part of society, and children should clearly know their own gender'.

- 'Childhood and adolescence are confusing; mixing up ideas about gender is only going to confuse young people more'.

- 'If we give children more options about their identity, they will take them for fun and for play and for sport. This will lead to a trivialisation of gender'.

- 'Boys should be boys and girls girls. Then we all know how to behave and what to expect, and how to be attractive and attracted to others'.

Gender is currently an important part of society, but it doesn't need to be this way.

James Acaster has an excellent part of a comedy set in which he takes apart a joke which mentions race. His important rejoinder – But is it *relevant?* – applies equally to gender. We've got so used to saying, 'this guy/man/woman/girl/lady/boy/girl' and 'my daughter/son' that we do it all the time, without much thought, and certainly without thinking about the consequences. I have two daughters versus I have two children. The girls versus the children. My mum and dad versus my parents. My nephews versus … I'm not sure what could go there in English. We need better words.

In the academic community, one of my favourite recurrent phrases is 'but it depends on which way you slice it'. In other words, we don't have to choose this characteristic to focus on. What would happen if we chose something other than gender? Do we even need to group pupils at all? (Inevitably, the answer sometimes must be yes.) Do we clearly understand the consequences when we do?

Gayle Rubin uses the term 'sex/gender system' (1975)[13] to designate the common assumptions that there are only two sexes, that there are only two genders and that sex automatically determines a person's gender. There are a generation of people who have grown up under this idea – some quite happily, others very much the opposite. I say a generation because there have been times and places in which the whole gender binary has been quite absent, allowing for at least one other designation. There are plenty of examples of this: Hawaiian *maju*; Najavo nádleehí; Albanian *burrnesha*.

Did you know that not every society, culture or age has had two genders?

But some have argued (quite rightly) that adding an 'other' gender to the two already acknowledged is not necessarily deconstructing the binary. What about ideas around gender fluidity? More on that later.

Mixing up ideas about gender is freeing and not confusing. It is a playful way to approach identity. Ever since I started wearing a suit and tie for (most) professional occasions, and especially since I have dyed my hair a multitude of different colours, I have found people to be very disconcerted by my appearance. Almost everywhere I go, I am greeted with the same response: 'But you look DIFFERENT!' (I'm pretty sure they mean 'from the last time I met you', not 'from everyone else'. I feel like that's something of a given.)

It is given, not with delight, but with accusation. And I get it – it's hard to remember the faces of acquaintances and professional contacts. I'm pretty terrible at it. But the lack of space for me to wear a men's suit (is it a men's suit if I'm wearing it?) one month and a long dress another, or to wear heavy makeup one day and none another, or to have long blonde hair and change it to short blue hair is somewhat puzzling. Is this related to gender? In the sense of fluidity of identity, I think it must be. It is abnormal to the point of comment that someone should be so metamorphic. Aside from the practical implications of recognition, it is something that we may feel uncomfortable with as a concept: we so often think people should remain in their boxes.

If you are familiar with the NB (enby/non-binary) community across the world, you may have a different perspective. All over the globe, people are happily changing the way they look and behave (and feel) to cross traditional gender norms and, in so doing, to cross boundaries of what is assumed to constitute masculinity and femininity.

I simply cannot tell you how happy this makes me on two levels. The first is aesthetic: I love the variety of looks, and I love the time and care people spend on creating them. Want to be a fluffy tutu-wearing, stubbled person with the leg warmers to match? Go for it. Feel like wearing your short hair femininely styled with goth makeup and a neck scarf? Knock yourself out. Turban and heels? Check. Plaid and heavy boots with exquisite nails? Check. As someone who delights in design, I'm totally inspired by these mash-ups, juxtapositions and creations, as well as enjoying immensely the powerful transformations of those who look traditionally feminine one day and masculine the next. I also find this variety interesting from the perspective of sexual attractiveness; the more I see, the more I find that I like. Surrounding yourself with images of people that break the stereotypes of conventional gendered attractiveness is a powerful thing to do, and I will expand upon it later in this book.

The second reason why I rejoice in open self-expresssion in the non-binary community is that it is playful, expressive behaviour – thinking actively about boundaries and barriers – and this almost always delights me. I'm a mathematician and artist, and you don't get very far in these two disciplines without such as approach – working with what you have, trying new ideas and analysing what works. Tinkering and pattern-sniffing and combining and evaluating and dismantling is intellectual and creative work, and watching people do it with their own identities makes me realise how healthy and important it is. We all have (or are) that friend who wears the same clothes every day, who has to have their hair just so, who is afraid to be seen without makeup and who obsesses about their body changing or their hair thinning. Our identity is mapped to our physical appearance, and like it or not, this changes over time in ways that we cannot control (ageing, illness). We have to learn to adapt, or suffer the mental health consequences. Why not own and control that process by being a joyful identity experimenter?

How would you feel if tomorrow you had to shave your head?

What if you woke up in the morning with (if you don't have them) breasts?

How would you feel about a great deal of facial hair sprouting (if you don't already have it)?

Creativity is literally the opposite of trauma. For many people, taking a body that does not match their 'inner' (if non-stable) identity and creatively changing its appearance is like making a phoenix rise from the ashes. It's powerful. It's strong. It's about control. It's also about problem-solving, working with what you have.

Questioning of gender identities might well be the opposite of trivialising them. Can you conceive of a world without gender (or even without its being so crucially important all the time), and can you imagine the amount of work we would have to do to get there – the questioning, the cultural work, the dealing with this fear and emotion that people cling to, the hearts and minds that would have to change? This is serious stuff, and people really care about it.

In the Simon Amstell mockumentary *Carnage*, we see this type of process in action – this time on the subject of veganism. Amstell presents a coherent vision of the change from a world that views animals as commodities, and complacently accepts the means of producing them, to one where people question these cruel practices and ultimately come to live without them. I highly recommend this documentary, not just because I'm all for veganism, but for insight into the way that people react against a change in mind from 'this is what we have always done' to 'but what if things could be different?'

I am not suggesting that we all bow down to the idea of gender fluidity as instinctively right, of course. Neither should we fear and dismiss it, particularly those of us who have been raised on a gender binary. The key here is to be informed, to understand the basis for questioning gender identities and the effects they may have on ourselves and our pupils. We, as teachers, need to understand gender fluidity, especially if we have never felt the need for it ourselves. (This is called cisgender privilege, and it's very much a thing.)

Far from trivialising it, I am advocating the questioning of gender precisely because it is important. At least it is a paradox, at once so important and so unimportant. Gender currently shapes our thinking about our *selves* and others so much that for many people, it is hard or impossible to untangle. But this is not true of everyone in every era; it does not have to be true. What might be the consequences if it gender didn't shape our thinking about ourselves? What if we didn't have to spend our lives negotiating and lightfooting around the gender order, but could just roll it up and put it out of sight unless we needed it, instead?

How will we navigate sexual attraction without gender? We already do. This brings me to what is often the central question of this debate.

It may be hard to imagine how to feel attraction, date, have sex and relationships with people if you don't immediately know their gender, if they don't have one, or if they move between genders (probably, but not necessarily, retaining the same genitalia throughout). This prompts people to suggest the 'boys should be boys and girls should be girls' argument, further maintaining that there are stable gender traits present in boys and girls, respectively, that make them attracted to one another.

I'm here to give a big wave to the non-hetero folk and to tell you that this attitude is particularly disrespectful to them.

Once you realise that our world is *heteronormative* – that is, built on the assumption that men and women find one another attractive and this is somehow 'normal' – then a lot of things fall into place. Questioning and challenging this – sometimes called *queering* – is pretty important, because without it, everyone who doesn't conform to this norm (and indeed, to every other norm, because the argument extrapolates) feels invisible and maybe even 'wrong'. Yuck.

I am a woman who finds women attractive. Most people take a beat when I tell them this, because they might have heard me talk about my current partner, who is the male, and my two children, and assumed I am straight. Of course! Why wouldn't you? And I am not blaming those people, or you, if that was your first thought. But there's that heteronormative thinking again. It's erasing to people; it's painful to our pupils who may have non-traditional families (more on that later); for me, it's *boring*. Assuming the pupils we come into contact with are growing up heterosexual and will be attracted only to the opposite gender is statistically incorrect (some will, some won't); morally incorrect (why is hetero love better than any other kind of love?); and socially incorrect (it puts people who are 'different' in the position of having to explain or justify themselves to us).

Sexual attraction without reliance on a gender binary has been happening, and will continue to happen, all the time. It works on the basis that we are honest with one another, but also that we don't need to define ourselves by a gender. Some people have frank discussions about what's in their pants on the first date; some people (aces, or asexuals) don't feel sex is part of their relationship repertoire, so that may be less important to them. Attraction is more than sex; love is more than attraction; supporting our pupils in navigating all these feelings is the particular privilege of being a teacher, and one that requires being well informed about the issues involved.

Another really important consequence of the 'boys should be boys and girls girls' argument is that women have been 'kept out' of curriculum areas like mathematics, science and computing, finding it hard or impossible to reconcile being good at these with being feminine. Those boundaries aren't there 'naturally' – we're keeping them there. Similarly, boys can feel the same way about textiles, fashion and cooking, or languages and humanities. Our pupils are then faced with a choice: minimise their skills and interest in the subjects they love or minimise their performance of their gender identity. For example, girls in one study said they 'acted dumb' about their mathematical proficiency to relate to boys[14]; girls in another study emphasised their 'masculine' characteristics to gain entry to a subculture organized around cars and racing.[15]

Now/later

Now: Think about the ways that gender identities are reflected in your school and your classroom. Think about the stereotypes that pupils might encounter and how these might affect their view of what men and women are and do. Put up a poster, an image or a quotation that challenges gender identity stereotypes in some way, and ask pupils to respond to it.

Later: Find out about your school administration's policies. Do pupils or parents have to choose a binary gender when they register? Does a non-binary option exist? Do other options exist? What happens if pupils feel uncomfortable with their gender and would prefer to use different pronouns (he/she/they/ze)? What about a pupil who is transitioning to a different gender? (See Chapter 9.) Under the Equality Act 2010, any young person has a right to be addressed in a manner that reflects the gender with which they identify, regardless of any diagnosis or medical intervention and irrespective of age.

Graham says

As educators we play a key role in how the children in our care grow up, in the messages they get and in the aspirations they may have. Our children – boys, girls and others – need to see a range of people in a range of roles. They particularly need to see men doing household chores, looking after young children and showing emotions. Unfortunately, the early years and the primary school setting aren't the ideal place for this, because men make up just 7.4% of the total childcare work force.[16] So how do we help our young boys with their emotional literacy?

We need positive male role models that can show boys it is ok to cry when feeling sad (or happy), that it is ok to talk about how we feel, that looking after babies is great and that wanting to care or be creative or sing or love unicorns are all normal things for all humans.

I recently saw a mum and son about 5 years old in a large store, and they were looking for a present for his birthday.

SON: 'Mum I want this', grasping a doll.

MUM: 'You can't have that – it's for girls, choose something else'.

Why not let the boy have the doll? What message is this refusal communicating to the boy about fatherhood and caring?

At a recent conference, one of the stallholders told me about a girl who was with her grandmother and wanted to buy a finger puppet. The young girl chose a footballer with a number 10 on his shirt.

GRANDMOTHER: 'Oh no, how about this one?' grabbing a fairy puppet.

GIRL: 'I really want this one'.

GRANDMOTHER: 'How about this mermaid? You love mermaids'.

GIRL: 'But I like this footballer'.

GRANDMOTHER: 'If you can't make up your mind, you won't have anything'.

Needless to say, the girl walked away without a puppet, because her grandmother wanted her to have a puppet that fit with her own stereotypes of what a girl should like. This makes me so sad.

People working in childcare settings have the perfect opportunity to challenge stereotypes; to share stories of princesses fighting dragons or boys wanting to dance all day; to inspire girls to want to be scientists by teaching about inspirational female scientists; and to show boys role models demonstrating the strength, power and grace they can have without worrying about their masculinity.

Tl;dr

Gender identities are often more rigid and stereotyped than we might like, and schools play a part in perpetuating this. Gender doesn't have to be binary, and many people feel more comfortable either without a gender or moving between genders in a fluid way. How can we make schools places that challenge the gender binary and its restrictive stereotypes and that support our pupils, and make them safe, as they ask healthy and important questions about gender identity?

References

1. National Education Union/Feminista. (2019). *Sexism in schools.* Retrieved April 13, 2019, from NEU website: https://neu.org.uk/advice/sexism-schools
2. National Geographic. (2018, October 22). *How science is helping us understand gender.* Retrieved April 13, 2019, from magazine website: https://www.nationalgeographic.com/magazine/2017/01/how-science-helps-us-understand-gender-identity/
3. Rutherford, A., & Roberts, A. (2018). *The Book of Humans: The Story of How We Became Us.* London, UK: Orion.
4. Perry, G. (2017). *The Descent of Man.* UK, London: Penguin.
5. Harari, Y. N. (2011). *Sapiens: A Brief History of Humankind.* Israel: Harper.
6. Francis, B. (2002). Relativism, realism, and feminism: An analysis of some theoretical tensions in research on gender identity. *Journal of Gender Studies, 11*(1), 39–54. https://doi.org/10.1080/09589230120115158
7. Alderman, N. (2016). *The Power.* Großbritannien: Penguin.
8. Brill, S. A., & Pepper, R. (2008). *The Transgender Child.* San Francisco, CA: Cleis

9. National Education Union/Feminista. (2019). *Sexism in schools.* Retrieved April 13, 2019, from NEU website: https://neu.org.uk/advice/sexism-schools
10. *No More Boys and Girls.* (2017). Outline Productions/British Broadcasting Corporation. Broadcast August 2017, BBC 2.
11. Perry, G. (2017). *The Descent of Man.* London, UK: Penguin.
12. Francis, B., & Skelton, C. (Eds.). (2001). *Investigating Gender: Contemporary Perspectives in Education.* Philadelphia, PA: Open University.
13. Rubin, G. (1975). The traffic in women: Notes on the "political economy" of sex. In R. R. Reiter (Ed.), *Toward an Anthropology of Women* (pp. 157–210). New York, NY: Monthly Review.
14. Sherman, J. A. (1982). Mathematics the critical filter: A look at some residues. *Psychology of Women Quarterly, 6*(4), 428–444. https://doi.org/10.1111/j.1471-6402.1982.tb01071.x
15. Lumsden, K. (2010). Gendered performances in a male-dominated subculture: 'Girl racers', car modification and the quest for masculinity. *Sociological Research Online, 15*(3), 1–11. https://doi.org/10.5153/sro.2123
16. *The early years workforce in England.* (n.d.). Retrieved April 13, 2019, from Education Policy Institute website: https://epi.org.uk/publications-and-research/the-early-years-workforce-in-england/

Expert view: teaching gender

Kath Tayler

Children don't live and grow in a bubble; they are influenced by the people around them and by society in general – but they can also exert influence, by expressing their thoughts and ideas, if we are willing to listen. Every generation experiences children and young people laughing at the bewildered older generation who fail to understand the things the young take for granted with ease. In modern society this may largely revolve around technology, but the young have always pushed boundaries in areas like clothing, music taste and language, and therefore they contribute to the changing and developing society around them. There is an important back-and-forth, a mutuality and reciprocity in relationships between children and adults, and between children and other children, that fosters innovation and independence.

When my daughter was born in 1988 there was still a long way to go in terms of tackling everyday sexism and the stereotyping of childhood experiences. As a feminist, and having worked in early-years education for many years, I had particular views about how I wanted to raise my child. I didn't want her vital formative years to be limited in any way by being a girl. I wanted her to be free to run, jump, climb, splash in puddles, get muddy, build, create and explore; to be tender, thoughtful and kind; to play with dolls, spaceships, cars, trains, teddies and tea sets; to imagine picnics and pirate adventures; to get lost in a world of books, listen to music, hear poetry, see plays, be brave, ask for help, shout loud and whisper secrets; to dress up as a princess, or a prince, or a frog or a knight in shining armour. I wanted to be a role model for my daughter too, and that meant she needed to see me cooking, cleaning, using a drill, putting up shelves, driving a car, going to work, having friends, reading, writing, listening and talking.

From the age of about 3, my daughter mainly wore her Postman Pat t-shirt and jeans by day and her Spiderman pyjamas at night. She had short curly hair and was constantly mistaken for a boy. At this time, much of her play was with cars and trains. For some people around her, this was challenging and undermined their concept of what a little girl should be. They would have felt more comfortable with the familiar trappings of mini-femininity. If I hadn't been willing to listen to my daughter's wishes regarding clothes and toys, and if she hadn't gone to an excellent nursery school (now, sadly, a rarity), we would have had daily battles, with me trying to put my unhappy child into dresses and ribbons. Battles over bath time or bedtime are a regular feature in family life for many, but this sartorial struggle just didn't seem worth the trouble.

It is easy to explain to a child that they need a bath to keep clean or need to go to bed because sleep is important for their health. While it might have been possible to find an explanation for opposing her choice of clothes or toys that would have satisfied some people ('Those are boys' clothes', 'Only boys play with trains'), these were not explanations I was happy with, and they were certainly not part of my parenting style!

Although children can be seen as co-constructors and as having voice and agency, it is crucial to acknowledge that in relationships with young children, adults are generally the more powerful and the better able to express their beliefs and to structure those beliefs in a way that makes them seem 'normal' to a young child. The argument that it is 'natural' for girls to like princesses and fairies, whereas boys like trucks and trains, is more a reflection of the society we have structured than of any innate gender expression.

It is important to recognise the changes that have happened through-out history that contradict the idea of these preferences being innate. At the beginning of the last century, it was common practice to dress baby boys in pink. Pink, seen as a version of red, was viewed as repre-senting strength and power. Meanwhile, baby girls were dressed in pale blue, which was seen as a colour of purity and delicacy. This means that in terms of early-years education, it is vitally important that practitioners be aware of their responsibility to allow all children to explore all options in terms of activities, toys, books, games and ways of behaving and expressing themselves. It is a helpful practice to provide resources that reflect a range of roles and ways of being, but these resources won't achieve much on their own – practitioners also have to be committed to using them in positive ways.

For example, in one early-years setting, a practitioner read a group of children a book that showed a female pilot in a plane. When a child commented on this, the practitioner responded by saying, 'Yes, it's unusual, isn't it?' and then continued to read the book. It might have been more helpful to engage the children in a discussion about how unusual it is, why this is so and what the barriers might be. This could lead to thinking about other jobs that are often performed largely by either men or women and what the reasons for this might be. Challenging any stereotypes that exist in relation to these jobs would help young children see that different possibilities are open to them and that there are new stories we can tell about women and men and others.

When my daughter went to drama school, she once again experienced the freedom she had had as a young child. Once again, she could be anyone (although there are still limits to this on stage and screen!). The first time I saw her in a student production she was a prostitute, the next time a Catholic schoolgirl. I've seen her in the role of a young child, a strident young feminist, a maid, a bride, a middle aged woman and many, many more.

This is what life is about – and it is particularly what childhood is about. Children need to try things out; they need to explore all the dimensions of life and to experience things first-hand in order to develop their understanding of them. This is not about a search for a true, fixed self – as if that self were sitting, fully formed inside us waiting to be uncovered. This is about exploring what sense of self might fit at a given moment, open to change and development. Having supportive and engaged adults around supports this process and makes this exploration possible. If a little boy puts on a glittery tutu and an adult tries to discourage this, he is getting the message that this is not appropriate behaviour for him. He may have been enjoying the feel of the material, the way it glitters in the light and the sound it makes when he brushes against something. All of these learning opportunities are lost if he is discouraged from playing in this way.

A girl 'dressing as a boy' or a boy 'dressing as a girl' is nothing more than a child wearing a particular set of clothing. It is our culture that identifies that clothing as 'appropriate' for a girl or boy. There is nothing inherently female or male about any clothing. Clothes have been invested with that status through our culture and through stereotyping. Throughout history and across cultures, the ideas about what women and men should or should not wear have changed. In some ways, women have had greater societal limitations on their clothing, and this in turn has limited their range of activities. However, at times, men too have worn long hair or wigs and high heels and been similarly encumbered.

This is also true of other activities in an early-years setting. In one setting, I vividly remember a little girl who liked playing with the bikes and climbing as high as possible on the climbing frame. She was happiest when outside and found it hard to sit still and concentrate inside. She was often told off for her behaviour, which was seen as disruptive and aggressive. A practitioner who was new to the setting noticed this and also observed that the boys who behaved in the same way were often praised for their bravery and skill. She brought this to the attention of the other practitioners, and they were shocked to realise how differently they treated the girl. They then made every effort to praise and encourage her, and they found she began to settle more and engage in a wider range of activities. Interestingly, this had an effect on some of the boys, who also began to engage in other activities. The broadening of expectations when it comes to children can benefit them all.

By narrowing the way children play and behave, we are limiting their choices, not only in childhood but also throughout life. We need girls and boys to grow up aware of the choices available to them. If we see a girl in a Postman Pat t-shirt as dressed 'like a boy', we speak volumes about what we think being a girl or being a boy means, what choices are open to them and what they can expect out of life. By limiting our expectations around gender in relation to what children should wear and how they should behave, we are prioritising our own comfort above children's wants and needs. We owe *all* our children better than that.

Gender identities: brains and biology

But chromosomes – sex verification – 'hair colour reveal party' – neuroplasticity and neurosexism – is science sexist? – bodily associations – hirsute but feminine Lettie – fat if you're funny – an inconvenience and an embarrassment – bleed out quietly – clitorises should not be need-to-know – who moves the chairs in your classroom? – gently high on lasagne – I wasn't suddenly beautiful – girls' body issues – the Pink Palace of Party – under the hood – my woman-brain – against all odds – a middle-aged Countdown champ – fetishizing gender – what if they get haemorrhoids – code-red situation – swellings that tumesce from us – friendly yet scientific curiosity

Stats

'The most thorough existing research finds intersex people to constitute an estimated 1.7% of the population, which makes being intersex about as common as having red hair (1%-2%)'.[1]

'17% of boys and 24% of girls were embarrassed/worried about body changes [during puberty]; 8% of boys and 10% of girls were really sad about becoming an adult or considered that something was terribly wrong'.[2]

The issues

By now you might be furiously demanding that I consider biological ideas of gender. 'But it's not in our imagination – boys and girls *do* exist!' you might be shouting. 'But chromosomes!'

Well, sure. But also, this is not as absolute, as defined or as definitive as most people think.

'The belief that *Homo sapiens* is absolutely dimorphic with respect to sex chromosome composition, gonadal structure, hormone levels, and the structure of the internal genital duct systems and external genitalia, derives from the platonic ideal that for each sex there is a single, universally correct developmental pathway and outcome'.[3]

In other words, the idea that people are all born with one set of chromosomes or the other, one set of genitals or the other and one set of hormone levels or the other may well be far from the demonstrable truth for some people. Ask people in the sports science world – sometimes it can be remarkably difficult to 'find' someone's sex by biological markers. This is called 'sex verification', and not only is it harder than it might seem, it's often regarded as humiliating, degrading and against someone's fundamental human rights. There are reports of genital mutilation and serious psychological harm caused by such practices. (More on the particularly tricky issues of gender in sports later.) It's also worth clarifying the use of the terms 'sex' and 'gender' here too: 'The term sex is used mostly to group people into females and males on the basis of an individual's reproductive system and of secondary sexual characteristics. Gender refers to the social roles based on the sex of the person or personal identification of a person's own gender'.[4]

Similarly, we'll look next at the idea of gendered brains and how contentious this issue is. We're dealing here with people's identities, with their lives and their bodies, and it's important to acknowledge the harm and difficulty this can cause. But it's also crucial that we talk about this stuff, in schools and classrooms and staffrooms and homes. So let's proceed sensitively, but honestly.

Finding out the gender. It is such an important part of having or, for some, adopting, a child – the breathless excitement and anticipation of finding out what the child's gender is. I remember looking forward to the scans of both my children with an enormous thrill, not to mention the endless questions of interested friends, family and strangers ....

But is it utter – not to mention harmful – rubbish?

Picture the scene. It's a 'hair colour reveal party'. Family and friends cluster around the cake as a smiling couple cut into it, revealing yellow sweets. A tiny yellow balloon shaped like a golden nightingale sails out of the cake and into the sky. 'Awhhh, a blondie!' coos the throng. 'They'll be so beautiful – but watch out for those brains, probably not the smartest!' Everyone laughs.

You may struggle to see the parallels – the stereotype about blonde people (women) being less intelligent is all about perception, surely? Whereas boys and girls have structurally different brains as well as bodies, which means we *can* say something about the different ways they behave ....

Except that this is very much a problem too.

Just as blonde people (women) who get treated in a certain way because of their blonde hair will adapt and grow into (or defiantly out of) the stereotype, we know that boys' and girls' brains develop in response to their experiences – something known as *neuroplasticity*. Experience shapes our brain – and is still shaping it in the here and now – in ways we are only just beginning to understand. Some (though not all) researchers in this area have suggested that 'neuronal plasticity is a crucial factor in elucidating the question of sex/gender differences in the brain'.[5]

While it is certainly true to say that, even from birth, the brains of girls generally tend to differ in some ways from the brains of boys, neuroplasticity means that studying adult brains and looking for differences doesn't solve the 'born or made' debate, because the two are very much linked.

In the previous chapter we talked about gender identities and social and cultural roles. You may have been thinking, 'But males and females are *different* in their bodies and their brains, and that's just biological fact!'

Of course, there are differences. There are physical differences – although they tend to fall on a spectrum rather than constituting a binary system – and, perhaps, some brain differences. However, saying these differences have a biological cause rather than a social or cultural one is a problem. Researchers don't currently agree on many ideas related to gender in neuroscience, because environment and social cues have an impact from the very start of life – in fact, from before a baby is born (if the parents know its gender, they give it different cues through touch and tone of voice). Knowing this, and knowing that both brains and bodies respond to environmental cues, it is difficult to find out exactly how the 'natural' brain structures of males and females differ, or indeed what this means.

Cordelia Fine, in their 2011 book *Delusions of Gender,* uses the term 'neurosexism'[6] to describe the explanations that various experts have created to describe differences between men's and women's behaviour that are thought to be brain-based. One of the issues they describes is the jump from brain structure to psychological function; the mere fact that there are some differences in one does not necessarily mean there are differences in the other. Even if we can see differences between male and female brains in neuroscientific pictures, the link between (images of) the brain and behaviour is not at all easy to see, and 'social subplots' are at work, even when these mechanisms appear to be observable (in rats at least). Experience alters the brain in ways we are only just beginning to truly investigate.

Explaining differences in the behaviour of boys and girls by simple reference to 'brain difference' is factually incorrect. The idea of inherent 'boyness' or 'girlness' that we invoke when we say, 'Oh, girls are just like that!' or 'Boys will be boys' (the perennial excuse for males treating other people inconsiderately) is a ghoul, a will-o-the-wisp, a fantasy. It's an irrelevant genderevenant, a weirdly spliced sex-difference-heist poltergeist. It's a femininomania, a nobsession, a sleeping dogma we should let lie because so much of it is based on a lie about the way we get a lay.

It's also a leftover from centuries of scientific thinking about gender, largely done by men, in a way that might in itself be sexist. This idea of a 'natural' essence of gender – biological sex as a basic, pervasive and powerful source of human outcomes – has also been used as a way of viewing and conducting research itself, so some of the scientific conclusions reached may well have been based on unconsidered assumptions about gender in the first place, calling them into question. (We have also only quite recently realised that most medical research has been done on men, and this too might present some issues.)[7] In other words, not only the idea of natural fundamentals of gender, but also our ideas *about* that idea, may well be flawed. It's no wonder we're in a period (pun bloody intended) of questioning about gender.

Let's talk about bodies for a second. We know that male and female bodies have some important differences and that many people are born intersex, with some combination of male and female bodily characteristics. However, it takes only a second of thinking to realise the enormous variety of bodies in humanity, and the next thought might be that these differences often go across, rather than with, the grain of gender. All genders can be fat or not fat, tall or not tall, muscular or not muscular, hairy or not hairy and can have a disability or not – and all these characteristics are spectra, not binaries. Some of them we consider it rude or offensive to classify by in some situations. Some carry incorrect or even downright harmful associations – that fat people can't be strong, that hairy people can't be feminine (um, hello gorgeous Lettie in *The Greatest Showman*), that tall people must be leaders – but gendering a body can be particularly harmful.

When you meet a person for the first time and you look at their face and body, you will often scan for gender first. Then come the associations:

Because she's female, she …

Because he's male, he …

Or even:

I can't place this person's gender and it's making me uncomfortable.

When we don't challenge gendered assumptions about bodies, we often betray fear of the unknown or unfamiliar.

Imagine a powerful, muscled woman or a gorgeous, flower-delicate man. Imagine a person whose gender is not immediately evident from their body. How do you feel about that? What if they were one of your pupils and you were meeting them for the first time?

In the TV show *It's Always Sunny in Philadelphia*, we are told that men have four acceptable body types: *skinny ripped, jacked ripped, dad bod* and *fat if you're funny*. Women have just one (and it's pretty aspirational): *skinny with big tits*. If you're not familiar with the show, it's diabolical satire, with some hard-hitting truths delivered right to the jugular. It's an excellent point – we need more body discourses for everyone. Women don't 'deserve' to be invisible if they aren't skinny with big tits. Neither do they 'deserve' to be grabbed, harassed or commented on. Bodies that aren't gendered may still function in gendered ways – erections and periods can be hard to ignore – but they can be freer to do all kinds of wonderful things they like, to explore and to interact. Often, not gendering bodies means we can take some of the pesky sexual stuff out of interactions where it is not needed, too (more on that in later chapters on relationships and sexualities).

When we teach children at school only about 'their' own gender's body, we are entrenching some weird stuff. We are also doing them a serious disservice when we assume they don't 'need to know' about penises or periods because (we assume) it is not something they will experience first-hand. I have had the benefit of living and working with men who understand clitorises and periods and breasts, and it has helped take the sting and the weirdness out of conversations about those things. But mostly, my body and your body are very similar and very much equally important.

Speaking of periods, they are one area of 'difference' that it is very much worth considering and demystifying.

Periods of questioning

If you are a uterus-owner with periods, how do they affect your life? If not, how might they?

'How was your period today?'

'Are you in pain right now?'

'Can I get you anything to help with your period?'

Have you ever asked these questions? I am surrounded by wonderful, caring men and non-men who regularly have these conversations with me. But many people don't. Many people see period issues as too dirty, embarrassing, shameful or disgusting to talk about. My youngest daughter shared some of her worries recently: 'People will try to embarrass me for having a period.' 'How will I hide my sanitary towels?' Hide them from whom? Why?

Recently, the public dialogue around periods has started to open up a crack. (No apologies, plenty more where that came from. The discussion has started to flow a little. Ha!) From menstruating athletes to tampon taxes, we are talking about periods a little more. But who is talking? Is it, as I suspect, still (some) women having these conversations, while others smile benignly and zone out or, worse, display disgust and revulsion and ask us to take it elsewhere? (It is worth noting here that not just women have periods, and not all women have them, obviously.)

I'm going to speak to those who haven't ever had a period now. Please, please don't zone out or disappear – this is for you.

Go back in time to your 11-year-old self. You are gauche and insecure; friends and relationships largely dominate your life. School is a social testing-ground. Your body, taken for granted for so long to be reliable when you need it, begins to betray you. Hair sprouts; parts enlarge; you morph daily and alarmingly. Embarrassment is a hot glow that pools around almost everything you do. You want so badly to be noticed, but also to be invisible.

So far, so genderless. Now add pain, the kind of pain you haven't felt before because it is neither injury nor illness. It is not the kind of pain that adults give you much sympathy for. There is no upside to this pain – no invalid treatment, no daytime TV and staying at home, no ice cream and indulgence. It is not the kind of pain that starts with a bang and slowly heals. It is the kind that lasts and lasts, that seems endless and wanes and then strikes again with no regular pattern. It is the kind of pain that inconveniences and embarrasses everyone around you and makes you an inconvenience and an embarrassment. Sometimes it brings you to your knees, sobbing; sometimes it is so distracting you cannot concentrate on anything else for days. Adults soon tire of reassuring you. It is not going away. It cannot be cured, and it must be endured.

With the pain comes the steady drip, drip, drip of bodily fluid. Like snot, earwax or vomit, it causes people to recoil in disgust, and you are required to remove it from sight immediately. If left, it congeals, crusts and smells. The fluid is red or brown and eye-catchingly obvious when-ever it leaks. The flow of it is unpredictable and difficult to anticipate, sometimes flooding with no warning. You are pierced with embarrass-ment that others might detect a stain or a smell. You are paranoid that you haven't been careful enough to cover it up. You cannot even tell people what is the matter, when they ask. If you speak its name, they look shocked and uncomfortable, and you know you have done something wrong.

This is our contemporary world in 2019. We have hardly moved on in decades.

I have had periods for 21 years of my life. By my calculation, I have spent around three and a half to four years' worth of time having a period. For roughly half of that time, I probably haven't noticed it too much – just a quick extra trip to the loo to change a tampon, a brief twinge every now and then, a noticeable temperature change in my body. For the rest – nearly two years – I have been doubled over and howling in private, grim and tight-lipped and on the verge of tears in public.

At the very least, we need to be able to talk about this. When some-one asks me if I'm ok, I need to be able to say, 'No, I'm not ok. I'm having a particularly brutal period'.

Which is what I do say, now. And note the reactions. Some people – kind, thoughtful, compassionate – swallow down their surprise, commiserate or give practical help. Many, many others are shocked and disquieted and even offended. They are not awful people; it's just that we don't know how to form a dialogue around periods in public, yet. Here are some handy suggestions from me:

- If you see someone (not just women get periods) clutching a hot water bottle or bent over in pain, ask them actively if they're having an awful period. Say the word 'period'.

- If you are the person above, and someone asks you what is wrong, say the word 'period'. Use an adjective if, like me, you feel you might not be taken seriously enough. 'Brutal, appalling, painful, savage and remorseless' are all nice and clear.

- If you use tampons, a menstrual cup or sanitary pads, don't hide them. If you see one, don't flinch or laugh or remark on it.

- If you're a parent or a teacher, talk to children – girls and boys and others – about periods. Normalise the topic and say the words clearly. Set a precedent for allowing children dealing with a period to have a hot water bottle, a blanket and/or a more comfortable chair if they need it. Make compassion more important than embarrassment in your reaction.

- Ask for a box of free sanitary products to be placed in your toilets at your place of work. Not in a drawer, or hidden in a cupboard, but arranged prettily in a basket and displayed prominently.

A period is – literally – a wound that never heals. For those who have never had one, I can understand the revulsion and embarrassment, the desire to ignore them and sanitise them and make them go away. But this reaction simply makes the wound a psychological one too. By reacting in this manner, we are telling those who are having periods that their pain and their fear are not important. We are telling them – some of them 8- and 9-year-olds – that they must prioritise being compliant and polite over getting help when they need it. Bleed out in the corner if you must, but do it quietly, please.

All bodies are important

'Students commonly report cases of male students exclusively being asked to undertake tasks involving strength, such as moving desks and chairs or sporting equipment. Female students frequently report that they ... dislike being perceived as weaker than the male students.'[8] Does this sound like your classroom? Are you making some unwarranted assumptions about who is strong and who is weak based on gender? When we look at deficiency models of bodies, through gender or otherwise, we are failing to help our pupils use and celebrate their bodies, and we are encouraging shame and limitation. From here, it is a small step for pupils with various disabilities to consider themselves weak, different and less than whole, too.

Fat positivity

We are living at a time where being fat or obese is increasingly prevalent, and these issues affect our pupils often. We may struggle, as teachers, to tread the line between criticising parents and encouraging pupils to be safe and healthy. Fat is so often a gendered issue, with different discourses surrounding ideas of fat among boys and girls, men and women, and other, non-binary folks. Susie Orbach, author of *Fat Is a Feminist Issue*, describes the relationship between women and food like this:

> Emotionally schooled to see our value as both sexual beings for others and midwives to their desires, we found ourselves often depleted and empty, and caught up in a kind of compulsive giving. Eating became our source of soothing. We stopped our mouths with food [instead of] ... words.[9]

For so long, overeating, undereating and just plain focusing on eating have been seen as a 'women's' issue, because women's bodies were under so much more scrutiny. Also because, as Caitlin Moran rightly says, women and girls who carry a heavy burden of caring for others can't afford to be wasted on drink or drugs, but they can still perform their responsibilities gently high on too much lasagne. Eating is the carer's drug of choice, and after we sadly eat – or don't – and find our quiet buzz, female bodies are so often judged and humiliated by that same society that calls violent alcoholic men 'tortured creative geniuses'.

Many studies have found results similar to this: 'Not only were girls more dissatisfied with their body, but they were more active in attempts to become and/or remain "thin".... [G]irls presented greater gaps between current body figure and perceived ideal figure.'[10]

Often, people comment that more boys and men nowadays are doing 'beauty work' – including the emotional labour of scrutinising their own weight and bodies, and that this is a marker of equality. Is it? Although being in control of our bodies and our health is important, the sense of obsession and fragility that comes with weight-watching often teeters on the brink, or downright drops into the chasm, of serious mental illness. Internalising judgement, failure and a subsequently stormy relationship with our own bodies is not good for physical or mental health.

If you've ever been on a serious diet or fitness regime and lost a great deal of weight, you may recognise the following sentiment: 'I was a lot slimmer, but I realised I wasn't a better person, I wasn't suddenly beautiful, I wasn't suddenly amazing. I was still the same person, but a lot less happy.'[11] We have been sold a lie about bodies that slim bodies are healthier, that slim people are happier, that fat people are greedy and disgusting and contemptuous and even subhuman. Some people spend their lives on hold, waiting to be that thin, fit, successful person that they feel is inside them, just waiting to be liberated from the fat prison that's holding them back. They are constantly trying to change their bodies to fit society, instead of the other way around.

Do you recognise some of these ideas?
Do you teach or work with anyone fat?
How do you feel about them?
How do you feel about your own body?

'But fat is bad!' you may be thinking. 'Obese children are unhappy and unhealthy!' Actually, the evidence surrounding fat and health assessment – for example, the use of BMI (Body Mass Index) as a 'measure' of good health – is surprisingly controversial. 'We have a problem in obesity research—clinical trials continue to prioritise weight loss as a primary outcome and rarely consider patients' experience, quality of life, or adverse events.' In this research paper, a patient is quoted who challenged simplistic views of weight loss; they concluded, 'It is inaccurate to assume that weight loss always means an improvement in health, even for someone with obesity.'[12] Fat positivity, without ignoring obesity and health issues, is an important principle for us to consider. Hating our bodies – these idiosyncratic fleshy bubbles we are encased in, for better or worse – is no way for anyone to live.

Girls' body issues are not confined to girls

While it is true that body/mind disorders are currently more prevalent among girls than boys, it is crucial that we, as teachers, understand that body issues can and do affect everyone. Anorexia, bulimia and body dis-morphic disorder (a mental health condition wherein a person spends a lot of time worrying about flaws in their appearance which are often unnotice-able to others) affect boys, girls and non-binary pupils too.[13] If we know this, we can watch for signs and symptoms in all pupils. Some helpful facts:

Anorexia is an irrational fear of food, as well as extreme, life-threatening weight loss caused by not eating enough. Bulimia is eating a large amount of food over a very short time (binge eating) and then ridding your body of the extra food (purging) by making yourself vomit.

Signs of eating or body disorder may include:

- Refusing to eat around other people
- Being very critical about one's weight and body shape
- Cutting food in small pieces and/or rearranging it on the plate in an effort to avoid ingesting it
- Straightforward refusal to eat
- Feeling guilty and ashamed, and behaving secretively
- Disappearing into the toilet after a meal
- Excessive exercise
- Sore throat from being sick
- Bloating or stomach pain
- Mood changes – feeling very tense or anxious, for example
- Use of laxatives, diuretics, diet pills, and other methods that may aid weight loss
- Severe muscle loss, thinning hair, brittle nails, extreme sensitivity to cold, and yellow, dry skin
- Cessation of menstrual periods

What needs to change

We emphatically need to stop explaining (or justifying) most behaviour on the grounds of the biology of gender. Once we understand that the effects of environment and biology are difficult to disentangle – and that there is no sound neuroscientific consensus that boys and girls (and others) learn differently – this frees us as teachers to stop focusing on gender. The benign end of this argument is that we have been preventing our pupils from being accepted, known and judged as themselves – not as a boy or a girl or a non-binary person. The malignant end is that we have been explaining away rape culture, violence and harassment in boys, and frozen compliance, acceptance of being ignored or responsibility for emotional labour in girls, as 'natural' for 'their gender'. I can tell you, there's nothing in my brain that makes me better at making you coffee, sir, just as there is nothing in yours that makes you worse at listening if I tell you I don't want you to touch me. Once we are freed from the 'boys will be boys and girls will be girls' paradigm, we can expect better of all our pupils (and our colleagues, and ourselves).

There is good research to suggest that, at least in the West, schools are masculinity- and femininity-making institutions[14]; that we are supercharging those tired old stereotypes until our pupils are so pumped up on them that they struggle to create different stories for themselves. I want to see girls who feel strong enough and brave enough to lift weights, to walk on their hands, to be as tall and wide and big as they want. I want to see boys who feel confident enough to be gorgeous, to strut around, to be as gentle and loving and creative as they please. I want to see my pupils delighting in their bodies and what they can do without worrying about their gender at all, even for a second.

We also need to use clear and better language to refer to our bodies, particularly our genitalia or areas we might feel shameful about.

They're just words.

They're just genitals.

However, hang around a primary school or other public place for long enough and you'll hear plenty of parents and children using 'willy', 'winky', 'front bottom' or 'foof', giggling or blushing or shushing (in-)appropriately.

I still meet 16-year-olds who don't know how to use a tampon, who do not realise that their urethra is a different tube/hole from the entrance to their vagina, who think they can have instant anal sex without lubrication or who believe liking anal stimulation makes you gay. I know this because I talk to them about these issues, and the more you do this, the more you realise how pent-up their questions are, how desperate they are to come to terms with sexual attraction, how interested in pleasure they are but how deeply ashamed and worried they are about that fact, partly because they lack the vocabulary. This has to stop.

Let's start, very simply, by calling it a 'vagina'.

(Although, technically, of course, it's a 'vulva'. One battle at a time.)

We also need to normalise 'clitoris'. So many people I meet seem to think that going into detail (as if 'clitoris' were unimportant!) about genitals perfectly equates to actual paedophilia. I have no idea why. Children should know the correct words for their bodies – they should also be washing themselves properly, which takes more than a rudimentary knowledge of 'under the hood' of their pant-parts. Will this make them fetishize genitals? It seems unlikely. It seems particularly unlikely that they could possibly fetishize them more than contemporary society does, and that's partly due to the fact that they get hidden behind a huge secret exciting door marked 'adulthood'.

The strongest counterarguments and why they're wrong

- 'Male and female brains are just different – they have different strengths and weaknesses, and that's ok'.

- 'But girls' and boys' bodies are so different! It means we should split them off for some things, to protect girls' bodies from the boys' aggressiveness'.

- 'Being fat is unhealthy and unattractive and girls should worry about it; they won't get a boyfriend otherwise'.

- 'Teaching boys about girls' bodies, and girls about boy's bodies, is weird and unnecessary, and it will lead to their having sexual contact earlier than we'd like'.

The 'brains are gendered' thing is controversial and may well prove impossible to prove. Dr. Gina Rippon, in *No More Boys and Girls*, states, 'Structurally, there appear to be very very few differences, which is quite a surprise to a lot of people who have assumed for thousands of years that because males and females are different, their brains are different.' She explains that the brain is not fixed; it's mouldable, plastic. Its development is very much entangled with experiences. The world instantly plunging it into a tsunami of pink and blue causes all kinds of structural changes we can't completely account for or explain in the detail that would be needed to definitely prove brains are inherently one way or a different way. And even if we could, so what?

Even if we had good scientific evidence that your man-brain was wired better for mathematics than my woman-brain, what then? Would you feel okay with telling me to give up my dream of becoming a mathematician and discovering (inventing) new mathematics, because other people might have more 'natural' advantages in my subject? Well, guess what? People have 'natural' advantages all the time. Some people grow up with a swimming pool, some have access to thousands of books. Some get to watch their mother operate on other people's brains, or their father make award-winning cakes. Those things affect their brains and their minds and often their bodies, too. The story of the 'against all odds' humans who find a way to do the thing they love will never grow old, because so many people just become more resolute when they find obstacles in their way. It's pretty much every film ever. But there's a difference between obstacles that come up as a result of chaotic differences – social and geographical discrepancies, types of bodily (dis)ability, economic disparities (though you may disagree with this on the basis of attacking capitalism, and that's acceptable to me) – and completely unnecessary obstacles that occur because unthinking people repeat thoughtless thoughts.

'Girls can't throw'.

'Boys are just stronger'.

'Are you sure that's for people like you?'

'She'll find that harder than he will'.

'He shouldn't do that'.

Tradition, it has been said, is 'the democracy of the dead'.[15] It's all too often a legacy that constrains our identities, and it is one that we don't notice or choose to question until so very late. No matter how much we may think that we are a complete, finished person, and that our identity is consistent, we are building and rebuilding our identity constantly. It is work that is never done. This is terrifying – we are only as honest as our last lie, perhaps – but also truly liberating. Were you terrible at PE at school? You can become a marathon runner in your forties, if you like. Did you hate maths in your misspent youth? You can be a middle-aged Countdown champ. Did you always think you just weren't creative? Here's a secret: You can take up candle-making, crocheting, metal sculpture, writing poetry or making your own clothes whenever you want. You are not defined by who you were yesterday, apart from the expectations of others and your particular circumstances (for example, it is important to acknowledge that poverty, abusive relationships and oppression are extremely confining). Break out of your male-ness or your female-ness and do something unexpected.

If we are performing and refining our identity, what does this mean about gender and sexuality?

Neither is part of a dichotomy. Both are a spectrum, upon which we may dance about as gaily as we please.

Imagine that.

Bodies are indeed different, but gender isn't as important as we might think. I often wonder whether an extra-terrestrial being might think we are somewhat fetishizing gender. Certainly, I feel as if people gender my brain and body much more than I would like. 'But Lucy!' you might be saying, 'You do that to yourself! You are always harping on about feminism and women's issues.' Indeed, sir, I am. (Although 'women's issues' are for everyone.) And these are the times we live in – the paradox of being female is that I am at once sighing with exasperation that everyone else seems to care so much about gender, and yes, also emphasising it myself in some ways while trying to fight the good fight. But I am sure of one thing. I know that the generations we are raising now are better at thinking about gender in a more nuanced, relaxed manner, and I wholeheartedly want to support this thinking with the best-informed teachers we can manage to provide. The evidence is out there to tell us that gendering bodies and brains in stereotypical fashion is harmful – we just need to use that evidence to inform our thinking.

'A well-established body of evidence confirms the importance of education – and secondary education in particular – in changing the damaging norms that shape, for example, the roles played by women and men in the home and community, women's work outside the home, child marriage and gender-based violence,'[16] says ALIGN, a global community of researchers on gender equality. UNESCO agrees: 'Creating a more inclusive, just and equitable world – the essence of sustainable development – means ensuring that all men and women, all boys and girls, can lead empowered and dignified lives. Ensuring an inclusive and gender-equitable education of good quality is a key way to achieve this goal.'[17]

A difficult relationship with one's body (and mind) is something we need to watch out for, in all genders. I hope I don't need to spend too much time debunking the myth that girls 'should' be obsessed with their bodies and their weight, and that this is to prepare them to be ready to meet the male gaze at any time. It is not 'normal' for girls to feel constantly focused on their body or face or to think they are fat all their lives. In one study, 80% of 10-year-old girls thought they were too fat; in another, 58% of the same age groups had been called 'too fat' by someone else, and this actually increased the likelihood of their becoming obese by age 19. As for boys, studies show that they are also obsessing about their weight, this time often focused on how muscular they are, but that this preoccupation may present as depression, binge drinking or drug-taking.[18] These are not 'different issues' – all involve a desperate attempt to reconcile the body they're in with the one they have been sold – but they are probably presenting differently sometimes because of social and cultural limitations.

We also have good evidence that 'LGBTQ+ people face unique challenges that may put them at greater risk of developing an eating disorder. Research shows that, beginning as early as 12, gay, lesbian, and bisexual teens may be at higher risk of binge-eating and purging than heterosexual peers'.[19] We need to make sure that those whose bodies may be giving them a struggle already are particularly supported. We also need to help them see that it's the perception of others that is the problem, not their bodies themselves.

I hope I don't need to remind teachers that their own body image and way of relating to their physical selves can have a powerful effect on young people. If you are suffering from issues in this area, please go to a therapist. Please, please, do not hate your body or punish yourself or unthinkingly demonstrate to pupils that it's ok to do that. We all need help and support loving our bodies more, and in the classroom it's important that we see a range of healthy bodies – differently abled, different weights, different skin tones and different gender identities. You are an important part of that richness.

We need to teach all genders about bodies of all genders. Some of the best and most useful conversations about periods in my house have involved – gosh darn it! – a man. One reason why is that he asked good questions. Another is that his sympathy, understanding and warmth over issues of pain and mess helped us all get along a little better in the same house. That kind of empathy between people whose bodies might work slightly differently could actually change the world. It also encourages conversations about other kinds of difference, like colostomy bags and breathing tubes and missing limbs and body hair and haemorrhoids. 'But – YUCK!' you might be thinking. 'Bodies are disgusting! I don't want my children talking about *haemorrhoids*!' But, I ask you, what if they *get* haemorrhoids? (Pretty likely.)[20]

Well, you might say, I'll talk to them about it *then* ....

I'll say it: Bodies are weird. Mine produces a particular kind of bloody gunk for about 7 days in every 25. If you lived with me, there's a good chance you'd find some of it in the plughole, on the inside of the toilet rim or smeared up the wall on occasion. Despite being quite the independent feminist, I might well call you for help if I got in a 'code-red situation'. I might also call for help if I got stuck in a slightly damp sports bra, which seems to be the worst voluntary prison a person can find themselves in. These are 'healthy' bodies. People also get sick and injured every day; some of them are so ill they die, and all of these processes can involve some serious mess and difficulty. How do we try to treat them with dignity, and how do we maintain our own dignity in such situations?

We teach children about bodies. All kinds of bodies, not just the ones we expect them to be in (bodies change, sometimes frighteningly quickly). Learning about erections and wet dreams helped me understand many things beyond the hydraulics of being a penis-owner; it helped me empathise with some of the ways sexual arousal might affect such a person, and it helped me see beyond my own point of view. In the same way, finding out that another person can bend their thumbs back, has a voice box for speaking or cannot see colour is endlessly fascinating to children; they will be talking about it without us if not with us. Why not guide the conversation in a helpful and empathetic direction?

We also need to teach in more detail about bodies, full stop, of course. It is fairly common to meet young women who don't understand where their urine hole is with respect to their vulva, or young men who think that clitoral stimulation is simply an added extra to sex (many, many women can literally not orgasm without it).[21]

We are made to feel that puberty is a time of embarrassment and shame, that these swellings that tumesce from us and hairs that sprout from us and liquids that pour from us are to be covered up with a squirm and a cringe. Why? We are like the unfurling buds of spring, the cracking earth after rain, the warm swollen bulbs of flowers in sunshine. We could not hide them, in any case. These feelings of shame need not be learned in school. If we approach our own and others' bodies with a friendly yet scientific curiosity, we can learn a paradigm that is non-sexual without being wholly clinical. Let's also teach children the correct medical terms for their bodies and others', so they can clearly communicate pain and consent (and joy) when they need to.

The argument that learning about others' bodies will encourage sexual ways of knowing them is easily exploded. Research suggests that teaching kids about sex does not make them have more sex or have sex at a younger age.[22] It is likely to decrease their risk of teenage pregnancy, if anything. It also helps to prevent sexual violence.[23]

Now/later

Now: I dare you to watch any TV show from, or set in, the fifties or sixties. Note the way that women and men's brains and bodies are referred to. (I recommend *Mad Men* or *I Dream of Jeannie*.)

Later: Begin your lessons with an 'assumption splurge'. That is, ask everyone in the room (including adults) to talk about their assumptions of who does and doesn't study that subject. Who is our archetype or stereotype for maths, French, drama, PE, or chemistry? Why? Ask the students to talk about times when they felt unwelcome in that subject, and why. If you can, invite someone who breaks that stereotype to talk to your class about their work.

Put up a range of images of bodies, and talk to pupils about strength, health, (dis)ability, fat and gender in the

(*continued*)

Now/later (*continued*)

context of our relationship with our bodies. Look at role models such as Jessamyn Stanley, Mama Cāx, Angel Giuffria, Kelvin Davis and Rebekah Taussig.

Find out whether your school policy on sex education or biology lessons related to puberty suggests segregating pupils by gender. If so, ask why.

Graham says

It still annoys me when I encounter people who say that regardless of the messages children receive, and regardless of what we do, boys and girls will always be different! I even met one of my childhood heroes at a recent conference after an amazing day of positive messages on gender. Sadly, my childhood hero threw this all out of the window by saying that boys' and girls', and women's and men's, brains are different, and it doesn't matter what we do. What made it worse was that when they were challenged and asked for evidence, they related some experiment from decades ago involving adult men and women drawing a bike. Because women were less likely to draw gears and machinery, they were considered less mechanically minded – and therefore less likely to be equipped to do jobs where things needed fixing. This conclusion is not warranted, of course, because ideas, thoughts and opinions in adults are part of a complex pattern of socialisation and enculturation. Let's just say that person wasn't the most popular speaker that day! Dr. Gina Rippon does much to debunk the obsolete theory in her recent book *The Gendered Brain*.[24] Go Gina!

It is important that we show our children a range of body types and different genders in different roles; we want our children to grow up with the idea that regardless of body shape, looks, blemishes, personalities, likes and dislikes, everybody is different, but everybody is awesome in their own way. The new 'She-Ra' cartoon does this brilliantly, showing heroes with a range of body types, relationships, personalities and problems to overcome (although the social media backlash at the change of look for She-Ra was pretty vociferous to start with, and that makes me sad).

So, in your classroom look at displays, posters, books and images. Are they showing a range of people? Do you have people of all shapes, sizes, colours, genders and so on? If not, I urge you to make changes, because children need to see variety as the norm. One of the most painful discoveries I have ever made was to find that two of the girls in my class perceived themselves as ugly. How can anyone 7 or 8 years of age have this perception of themselves? Messages from magazines, TV shows, the internet, films and books should not influence our children this much – but they do, and we need to do what we can as educators and human beings to counteract these messages.

Tl;dr

There is no clear research consensus as to how, exactly, brains might be 'gendered' – except that it is difficult, and perhaps impossible, to disentangle social, cultural and psychological effects of experience on brain structure. Bodies have some sex differences, but there are people born intersex, and there are those who feel that their gender is not the same as their sex, and we should be mindful of the way our gendering of others can be harmful and unnecessary. We may wish to reconsider many topics that we have approached as just 'for' boys or girls, or that we have traditionally taught in gender segregated groups. We all need help loving and accepting our bodies more – let's talk about them clearly and without shame.

References

1. Intersex Campaign for Equality. *How common is intersex? An explanation of the stats.* (n.d.). Retrieved April 14, 2019, from https://www.intersexequality.com/how-common-is-intersex-in-humans/
2. *Global early adolescent study.* (2018). Retrieved April 14, 2019, from Global Early Adolescent Study website: https://www.geastudy.org/
3. Blackless, M., Charuvastra, A., Derryck, A., Fausto-Sterling, A., Lauzanne, K., & Lee, E. (2000). How sexually dimorphic are we? Review and synthesis. *American Journal of Human Biology, 12*(2), 151–166.

4. Jäncke, L. (2018). Sex/gender differences in cognition, neurophysiology, and neuroanatomy. *F1000Research*, *7*. https://doi.org/10.12688/f1000research.13917.1
5. Kaiser, A., Haller, S., Schmitz, S., & Nitsch, C. (2009). On sex/gender related similarities and differences in fMRI language research. *Brain Research Reviews*, *61*(2), 49–59.
6. Fine, C. (2011). *Delusions of Gender: The Real Science behind Sex Differences (Repr)*. London, England: Icon Books.
7. Dresser, R. (1992). Wanted: single, white male for medical research. *The Hastings Center Report*, *22*(1), 24–29. https://doi.org/10.2307/3562720.
8. National Education Union/Feminista. (2019). *Sexism in schools*. Retrieved April 13, 2019, from NEU website: https://neu.org.uk/advice/sexism-schools
9. The Guardian. (2018). *Forty years since Fat Is a Feminist Issue*. Society. Retrieved April 19, 2019, from https://www.theguardian.com/society/2018/jun/24/forty-years-since-fat-is-a-feminist-issue
10. Golan, M., Hagay, N., & Tamir, S. (2014). Gender related differences in response to "In favor of myself" wellness program to enhance positive self & body image among adolescents. *PLoS ONE*, *9*(3). https://doi.org/10.1371/journal.pone.0091778
11. *Why we're proud of our fat bodies*. (2018). Retrieved April 19, 2019, from BBC News website: https://www.bbc.co.uk/news/resources/idt-sh/why_we_are_proud_of_our_fat_bodies
12. Sturgiss, E., Jay, M., Campbell-Scherer, D., & van Weel, C. (2017). Challenging assumptions in obesity research. *BMJ*, *359*, j5303. https://doi.org/10.1136/bmj.j5303
13. Phillips, K. A., & Diaz, S. F. (1997). Gender differences in body dysmorphic disorder. *The Journal of Nervous and Mental Disease*, *185*(9), 570.
14. Kessler, S., Ashenden, D. J., Connell, R. W., & Dowsett, G. W. (1985). Gender relations in secondary schooling. *Sociology of Education*, *58*(1), 34–48. https://doi.org/10.2307/2112539
15. Chesterton, G. K. (1908). *Orthodoxy*.
16. Align Platform. (n.d.). *Education and gender norms*. Retrieved April 19, 2019, from https://www.alignplatform.org/education
17. UNESCO. (2018). *Gender review: Meeting our commitments to gender equality in education*. Retrieved from http://unesdoc.unesco.org/images/0026/002615/261593E.pdf
18. Field, A. E., Sonneville, K. R., Crosby, R. D., Swanson, S. A., Eddy, K. T., Camargo, C. A., … Micali, N. (2014). Prospective associations of concerns about physique and the development of obesity, binge drinking, and drug use among adolescent boys and young adult men. *JAMA Pediatrics*, *168*(1), 34–39. https://doi.org/10.1001/jamapediatrics.2013.2915
19. *Eating disorders in LGBTQ+ populations*. (2017, February 25). Retrieved April 20, 2019, from National Eating Disorders Association website: https://www.nationaleatingdisorders.org/learn/general-information/lgbtq

20. Lorenzo-Rivero, S. (2009). Hemorrhoids: Diagnosis and current management. *The American Surgeon, 75*(8), 635–642.
21. Puppo, V., & Puppo, G. (2015). Anatomy of sex: Revision of the new anatomical terms used for the clitoris and the female orgasm by sexologists. *Clinical Anatomy, 28*(3), 293–304. https://doi.org/10.1002/ca.22471
22. Kohler, P. K., Manhart, L. E., & Lafferty, W. E. (2008). Abstinence-only and comprehensive sex education and the initiation of sexual activity and teen pregnancy. *The Journal of Adolescent Health: Official Publication of the Society for Adolescent Medicine, 42*(4), 344–351. https://doi.org/10.1016/j.jadohealth.2007.08.026
23. Raphael, D. A. (2015). The effect of sexual education on sexual assault prevention. *Beijing +20: Violence Against Women CEDAW: Articles 6, 10 - Trafficking, Education.*
24. Rippon, G. (2019). *The Gendered Brain: The New Neuroscience That Shatters the Myth of the Fema le Brain.* London, England: The Bodley Head.

Expert view: gender from an early age

Jayne Osgood

In 2018 Deanne Carson, an expert in sexuality, was the subject of a Twitter storm following a TV interview she gave on ABC News about the issue of children's consent. Her insistence that children, at the youngest of ages, should be invited to participate in developing 'cultures of consent' was viciously ridiculed.[1] She suggested that nappy changing is an intimate moment requiring respect and care, that a dialogue with babies is essential and that modelling conversations about consent can never start too young.

In research I have undertaken about the benefits of music in the early years,[2] mothers have reported that playing music to their unborn child has provided an important means to connect and that, once in the world, children are soothed or stimulated by the music and sounds they encountered in utero. Playing music, reading stories and generally chatting to babies in the womb, from around the second trimester onwards once babies develop the capacity to hear, underline the importance of nurturing a connection from the earliest stages. This is generally viewed positively, and yet, bizarrely, the very idea of talking to babies throughout an intimate moment such as a nappy change is met with derision. Engaging in respectful dialogue with the very youngest of children should be recognised as crucial to their well-being and to the sense they come to make of themselves and their rights. To the majority of early childhood educators and researchers, this is not 'lefty lunacy' but rather a perfectly reasonable means to explore ideas about children as people with rights, starting in babyhood.

Issues of touch and consent in early childhood contexts have long generated anxiety in the public psyche. But there is much to be learned from a long tradition of feminist research on the topic. Deborah Price, senior lecturer at the University of Brighton, has written extensively over the past 40 years on this topic, offering practical guidance about how to address gender diversity and sexuality in the early years. She is among many researchers in the field of early childhood to argue that children should be understood as individuals with rights, who must be listened to and respected.

Of course, this is not to suggest that children do not benefit from the comforts offered by clear boundaries, but alongside this, as citizens with rights, children should become actively engaged in identifying, negotiating and setting those boundaries. Adult–child relationships, as suggested by Deb Albon and Rachel Rosen,[3] must be negotiated – they are not a given. The oversimplified paradigm of thinking that the adult always knows everything, including what is best for the child, is rightly being questioned.

Child-centred approaches to both early years education and parenting over the past couple of decades are challenging ideas about how children should be treated, nurtured and educated. The degree to which individual early years settings and parents embrace a child-centred approach varies depending upon the underpinning values, beliefs and philosophies that these institutions and adults adhere to. However, the official line, as articulated within the Early Years Foundation Stage Curriculum, and related guidance on supporting the development and well-being of young children, espouses child-centred approaches. There is a wealth of international evidence and policy, spanning decades, that promotes child-centred practices (e.g., the Anti-Bias Education movement and the Organisation for Economic Co-operation and Development [OECD]). In many senses the early years are a unique time when children are developing at an astonishing rate, and recognising the ways in which they make sense of themselves and the worlds in which they are located is a really important opportunity for adults to re-evaluate their ideas about rights and boundaries.

Nursery contexts offer the space and opportunity to tell different stories than just 'adults know best' – to cultivate other narratives and experiences in early childhood that recognise that children are knowing subjects, exhibiting incredibly interesting ways of being in and experiencing the world around them. Adults have an enormous amount to learn (and unlearn and relearn) from being with children and taking them seriously.

By observing the youngest of children very closely, it is possible to discern that gender is not fixed, and that ideas about diversity, consent, what is 'normal' or deviant are always in the process of being formed and then changing again. Through my research over the past 20 years, I have been profoundly struck by the ways in which gender and ideas about sexuality are often much freer in early childhood than at later points in childhood. Very young children are – when allowed – routinely experimenting with ideas about gender (from dress-up, to role-play, through choice of toys, and peer-group formations and fallouts[2,4,5]). When this fluidity and curiosity are supported, early childhood is a time, and nurseries are places, where good equality and diversity practices can provide wholly inclusive experiences for all children. Cultivating the 'culture of consent' promoted by Carson and generating acceptance of diversity is a core part of the project for families and early years settings.

Practically, there is a great deal that early childhood providers and families can do. The environments in which children spend much of their formative years, i.e., the nursery and the home, are crucially important. We should endeavour to ensure that these spaces reflect diversity and a critical engagement with the wider world. Price (2017) recommends an 'equalities audit' of the play and learning environment, an idea that holds true for the family home also. What do children see when they look at the environment? Are there things that reinforce gender stereotyping? What aspects are neutral? What is there that might offer opportunities for questions and discussion?[6]

Go into any nursery, and you will most likely be confronted with bright, eye-catching images on the walls. Similarly, many fridge doors are adorned with the latest artwork of the youngest members of the family. There is a great opportunity here to engage children in the production of images and artwork that says something about them, their likes and dislikes, and about their families and the wider world and lives of families that might not be so familiar (especially where there is not much diversity in the nursery community or the local neighbourhood). Ensuring that wall displays actively involve the ideas and activities of children and speak to families in ways that generate curiosity and conversation is the goal.

For example, a display that illustrates boys and girls engaged in non-stereotypical activities (e.g., girls and boys constructing together, girls playing football, boys washing up and cooking) will send powerful messages and also provide a talking point for staff, families and children. As simple as this sounds, it is an effective means to think deeply about what we do with children, and it can generate ideas about what is possible for girls and boys, women and men. It also provides opportunities to recognise gender as fluid and non-binary. Price (2017) also highlights the importance of acknowledging and celebrating non-normative and diverse family formations.[6] It is vitally important that children's curiosity about diversity and difference be satisfied through effective pedagogical practices and meaningful discussions.[4,7]

Returning to nappy changing, the toilet area provides another crucial space and opportunity to address issues of gender. Along with cultivating cultures of consent and respecting the rights of very young children by engaging them in dialogue about what is happening throughout the nappy change, ensuring privacy and a pleasant environment is important. But it is often in and around the toilet area within nurseries that ideas about gender conformity emerge – with segregated toilets and narrow expectations (often parental) about the suitability of specific staff to change nappies. Research with and about male nursery workers[8–10] underlines the persistence of problematic stereotypes about men in childcare and the implications of this for recruitment and retention. Male workers are often viewed with suspicion and, as a consequence, are routinely discriminated against.

The government has long called for an increase in men in the early years workforce[11] to provide role models and convey a better sense of gender equality, but the proportion of men remains tiny (the 2018 statistics reveal that only 2% of the workforce is male).[12] The same story is widely replicated across the globe. Addressing the shortage of men in the early years and promoting the more hands-on engagement of fathers in all aspects of parenting – including nappy changing – is desperately needed, but it is chronically undermined by conservative and regressive ideas about what men can and can't, should and shouldn't, do in the care and nurturance of young children.

Another important issue to consider is gender delineated coat pegs. It is very easy to unwittingly slip into reinforcing gender stereotypes with the use of gendered colours and gendered motifs (flowers and trucks, butterflies and diggers); much better to invite children to design their own coat peg, for example. This is another seemingly insignificant, mundane element of early childhood, but it can be seized as an important opportunity to challenge the ways in which gender stereo-types are so ubiquitous and appear so regularly that they become almost invisible (but remain deeply entrenched). The coat peg becomes a 'teaching moment' when child and adult can reflect and resist the unconscious slip into reproducing symbols that limit ideas about what girls and boys are allowed to be.

Another core staple in early childhood includes dress-up and role-play. Children are magnetically drawn to the dress-up box, and research has identified the multiple benefits that are gained through this form of play, as children develop cognitive, fine-motor, communication, social and emotional skills. However, such play has also been the subject of much consternation and criticism by feminist researchers, who are con-cerned that it provides fertile ground for reinforcing gendered divisions and stereotypes.

My observations[13,14] reveal that children's engagements with dressing up may offer us some interesting surprises – but only if we are prepared to observe what is going on without jumping to imme-diate conclusions. I have found that children play with the available materials within those spaces in unexpected ways, ways that often challenge what we think we see (the hyper-feminine princess, the super-butch boy builder); there is often much more going on. Price (2017) argues that small adaptations to the dress-up repertoire can reap enormous benefits.[6] For example, including the widest possible range of dress-up outfits (but not banishing the *Frozen* dresses either) and ensuring the availability of wings, hats, scarves, suitcases, tool-boxes, large sheets of material and other items that can be 'fashioned' by the children (with the help of adults when necessary) open up the possibilities for how children re-create and enact gender through their play.

The book corner is also a mainstay within many early childhood con-texts (and books are likely to appear in the family home as well), so it is worth giving careful consideration to both the environment (i.e., where reading and storytelling takes place) and the books that are made avail-able. Making the reading space comfortable and relaxed and locating it somewhere that children can visit of their own volition are important matters to consider. Then, deciding which books to include in the col-lection requires some forethought and investigation. Thankfully, there is a growing body of children's literature that addresses issues of gender diversity, non-normative sexualities and issues of consent in an age-appropriate way. For example, Letterbox Library offers an extensive collection of books that have been critically appraised by experts and deliver positive messages to children.

Ensuring that a wide range of books are available to form the basis of project work and ongoing discussions is an incredibly effective way to challenge stereotypical ideas about gender and promote more inclusive ideas about diverse family formations. There are a wealth of picture books to choose from. Some exemplary texts are *This Is Our House*,[15] *The Rainbow Stick*,[16] *We All Sing with the Same Voice*,[17] *Be Who You Are*,[18] *And Tango Makes Three*[19] and the *Rebel* series of books such as *Goodnight Stories For Rebel Girls*.[20] They all feature ideas and stories about gender and sexualities that can be explored and debated within early childhood contexts in a way that embraces children's innate curiosity. The power of a book should never be underestimated. It is crucial to introduce books illustrating that boys and girls are not limited by their gendered identities and that they have rights and opportunities to experiment and play with gender.

As research by the National Literacy Trust attests,[21] children often grow strong attachments to particular books, and that affinity can become quite fanatical for some. Very young children are drawn to characters, illustrations, storylines and dramas that unfold within picture books. The exemplary texts mentioned above offer a level of nuance, sophistication and humour that will appeal to adult readers time and time (and time) again, as young children insist on reading them over and over. The subliminal messages conveyed through these books work to provoke reflection among the adults reading them, and they also offer opportunities for debate and discussion about issues that might otherwise be regarded as taboo or off-limits. Books are celebrated in the early years for their potential to support the development of young children's language and literacy skills, and they also have significant potential to achieve so much more with respect to gender, equality and diversity.

Through these very practical examples, it is clear that the smallest of interventions can bring about massive changes in the ways in which children's curiosity (about themselves and the world around them) can be supported. Also important is what adults can learn (unlearn, relearn) from a more critical engagement with seemingly unremarkable and everyday objects, practices and spaces within the nursery and home. Thinking about what the world is like from a child's perspective, and initiating a few adaptations, can reap real benefits for us all.

References

1. Fact Check. (2018). *Did a sexuality educator say parents should ask babies' permission for diaper changes?* Retrieved April 20, 2019, from Snopes.com website: https://www.snopes.com/fact-check/did-educator-say-ask-babies-permission/

2. Osgood, J., Albon, D., Allen, K., & Hollingworth, S. (2013). *Engaging 'Hard to Reach' Parents in Early Years Music-Making.* London, England: Youth Music. Retrieved from https://network.youthmusic.org.uk/sites/default/files/users/Research/Engaging_hard_to_reach_parents_in_early_years_music-making.pdf

3. Albon, D., & Rosen, R. (2014). *Negotiating Adult-Child Relationships in Early Childhood Research.* London, England; New York, NY: Routledge.

4. Robinson, K. H., & Jones-Diaz, C. (2016). *Diversity & Difference in Childhood: Issues for Theory & Practice* (2nd edition). McGraw-Hill. Maidenhead: Open University.

5. Robinson, K. H., & Lyttleton-Smith, J. (2019). 'I like your costume': Dress up play and feminist trans-theoretical shifts. In J. Osgood & K. H. Robinson (Eds.). *Feminists Researching Gendered Childhoods: Generative Entanglements.* London, England: Bloomsbury

6. Price, D. (2017). *A Practical Guide to Gender Diversity and Sexuality in the Early Years.* London, England: Jessica Kingsley.

7. Scarlet, R. R. (Ed.) (2016). *The Anti-Bias Approach to Early Childhood Education.* Sydney, Australia: Multiverse.

8. Cameron, C. Moss, P., & Owen, C. (1999). *Men in the Nursery: Gender & Caring Work.* London, England: Sage.

9. Cameron, C. (2006). Men in the nursery revisited: Issues of male workers and professionalism. *Contemporary Issues in Early Childhood, 7*(1), 68–79.

10. Osgood, J. (2012). *Narratives From the Nursery: Negotiating Professional Identities in Early Childhood.* London, England: Routledge.

11. Osgood, J. (2005). 'Who cares?': The classed nature of childcare. *Gender and Education. 17*(3), 289–303.

12. Department for Education. (2018). *Statistics: Childcare and early years provision for children who are 5 years of age or younger.* Retrieved from https://www.gov.uk/government/collections/statistics-childcare-and-early-years

13. Osgood, J. (2014). Playing with gender: Making space for post-human childhood(s). In J. Moyles., J. Payler., & J. Georgeson (Eds.), *Early Years Foundations: An Invitation to Critical Reflection* (pp. 191–202). Milton Keynes, England: Open University.

14. Osgood, J. (2015). Reimagining gender and play. In J. Moyles (Ed.), *The Excellence of Play* (4th edition, pp. 49–60). Milton Keynes, England: Open University.

15. Rosen, M., & Graham, B. (2008). *This is our house.* London: Walker.

16. Santolini, M. (2012). *The rainbow stick boy.* Scotts Valley, CA: CreateSpace

17. Miller, J. P., Greene, S., & Meisel, P. (2005). *We all sing with the same voice*. New York, NY: Harper Trophy.
18. Parr, T. (2016). *Be who you are* (First Edition). New York ; Boston: Little, Brown and Company.
19. Richardson, J., Parnell, P., & Cole, H. (2015). *And Tango makes three* (First Little Simon board book edition). New York: Little Simon.
20. Favilli, E., & Cavallo, F. (2016). *Good night stories for rebel girls: 100 tales of extraordinary women*. Venice, CA: Timbuktu Labs.
21. *Research reports*. Retrieved April 20, 2019, from National Literacy Trust website: http://literacytrust.org.uk/research-services/research-reports/

Gendered expectations

Bright rats – blooming kids – a constipation of children – high heels for manliness – gendered adjectives – non-vaginal needlework – daddy-babysitting – women as sugar – emotional work – bumping against a dark spot – a big ol' pair of boobs – leaders – adorning the place – a wonderful all-weather cunt – a limit from within – archetypes hold us back – my agenda – husbands are overestimated – I see sexism – we're all learning

Stats

With the exception of China and parts of India, the rate of death by suicide is higher for men than women in almost all parts of the world by an aggregate ratio of 3.5:1.[1]

Eighty-seven percent of people surveyed saw a difference in the way men and women expressed their feelings, and 42% of these people thought that difference was biological.[2]

The issues

In previous chapters we examined ideas about biology, psychology and socioculture around gender. When you add these up, you get powerful *expectations* about students based on (our perceptions of) their gender, and those expectations can be incredibly limiting. Don't believe me?

Once upon a time, there were two groups of rats. One group was labelled 'dull' and the other 'bright' (don't worry, rats don't speak English, as far as I know). The rats were given that staple task of rat research: finding their way through a rat-sized maze. Rats need humans to put them into mazes and give them rewards and such, so each group had a few students who worked as rat-handlers. The handlers with the 'dull' group of rats (poor things) reported slower times, as you might have expected. The lucky handlers with the 'bright' rats had the joy of recording much faster times, just as you (and they) expected. Bright rats are bright, after all.

But the two groups were not 'bright' or 'dull' by any measurable means. They were *one single group of rats that had been randomly allocated to one category or the other.*

This is a real experiment that was conducted in the 1960s.[3] The suggestion is that the expectations of the handlers, who believed that the rats were smart or not-so-smart, somehow influenced the 'performance' of those rats. And yes, rats are not humans. So, later that same decade, Rosenthal and Jacobsen did the same sort of thing with humans.[4] They told teachers that some 20% of the students in their class were expected to do very well that year – 'blooming' – and looked at the effect on their academic performance, as measured by an IQ test. Once again, they did unusually well, suggesting that teacher expectation has an effect on student performance. Interestingly, their research showed that the gains made by the 'blooming' students were not at the expense of other students – all students did pretty well. Expectancy had a greater effect on younger children.

I hope you are thinking critically at this point –and yes, there are some problems with this study. Only 95 students were used, for example, and measuring IQ is notoriously problematic.

Another set of researchers in 1969 looked at the other side of things – what happens if you label students 'late bloomers'?[5] In this case, labelling seemed to make the teachers kinder, more supportive and encouraging, and the students did *better* than predictive measures might suggest. This study is interesting because it was conducted only with girls, and girls who were 'institutionalised offenders'. Once again, we can't necessarily generalise these results.

So what's the big deal?

Our expectations of pupils have huge implications. An inconsistent picture of gendered expectations across schools, across teachers and across districts adds up to a whole heap of chaotic and totally unfair dis/advantage for our students.

We know that social and cultural traditional discourses, rituals and often just great big myths – and not biology or brains – define expected gender roles, rights and duties. What does this mean? It means you might expect boys to be 'tougher', to cry less or to fight more. It means you might expect girls to be more compliant, to cry more or to fight less. Why does that matter? Because when boys feel the need to cry, or girls feel the need to be angry, there is no social and cultural space in our schools for them to do so. They cannot know what they know, or feel what they feel. They are conflicted and isolated, unable to express their emotion in an acceptable way. Obviously this has implications for learning. Some of them are pretty huge.

Have you ever been in a severely restricted physical space? When was the last time? How did it make you feel? (I have a recurring dream about being stuck in one of those children's soft play areas; blocked and blocking, with a constipation of children building up behind me as I frantically struggle to free myself. I know.)

Have you ever felt socially, culturally or psychologically constrained? Felt the need to cry, but knew it would be judged to be inappropriate in the circumstances? Been bursting with laughter, but couldn't let it out? Desperate to say something, but felt your opinion would be overlooked, or misunderstood, or ridiculed?

> The feeling of a lack of autonomy and control over one's life is known to be associated with depression. Socially determined gender norms, roles and responsibilities place women, far more frequently than men, in situations where they have little control over important decisions concerning their lives.[1]

Are we raising compliant, passive, depressed girls?

> The socialisation of men to not express their emotions and to be dependent on women for many aspects of domestic life may contribute to high levels of distress among them when faced with situations such as bereavement.[1]

Are we raising tough, broken, traumatised boys?
  Is there another way?

It is the work of a moment to remember that gender roles vary hugely in different cultures and different times. There was a time when men paraded around with wigs on, flamboyantly decorated with jewels, wearing high heels, to prove their 'manliness'. There are cultures where women are expected to show considerable physical prowess. Even in our familiar Western contemporary world, where the stories we tell are about men being better at dealing stoically with pain – be it physical or emotional – we forget that women bear considerable pain from periods and from heartbreak and from childbirth, often with great dignity and at minimal cost or dependency on those around them.

As with many things, the ability (and willingness) to step outside our paradigm is crucial.

Take a second – just see if you can – and list a few words that are generally used only to describe women. Then do the same for men.

I got: sassy, butch, feminine, bubbly, feisty, prudish, plump, pretty/ Handsome, hench, tough, camp, chiselled, absolute unit. Just thinking about these makes me feel faintly sick. It's not the way I want to categorise people.

If you were explaining to someone learning English, would you call these adjectives 'gendered'? Does it matter that we use words in this way? What does it say about our cultural expectations of women and of men? How does it reflect our vision of them and our view of them in comparison with one another?

How might these ideas have changed over time and cultures?

I've just been watching the TV show *Couples Come Dine with Me* (the couples, predictably, are almost exclusively heterosexual). I should have seen this coming. The 'ladies' (women are so nosy and gossipy, aren't they!) go and poke around upstairs, while the men stay and talk about video games. Finding a pair of crocheted slippers, the women assume them to be the work of the female partner. Not so. In an amazing twist, we find out – golly gosh – the *man* made them. Without even owning a vagina (traditionally used for all forms of needlework, knitting and crocheting), he managed to make himself a pair of slippers – goodness!

The reactions are interesting. Two different schools of thought emerge. One: that he is 'in touch with his feminine side', said with faint distaste (a feminine man seems to hit people's disgust buttons with alarming frequency; more on that later). The other: that this somehow makes him immensely more attractive. 'Who *wouldn't* love a man who crochets?' we are asked, brightly.

Um, me?

I'm pretty open-minded when it comes to traits I find attractive, but I'm also pretty sure loving someone solely on the basis that they can perform a particular skill isn't something I'd subscribe to. It seems like a terrible plan to me. Is it ok that he's more attractive to some people? Sure, there's a suggestion here that he isn't limited by other people's definitions of what is gender-appropriate, and that's great. But a one-dimensional conclusion that *man* + *crochet* = *love* is not the sort of analysis I want my children (my partner, myself) to be routinely con-suming without spitting out some bones afterwards.

We are veering towards Daddy-babysitting territory here, of course – the harmful idea that mothers have full responsibility for the child/ren at all times, whereas fathers, when they choose, 'babysit' temporarily and get extra cookies and praise for doing so. It's infuriating and incred-ibly disrespectful to the fathers involved.

You see a man out and about with a baby in a sling, or pushing a pram. Do you perceive him as competent, confident, caring? Do you think it is attractive? Are you impressed? Examine your reac-tion in the context of how you might feel if he were female.

A recent Twitterstorm surrounding Piers Morgan (as so many of them are) provoked many fathers to react angrily to Piers calling Daniel Craig 'emasculated' for carrying his baby in a sling on his chest. Fathers everywhere tweeted pictures of themselves caregiving, with responses about their notions of masculinity being inclusive of loving their off-spring. Radical, huh? But we are only decades away from a time when fathers typically didn't attend the birth of their children, saw them briefly once a day if they were lucky, had a hard time expressing love for them and reconciling it with being a man. Parenting – by which I mean meaning-making in terms of relationships with children – is a balanced diet of privileges and responsibilities, and for too long men have been confined to doler-out of punishments or provider of money, pushed out of nurseries and playgroups and middle-of-the-night feedings.

Men who care are often forced to reconceptualise their masculinity; others force stories on them of being emasculated or limited.[6] We need different scripts for men and boys that include loving others in all the ways they feel comfortable – truly free choices that allow them to enjoy the rich pleasures of parenthood (nuzzling infants' heads, napping with toddlers, comforting hurt little ones, baking messily with their tots) and to also experience the weighty responsibilities that come with it (being thrown up on, horrendous sleep deprivation, creating healthy meals that get dribbled straight onto the floor with an adorable smile).

But parenting is not the only meaningful care work we do, and fatherhood is not the only time men should be able to freely express love for others.

One of the most harmful expectations of gender out there is that women do emotional work, and men don't (need to). Emotional work (sometimes called emotional labour) could be: caring for people; anticipating others' needs; preparing and/or fetching and carrying practical things necessary for a task; checking on people to see if they're ok; listening and offering advice; making sure people get credit for their ideas; encouraging people; providing minor medical care; bestowing hugs and pats and wiping away tears; cleaning, cooking and preparing food and drink; anticipating danger and warning people of it; taking responsibility for solving problems and much more. (This is only one definition; others have defined it more narrowly as simply managing emotions and expectations in the workplace.)[7]

This, to me, looks suspiciously like a list of 'stuff teachers are really good at but not generally paid for'. In the hit TV series *Mad Men*, set in the 1960s, it is smack-you-in-the-face noticeable how obviously these crucial but unsung tasks fall to women nearly all the time. Women take men's coats and hats as they come in the door; they fix them drink and food; they buy presents for the men's children and send their wives flowers and set up their meetings and sit on their laps to cheer them up and clear up any and all mess going and *smile the whole time*. This isn't the distant past; it is within the lifetime of many people working in schools, or within the lifetime of their parents. Women are the water in the wheel; the petrol in the engine; the grease to the hinges. The constant attendant and companion to those who do the *real* work. Nothing works without them. One of the central plot arcs is that Don Draper, the charming-if-nauseating protagonist, literally cannot take care of his three children without a woman's help (and almost always ends up sleeping with that woman). Women are the sugar he takes with the medicine of parenthood, and he simply cannot bear to drink it without them.

Women as the sweetener-in-the-deal, the honey(s), the bon-bons, the treat at the end of the meal, the reward and the motivation and the impetus and the catalyst, but never the thing itself. Women, like sugar, make the world go around and, again like sugar, serve as the frivolous but necessary foil to the serious, meaty, fibrous men doing the bulk of the work, so full of their own importance that they value only what they can see and digest. Great big powerful carby salt-of-the-earth men, puffed up like wheat with their own importance which so often turns out to be a Rice Krispie full of hot air, a funny little *snap, crackle, pop!* that means nothing at all.

Joanna Russ in her book *The Female Man* explores it like this: 'you want a devoted helpmeet, a self-sacrificing mother, a hot chick, a darling daughter, women to look at, women to laugh at, women to come [to] for comfort, women to ... keep your children out of your hair, to work when you need the money and stay home when you don't.'[8] Women as the 8-in-1 tools, the ultimate adaptors to work around men and their needs.

Women – and some non-women – mediate relationships like this all the time. Often, patterns of behaviour emerge in institutions where this emotional labour is so invisible you might be forgiven for not seeing it at all. But those people are there, making the coffee and drying the tears and handing out the paracetamol and moving the chairs and tidying the papers and fetching the dustpan and brush and knowing where to find things and taking responsibility for problems and solving them, quietly, so the organisation can function.

Schools, like any other organisation (including the home), run on emotional work, and our pupils notice it.

Who does the majority of it in your school?

Self-expectations and confidence

It is a well-replicated result that boys are more confident in their own abilities than girls, as are men than women.[9] 'As we talked with women, dozens of them, all accomplished and credentialed, we kept bumping up against a dark spot that we couldn't quite identify, a force clearly holding them back', write the authors of *Womanomics*, Katty Kay and Claire Shipman, concluding that 'power centers of this nation are zones of female self-doubt—that is, when they include women at all.'[10]

Women all over the world – successful, intelligent, competent women – consistently give external reasons for their success – or just plain deny it at all. 'I was just lucky'; 'people think I'm better than I am'; 'I didn't really deserve it'. That's a failure in our – and their – expectations.

How do you feel about success? To what do you attribute it? How do you measure it?

If we want girls to be more realistic about their own abilities, we have to expect them to succeed. We also have to tell them that their value lies in their brains and their work ethic more than in their bodies. That they can make things – incredible things – that aren't babies or erections or hot dinners.

Like many girls, I hit puberty and got myself a big ol' pair of boobs. I didn't ask for them. I didn't do anything – besides exist – to get them. Bet let me tell you, I've had more attention my entire life – starting that very moment, aged 12 – for my breasts than I have ever had for what has come out of my mouth or my pen, however accomplished.

I'm not saying bodies aren't important or can't be amazing – see later chapters on sex. I'm also not saying I want the world to ignore my breasts (they're pretty good; I like them) or ignore all breasts (I am a huge fan of breasts). But listen to conversations around girls and young women. Listen to what people say to them and ask them about. Look at the way they are portrayed, all day long: sexy, demure, innocent, materialistic, make-up-obsessed, weak, coy, shallow, vain. Undoubtedly some of us are those things some of the time. But we have got to make space for women's ideas, for their words and their thoughts and their passions and their talents. I mean this in the nicest possible way: step the fuck aside, and stop talking about my shoes.

Leadership/mothership

Imagine a great leader. Think about their leadership qualities that you admire. Picture iconic images for them.

Whom did you think of?

54 percent of people said that they had no preference regarding male or female bosses; of those remaining participants who expressed a preference, however, twice as many preferred to work for a male leader.[11]

It's not surprising that we struggle to reconcile 'female' with 'strong leader' at times. It's 2019, and a person without a penis has never been president of the United States, not in its 243-year and 44-president history. Women leaders currently represent fewer than 10% of the 193 United Nations member states.[12]

I was at an event recently in a room full of portraits of great leaders. Guess how many of them were women? It doesn't rhyme with 'heroine'.

Researchers investigated a situation where people were asked to give scored speeches in a room where portraits of famous people were placed at the back in their eyeline. 'Where the image at the back of the room matched the basic identity criteria of the speaker (mostly gender and ethnicity), they received higher scores from their audience. Their performance, demeanour and confidence all improved because they saw themselves reflected in the images'.[13]

People often have opinions about 'male' and 'female' ways of working, and gendered ideas of leadership. Organisations may have these ideas embedded at various implicit and explicit levels (as I wrote this, someone just tweeted that the Barclaycard admin process doesn't allow her to tick both 'Dr.' as a title and 'female' as a gender option).

I have heard people tell me 'men are just better leaders' more times than I can count, using this 'fact' to account for the statistics. The research is clear: 'This consistent disparity needs to be addressed by identifying the underlying mechanism embedded in organizational structures that portrays women as less suitable for senior leadership positions than their male counterparts ... evidence suggests that there is no substantial gender difference in leadership styles or behaviors'.[14]

Our environment is literally built for and often by (wealthy white) men.

I've just had a health and safety representative in my work office. 'Did you know', he said, 'that office temperatures are built for men?

Women are typically around 3 degrees colder than men, but we set the temperature to suit men, so [women are] nearly always cold. Mad, isn't it?' He shrugged and left, remarkably chipper about this casual built-in corporate sexism.

Caroline Criado Perez, in her book *Invisible Women: Data Bias in a World Designed for Men*, explores why: 'so much data fails to take into account gender, because it treats men as the default and women as atypical, bias and discrimination are baked into our systems. And women pay tremendous costs for this bias, in time, money, and often with their lives'.[15]

The Museum of Modern Sexism: 'It turns out, the world we live in was designed by men. Our economic structure, societal rules, government, social norms, and the very architecture we live in: all made by and for men. The rest of us are just walking around in it ... adorning the place'.[16]

Men represent humanity, with a 'gender data gap' where women should be. Absence versus presence. Sometimes, it feels like women don't even exist. That our being here is a privilege, not a fact. That we have to continually adjust to the world instead of the other way around. Don't let that world be your classroom.

What needs to change

It is time to challenge our expectations of boys, girls and any variations thereof; to turn off what Dr. Gina Rippon refers to as the 'Whack-a-Mole' myths based on entrenched beliefs that just keep popping up, despite a singular lack of evidence to support them. I don't know why we're surprised. There are more buses with gendered messages plastered on them, by a factor of hundreds, than there ever were for certain claims about how much the EU 'cost' the UK, and that misconception entered the minds of the public at a frightening speed and stayed there with a fascinating tenacity. But there are hundreds of thousands of teachers in the UK alone, and thousands of hours with pupils at their disposal, and our pupils trust and sometimes even love us. What a wonderful and terrible responsibility and opportunity we have before us.

Stephen Jay Gould wrote that there are 'few injustices deeper that the denial of an opportunity to strive or even to hope, by a limit imposed from without, but falsely identified from within'.[17] If we care about our pupils, we cannot constrain them with our gendered expectations – and in fact, we must do more. They will no doubt, as they move through the world, encounter the weight of limited expectations from others based on their (perceived) gender, and many other things they did not choose – their appearance, their sexuality, their background. We have to be the immunising shot of confidence that they can be bigger than those bigoted expectations. We have to sow the seeds of awareness about how discrimination works, take it apart, show them how to think beyond and sideways through paradigms like examining the thickness of a pair of spectacles. We have to show them how to react critically, how to examine and weigh evidence and how to view and value different types of knowledge differently. One might say this is the most important work of education. It's certainly one of the most important parts of being a thoughtful human.

The strongest counterarguments and why they're wrong

- 'Males and female are just different – we should accept this and play to their strengths, not try to change them'.

- 'Stop trying to push your agenda of equality all the time! Things are fine, we have achieved great strides, and we don't need to change any more'.

- 'We can't change everyone's mind – what about parents? It's too hard a job, and we've got more important things to be doing in schools'.

The evidence is complex, but it points to a vicious cycle.

Beyond the genital, sex is surprisingly dynamic, and not just open to gender influence from gender constructions, but reliant on them. Nor does sex inscribe us with male brains and female brains, or with male natures and female natures.[18]

Males and females aren't just seen as 'different', but females are seen as inferior in almost every arena, except a few where the order is reversed. What if we are perpetuating a vicious cycle effect where our expectations are determining successive generations to be constrained, unequal and destabilised by gendered messaging? By accepting the basic assumption that 'males and females are different' – categorising by gender – we are building all kinds of faulty reasoning on top. We are laying the groundwork for biological determinism, the idea that our behaviour is controlled by our physiology and not our environment. I'm sure you don't need me to tell you that kind of thinking is danger-ous, and potentially pretty harmful. Let's pause for a moment and con-sider what it might look like in a classroom.

'Boys are stronger, so …'

'Girls are just more emotional, it's in their nature, so …'

'No, boys aren't caring and loving, so …'

'Girls don't have any aggression, so …'

'Boys can't …'

'Girls like you shouldn't …'

How might boys, girls and others be sentenced by these sentences?

Can you see how this kind of thinking leads to a serious narrowing of expectation? What if I am a girl who wants to pursue gymnastics or horse riding or rugby, to develop muscles, to find my strength? How might I react to being continually told that boys are strong(er)? How long before I give up the struggle to find *my* space to be strong?

What if I am a boy who is sensitive to others, who loves and cares deeply and who has just acquired a new baby sibling? How might I react to being continually told that boys are not (good at being) caring and loving? How long before I give up the struggle to find *my* space to adore, love and express my deep feelings for the new baby in my family?

High –and almost always equal – expectations solve all these problems.

Do you really think we are giving everyone equal opportunities now?

Have you heard of the wage gap (in the UK, this is currently esti-mated at an average of 13%-19%)?[19] Ever stopped to think about whether women are seen as less worthy, less of value, than men? Ever measured who talks in meetings, conferences and discussions; who asks questions publicly; who is viewed as an 'expert' on TV and radio and across social media? Who is an MP? All these things offer clear evidence of what many have been feeling all their lives: the rhetoric may be there (though not always) but in reality, gendered expectations are still getting in the way of ideals of equality for many, many people. People who venture 'out of' expected areas – women in maths or motor engineering or computing, men in childcare or midwifery or textiles – still feel discriminated against, out of place, discouraged by both institutionalised and individualised prejudice.

Asking what 'men's' and 'women's' roles are in our world is in itself the wrong question. So often we have peremptory discussions that modify, that expand slightly or creep at the boundaries of gendered roles. What we should be doing is exploding the whole thing and starting again.

Have you ever seen young children's drawings of human faces?

You can predict with some accuracy the stages they go through – even the most talented artists – because it is about 'seeing' with the eyes and the mind in structured stages. People are almost always 'tadpole' shaped to begin with. Hair is too small; ears don't exist for a while. Eyes are always too high at first (they're actually about halfway down from the crown of the head). When I was learning to draw, one thing my art teacher kept telling me was to stop seeing what I thought I saw, and to draw instead what was in front of me. We all have an archetypal 'nose', a set of 'lip shapes' that we doodle, a preconceived idea about the look of eyes. This is why what we think we see holds us back from seeing the true geometry of light and shadow, space and content, absence and presence, that makes for a beautiful and accurate drawing.

Women 'do' what they do in real life, not what we think we see. So do non-women. Open your eyes and mind, and see what is there, not what you expect or want to see. A woman's role is what a woman does; what she chooses to do; what her passion, her skill and her enjoyment dictate. It is as fluid as the coffee she may choose not to make, and as resistant to your vision of her as the diamond she may decide not to wear.

Some sex differences exist, but here are no excuses for sexism, and we'll never agree how they got there. We've got to stop putting them there ourselves, is all.

[T]here is an issue with some researchers wanting to see sex differences, and going out of their way to see [them]. [A] study ... may show, for example, small structural [brain] differences. [But it is faulty to] infer from [this] ... that women are better at multitasking, ... or that men are more rational. We can't do that.[20]

Yes, I have an agenda.

Can we all just stop feminism now? When will we know when it has been successful? Are you just complaining about perceived inequality because you've got into a habit, and you don't know how to stop? These are crucial questions, and I wouldn't want to deny them. If you are interested in this point of view, Joanna Williams's book *Women vs Feminism*[21] is a great read; she says that we're all so caught up in our indignation that we've forgotten to stop, and that feminism has hurt men. Indisputably, feminism has hurt men's *privilege*, which a wise woman once told me can feel like oppression. But if you don't see life as a zero-sum game (and it's so often not), then this doesn't make sense. In a classroom, expecting both boys and girls (and others) to achieve highly doesn't hurt anyone unless you are grading in some kind of norm-referenced bell curve, and even then it emphatically shouldn't be a sexist one. Later in this book, I'll talk more about male privilege and the pain it can cause to level the playing field in a multitude of ways that cross ethical boundaries for many people. These are not easy questions, but not tackling them is worse than avoiding them.

Yes, we have come so, so far. If you want to take a moment to appreciate that, please do. I am no longer told that studying mathematics will make me infertile, or riding a horse astride will stop me getting a husband. (Got one. Got rid. They're not all they're cracked up to be.) Hurrah. I feel like that's a baseline, if anything.

So where are we? Why can't we stop?

From 2007 to 2017, women's board representation in FTSE 100 companies in the United Kingdom increased from 11% to 28%. Around 36% of legislators, senior officials and managers are women.[22]

But almost four in ten businesses in G7 countries have no women in senior management positions. Globally, the proportion of senior business roles held by women stands at 24%, up slightly from 22% in 2015. However, this minor uplift has coincided with an increase in the percentage of firms with no women in senior management, which stood at 33% in 2016 compared to 32% in 2018.[23]

I know that measuring this with numbers, research and stats is not perfect. I know that perfect 50% parity doesn't represent everything and may not always be necessary, possible or even desirable. I also know that qualitative studies consistently show that women feel undervalued, discriminated against and sexually harassed – not everywhere, not all the time, but enough. What is enough, and how will we know when things are equal?

I don't honestly know. This stuff is tricky, because it is true: I have got an agenda. Sometimes, as in an M. Night Shyamalan movie, I see things where no one else sees them. Sometimes I expect to see gendering and I get it. Am I right, or is someone who says they didn't intend sexism right? Is entrenched sexism invisible sometimes, or is it just not there? I don't know the answers to these questions. I cannot know them. I know that I desperately want feminism to win, and for things to be better for everyone, and I believe that a rising tide will raise all of our boats in this respect. Ultimately, I can only raise these issues and ask that we have an honest, productive and thoughtful discussion about them. A dear friend once said to me that I question him all the time and that, far from making him defensive or angry, it just makes him want to be better, to live up to my expectations. I wish that we could all have such relationships, where we can question with love and challenge with respect, but I know that it can't always happen. Feminism is dreadfully and powerfully and sometimes dangerously emotive, and this can be great, and it can be terrible. But really, we all just want to build a better world for our pupils and our children, and we are often just disagreeing on the details.

Now/later

Now: Film, record or ask someone to observe you teaching with a specific eye on gendered expectations. Do you say or do anything that looks gendered? Do you choose pupils for specific jobs based on gender? Do you use gendered language?

Later: Audit your school for emotional work, explicitly involving others in the conversation, if you can, and asking what they think. Consider your expectations of other members of staff and how those expectations might look and feel gendered. Ask someone to do something that might not be expected from a person of their gender. Notice evidence of strong females and caring males.

Graham says

Unconscious bias is a huge factor in shaping the way our children see themselves and each other, but it can also be the hardest to address because we are not always aware of it. My harmless (or so it seemed to me at the time) use of terms of endearment in the classroom had a huge bearing on how the children saw themselves and their relationship with me. You only have to watch the scene from *No More Boys and Girls* where Javid asks the boys if it would be ok to be called 'sweetpea' and is met with a chorus of 'no way' and 'that's for girls' (and similarly, calling everyone 'mate' couldn't be done because that was 'just for boys') to see that such nomenclature really did influence their perceptions. Every time I used a gendered term of endearment, I was telling the children that they were different and that I also perceived them differently – lesson learned.

Look for unconscious bias in classroom interactions; listen to how you talk to your pupils. Do you choose boys more than girls to answer questions (perhaps because they have their hands up more)? Do you ask them to do different tasks as a consequence of their gender? Do you segregate boys and girls for lines or in groups? If so, I recommend that you try and if you see others doing it, challenge them – it *does* matter.

Something struck me recently: I have never been a parent and I'm not likely to be now, but being a parent must be hard. We try to do what we can to help our children, but I feel that when it comes to boys, we sometimes help them too much. I was at a recent residential with my class, and they were encouraged to abseil (rappel), climb walls and make fires. Generally the girls climbed higher, and they abseiled and pushed themselves more than the boys, which interested me. Despite boys' initial bravado before the activity, when they came to do it, they often fell short of completing the task or getting to the top.

'What does this have to do with me?' I hear parents up and down the land saying. As I talked to another teacher in the evening about it (a parent with both a boy and a girl), we came to the conclusion that it could perhaps come down to 'over-mothering' our boys. Because they are boys, we may expect them to do less for themselves, so we tidy up after them, we prepare food, we get them dressed. Thus, when Mum or Dad is not there to do it, they don't know what to do. We are in a basic sense taking away their independence, and when it comes to doing things themselves without the parent being there, they may struggle. Girls, of whom we often have different expectations, may have more independence in some areas and therefore may cope better when faced with a challenge by themselves.

Maggie Dent, author of *Mothering Our Boys*,[24] surveyed 1600 men for her book and asked the question 'What is it you wished your mother hadn't done?'

The most common answer was that they wished their mothers had 'done less for them'. This makes sense to me. The more we do for our boys, the less they will be able to do when they are older, and the harder those lessons may be to learn later in life.

I think we should expect the same from both boys and girls, and especially give boys their independence by expecting that they will do domestic things for themselves. Just because they are boys doesn't mean they cannot (or should not) wash, clean, cook and look after themselves.

Tl;dr

Our expectations matter, powerfully. To create the kind of classroom that breaks rather than perpetuates stereotypes takes self-examination and habit-breaking, because we're all of us to some greater or lesser degree stuck in sexist paradigms. We're all learning.

References

1. WHO. *Gender and mental health.* (2002). Retrieved April 20, 2019, from https://www.who.int/gender-equity-rights/knowledge/a85573/en/
2. Pew Research Center. *On gender differences, no consensus on nature vs. nurture.* (2017, December 5). Retrieved April 20, 2019, from https://www.pewsocialtrends.org/2017/12/05/on-gender-differences-no-consensus-on-nature-vs-nurture/
3. Rosenthal, R., & Fode, K. L. (2007). The effect of experimenter bias on the performance of the albino rat. *Behavioral Science*, *8*(3), 183–189. https://doi.org/10.1002/bs.3830080302
4. Rosenthal, R., & Jacobson, L. (1966). Teacher's expectancies: Determinants of pupils IQ gains'. *Psychological Reports*, 19, 115–118.

5. Meichenbaum, D. H., Bowers, K. S., & Ross, R. R. (1969). A behavioral analysis of teacher expectancy effect. *Journal of Personality and Social Psychology, 13*(4), 306–316. https://doi.org/10.1037/h0028470

6. Locke, A. (2017). *Rules of "how to be a dad" are changing as gender roles continue to blur.* Retrieved April 20, 2019, from The Conversation website: http://theconversation.com/rules-of-how-to-be-a-dad-are-changing-as-gender-roles-continue-to-blur-72907

7. Junwu, D. (2011). Research on emotional labor: Review and prospect. In Q. Zhou (Ed.). *Advances in Applied Economics, Business and Development* (pp. 572–578). Springer Berlin Heidelberg.

8. Russ, J. (2010). *The Female Man.* London, England: Gollancz.

9. Heath, V. (2018). *Addressing the gender confidence gap.* Retrieved April 20, 2019, from Gender and the Economy website: https://www.gendereconomy.org/addressing-the-gender-confidence-gap/

10. Shipman, K. K., & Shipman, C. (2014). The confidence gap. *The Atlantic.* Retrieved from https://www.theatlantic.com/magazine/archive/2014/05/the-confidence-gap/359815/

11. Gardiner, R. A. (2015). Gendered expectations. In R. A. Gardiner (Ed.). *Gender, Authenticity and Leadership: Thinking with Arendt* (pp. 39–56), London: Palgrave Macmillan.

12. *Reality check: Do female leaders improve women's lives?* (2017). Retrieved from https://www.bbc.com/news/world-41258332

13. Barnes, E., & Carlile, A. (2018). *How to Transform Your School into an LGBT+ Friendly Place: A Practical Guide for Nursery, Primary and Secondary Teachers.* London, England ; Philadelphia, PA: Jessica Kingsley.

14. Seo, G., Huang, W., & Han, S.-H. C. (2017). Conceptual review of underrepresentation of women in senior leadership positions from a perspective of gendered social status in the workplace: Implication for HRD research and practice. *Human Resource Development Review, 16*(1), 35–59. https://doi.org/10.1177/1534484317690063

15. Criado Perez, C. (2019). *Invisible Women: Exposing Data Bias in a World Designed for Men.* London, England: Chatto & Windus.

16. *The world is built for men.* Retrieved April 20, 2019, from The Museum of Modern Sexism website: https://www.museumofmodernsexism.com/the-world-is-built-for-men

17. Gould, S. J. (1996). *The Mismeasure of Man* (Rev. and Expanded). New York, NY: Norton.

18. Fine, C. (2018). *Testosterone rex: Unmaking the Myths of our Gendered Minds.* London: Icon.

19. Olsen, W., Gash, D. V., & Zhang, D. M. (n.d.). *The gender pay gap in the UK: evidence from the UKHLS.* 36.

20. Schulte, B. (2018, February 20). *How different are men and women, really?* Retrieved April 20, 2019, from Slate Magazine website: https://slate.com/human-interest/2018/02/an-interview-with-angela-saini-author-of.html

21. Williams, J. (2017). *Women vs Feminism: Why We All Need Liberating from the Gender Wars* (First edition). London, England: Emerald.
22. *Quick take: Women in the workforce—UK.* (2019). Retrieved April 20, 2019, from Catalyst website: https://www.catalyst.org/research/women-in-the-workforce-uk/
23. *Today's Gender Reality in Statistics, Or Making Leadership Attractive to Women.* (2016). Retrieved April 20, 2019, from https://www.forbes.com/sites/dinamedland/2016/03/07/todays-gender-reality-in-statistics-or-making-leadership-attractive-to-women/#75606f86883d
24. Dent, M. (2018). *Mothering our boys: a guide for mums of sons.* NSW, Gerringong: Pennington.

6 | Toys

Stop playing with that – a passive, pretty thing – irons as presents – a bizarre battleground – playing around – childlike not childish – I'm scared of drumkits – props – decisions as curriculum – pipelines – *corrupted into gayness* – innately good at sewing – a social interface – poop sandwiches – preferences – that avalanche of pink – a teddy bear with eyelashes

Stats

Children start to make gender related decisions on toys from around 18 months, and they focus on toys suited to their gender by 3 years old.[1]

'When Action Man came out it was the laughing stock of the 1966 toy fair ("a doll toy for a boy? You'll be laughed out of the industry"), and of course it was the toy of the year for the next 10 years'.[2]

A survey carried out in December 2013 showed a 60% reduction in the use of 'Girls' and 'Boys' signs in shops compared with the same time in 2012, dropping from 50% of shops to just 20%.[3]

The issues

Think about your favourite childhood toys at different stages of your life. What did you play with at age 2 or 3? (Can you remember?) Was there a particular colour, shape, texture or music associated with it? What did you play with at 5 or 6 years? Did you like construction bricks, Barbies, toy cars on a mat, a doll's house, calculators, Spirographs, play dough or paint? Did you enjoy toy instruments?

Later, did you like yo-yos, silly putty, jacks, or cat's cradle? Did you like to play in cardboard boxes? Climb trees? Make dens with pillows and blankets?

There's usually a warm feeling associated with these childhood play memories. Thinking about play when I was a child is largely positive and nostalgic. Those times feel safe and cosy. And yet, for many of us, there was something sinister at work beneath those choices – maybe not intentionally, but something that might be (generously) called 'benevolent sexism'. Girls need protection from muddy, messy, noisy things (maybe, including boys). Boys need proper manly toys, not sissy little dolls and frilly things. Everyone must play with things and people that fit the category of 'appropriate'. Don't touch that; don't play with him; that's not for you; that's dirty; that's wrong; put it down. I hope that in 2019 we don't overtly feel like this, or express these views, but we sure as heck make choices based on them often enough.

> Males are supposed to be masculine and like masculine things; females are supposed to be feminine and like feminine things: ... [an] active/passive divide. Physical, active and aggressive things are branded masculine; while passive, pretty things are branded feminine.[4]

I am not a passive, pretty thing. Your female pupils are not passive, pretty things.

Similarly, your male pupils are not active, aggressive things.

Our toy biases reflect our inherent sexism, and it stinks.

Play begets curiosity, learning and interest. I remember women in my parents' generation receiving tiny toy irons and ovens as children and, 20 years later, getting real irons and microwaves as actual 'presents' that they were supposed to be happy about. 'That's you', those gifts say. 'That defines you'. When we are children, we are unwritten books, waiting to find out what captures our interest and inflates our imaginations. This isn't just about gender – this is about teaching young humans that they can reinvent themselves and encouraging them not to narrow their focus too early. (And please, let's not make that focus ironing boards.)

It seems obvious, but if you want boys to know they can be pretty and caring if they choose, and girls to know they can be active and strong if they choose, you have to let them explore those identities through toys. You have to give them a wide range of toys so they can figure out what they like.

Once you provide this range, you then have to provide the non-judgemental attitudes that go with it – otherwise, you are just doing the stereotyping implicitly instead of explicitly. You have to let them really choose – no matter how many girls-climbing-trees or boys-playing-with-toy-kitchens you get, you have to support their freedom in this way. It might be a phase; it might be their future career. Guess what? That's not up to you, and neither is their sexuality or gender expression. That will happen either way, regardless of you; you simply have the means to support them and make them feel better about it.

There is a clear link between stereotyping toys and stereotyping interests and stereotyping jobs. Between selling little girls the 'dream' of pink ironing boards and insisting that ironing is 'women's work'; between selling little boys dinosaurs and encouraging them towards science. A research report found that toys with a science, technology, engineering and maths (STEM) focus were three times as likely to be targeted at boys than at girls; women account for around 9% of engineers in the U K.[5] These are not coincidences.

Parents take more risks with boys, encouraging them to be more adventurous, from the time they are infants. They expect girls to be quieter, more compliant. Boys play with trucks; girls wear tutus. Ever climbed a tree in a tutu? We are telling our children who to be by telling them how to play and what to play with.

> One of the earliest manifestations of childhood sexism is the almost surreal segregation of children's toys...the briefest glance around almost any children's toy store reveals a bizarre battleground. Bright hothouse pinks face off against defiant blues across a strip of notably empty no-man's land.[6]

Do you recognise this image of a 'bizarre battleground'? Does it bother you?
What do you like to play with, as an adult?
I'm very curious about the term 'creative' and how it is used by adults. In my experience, people often use it to describe the way I like

to play around with things to make other things (often a mess), also sometimes adding that *they're* not creative at all. It's like it's seen as a personality trait that people simply have or don't have.

I'm bemused. Playing around with things to make other things isn't just the basis for art. It's also the beginnings of science: engineering, chemistry, mechanics. It's also, when abstracted, a powerfully mathematical behaviour. It contains the seeds of generalisation, prediction and hypothesis-testing. In other words, for me, this playful behaviour that others might see as creative or risk-taking is in fact a very wide-ranging curiosity about how the world works or could work in a huge range of disciplines. I like to play with stuff, and I don't limit my ideas of that stuff to a particular type of stuff (although I do tend to stay away from dangerous chemicals, fire and sharp things, as a rule). I like to explore things and find boundaries, and I'm happy to make things that don't seem to have a function or could be seen as valueless. This is an emotional thing too – it's a form of intimacy. It's also the basis for comedy. In other words, I'm a huge child.

I don't mean this pejoratively – the way that children play is something I'm happy to be associated with. It's *childlike*, not *childish*. I've been fascinated with the way that my children have evolved through different stages of play, and with how predictable and generalisable those stages are on the one hand (nearly all English-speaking, TV-watching kids do imaginary character-based play with American accents, for example) and, on the other, with how idiosyncratic the specific games they invent can be. One daughter, whose hatred of vegetables was a cause of much confrontation at mealtimes, was found one day with her head through a clothes airer, happily munching on a carrot because she was a 'horsie'. Another of my children had a pair of imaginary friends who seemed to constantly switch gender, called 'Woggle and Bang'. At the time of writing, they are both (my children, not Woggle and Bang, although who knows?) enjoying a popular trend known as 'making slime', which seems to be the modern equivalent of alchemy and is deeply, deeply satisfying to watch.

I am a feminist, and I reluctantly bought one of my daughters an electronics set three years ago. It's been a huge hit and the source of much joy in our household – we have had helicopters and radios and buttons and buzzers and bulbs and circuits. Why reluctantly, then? Because I'm scared of it.

I'm not scared of electricity, or of toys. I'm scared of this 'male' domain. I'm scared that when she asks me how a resistor works, I won't know. I'm scared of physics, because despite being a mathematician, it's filed away in my head as 'male and scary'. I only figured all this stuff out when I sat down and thought really hard about it, and it knocked me over with how weird it was. Ditto stuff to do with aeronautics, plumbing and loads of other things, too. I've grown up with chemistry sets and calculators and paint and plasticine, but some things still seem filed off in a corner marked 'not for you', even now. Drumkits, too. I'm a grown woman and I'm scared of drumkits.

Think about the types of toys you wouldn't play with, and the types of toys you see as 'not for you'. Can you articulate why? Do you feel any strong emotions about them?

The very point of play is exploring boundaries, but it rapidly becomes dull if the limits are too narrow. Similarly, the messages we send about play – what is ok and what is frowned upon – crystallise into guidelines, parameters and values as children grow into them. While we know that children will play with almost anything (parents of toddlers know this all too well), they have a special place in their heart for toys we buy them, those first possessions that foster a burgeoning sense of *belonging* and ownership and are all too hard to share. Parents and carers may also know the frustration of other people buying toys for their little ones that are loud, irritating or impractical (often the most beloved in our house, and always the most likely to disappear inexplicably after a few months). To some extent, we are the gatekeepers of toys for early childhood, and the passers of judgement on them as children grow up and come to exercise more freedom of choice. What we say and do about toys really matters, because in these imaginary worlds, toys are the props in the theatre, which stimulate a way of understanding real-life contexts in the safe space of play.

'Some of the toys that look most interesting to adults are not particularly effective in promoting development. This suggests that teachers can make decisions about toys as thoughtfully as they do when making decisions about any other area of the curriculum', says Professor Trawick-Smith, professor of early childhood education at the Center for Early Childhood Education at Eastern Connecticut State University.[7]

I'd go even further: The decisions we make about what is available to students *are* the curriculum. If we aren't being thoughtful about the materials, we aren't designing that curriculum, and if we aren't challenging stereotypes, we're perpetuating them. Excluding girls from visuospatial toys like Lego or Rubik's cubes by implicit assumption, by subtle cues and expectations, is like telling them at age 4 or 5 that they'll never be any good at (this sort of) maths. Excluding them from adventure of every sort – telling them girls get rescued or play house for their husbands instead – is unforgivable. Too many women in our crazy world have lived their whole lives terrified, waiting or compliant. Some of those women undoubtedly would have changed it for the better if they had had the chance.

What toys or objects of play and exploration are available in your classroom, in your school?

Are they for everyone?

How do you communicate who is 'supposed' to use them?

The pipeline goes all the way from girls playing with toy cars to feeling they can change their own flat tyres to becoming racing drivers; from boys playing with dolls to feeling they can change their own child's nappies to becoming full-time carers. All toys are for everyone. This has to be the explicit and the implicit message. Even something as subtle as a raised eyebrow, a note of surprise in the voice or an awkward smile will hit home for the child who is scared that they are out of their lane anyway.

Boys who love glitter

I'm going to confront this one right now: If you are on any level worrying that the boy who wants to play with glitter, dress up as a princess or sing and dance to 'Frozen' all the livelong day is going to be somehow *corrupted into gayness* by these things, it's time to stop and think. Hard. That's a surprisingly pervasive idea, and one we'll deal with in more detail in later chapters.

Being gay is not a choice. Being fabulous is, and I'd take a world full of confidently fabulous men over a world full of sad, aggressive, frustrated ones any day. If you see dangerous dynamite in the heady combination of maleness and glitter, check yourself. If you are embarrassed by males wearing 'feminine' clothing or playing with 'feminine' things, go away and watch all 11 series of RuPaul's *Drag Race* and educate yourself [dabs self with tiny sponge in disbelief].

Think about boys exhibiting enjoyment of 'feminine' things: baking, pink and glitter crafts, princesses, musical theatre, crochet, fashion. Picture them bringing their hobbies and their questions to you. How might you react? How does it make you feel?

I am someone who enjoys making things. I have drawers full of buttons and candle wax and scraps of material and a soldering iron and God knows what else, in case the mood takes me. I'll knit for a time, when the mood is upon me. I'll crochet. I'm not very competent at either. I'm ok at sewing, but not great, and I like to tie-dye or play with clay once in a while. I love pens and almost any kind of stationery. I love colour, full stop. I like fiddling with new materials.

If I had been born male, do you think I would still be interested in all those things?

I sincerely hope so, but I also know that men who knit are still rare enough to be remarkable in our particular time and place (in fact, the history of knitting is fairly male-dominated). I know that sewing on a button is almost always seen as innately 'female' somehow, and that if there's a woman available, she's usually the one who gets asked to do it. Someone I spoke to about this told me that he thought women were 'innately' good at sewing, and that was why midwives were better at sewing women up after childbirth than doctors. That last one is problematic in many ways for me, starting with the assumption of gender in the careers, the absurd notion of 'innate' sewing skills; try giving a 2-year-old girl a needle and we'll see. (Actually, please don't!) But more than this, I am disturbed by the total failure to see that some women have grown up gaining and passing on these skills to successive generations because *someone bloody had to*. There's not really much art to sewing on a button. I wouldn't like to dismiss the skill of those who do it particularly well, but it's hardly craftspersonship. It's often been (seen as being) done by women not because they have a weird needle gene inside them but simply because it needed doing, especially if money was tight, and if the men were too busy working or fighting or socialising or telling women they should be in the kitchen. In other words, it simply fell to the women to do it. That's it. It's not a particularly fun job, either, I'd say. I'm not rushing home after work with glee in my heart to take up my children's school uniforms and joyfully attach their missing buttons, and neither would I expect many other people to.

Similarly, tinkering with engines, machines and working parts is still seen as so very 'male'. How things work scientifically, mechanically and spatially is still seen as so very masculine.

> Girls are not only being denied access to scientific and adventurous toys; they're also presented with such a narrow range of options that domesticity and typically 'female' duties are shoved down their throats before they've even reached the age of five.[6]

Is it, then, such a surprise that women like me are scared of taking things apart to see how they work?

> For boys, a wide variety of activities and interests are represented, from Doctor Who to building, dinosaurs to architecture. There is choice, and with it a platform on which boys may build their identity. But for the girls the shelves overflow with pink, and all that pink represents.[7]

We've already talked about neuroplasticity – the idea that developing brains respond to social and environment cues and that changes happen during this response. Not only do we need to give children wider, stronger and broader platforms on which to build their identities, we also need to make sure those platforms are free from gendered wobbles, so that their identities are less fraily balanced on them.

In *No More Boys and Girls,* Dr. Gina Rippon explains that one of the things teachers often note is that girls are not as good at visuospatial skills as boys are. She thinks this is likely to be a consequence of the types of toys that the different genders play with when young. In the show, we see her discussing how playing with Tetris changed girls' brains.

Toys matter.

What needs to change

'[I]f you give a very young child mechanical toys to play with, stuff that exercises their ability to build things and make things, they will be better, biologically better, at making and building things because of the experiences they've had. So a social interference produces a biological effect'.[8] It's really that simple. Our choices about toys matter.

The strongest counterarguments and why they're wrong

–   'But my daughter loves her tiny ironing board/doll! She just natu-
    rally prefers it!'
–   'Boys just like dinosaurs more, that's all there is to it'.
–   'Other people have bought these toys for my child/classroom/
    donated them to my school, am I supposed to throw them away?'

*Your daughter might love playing with matches, but that's not really
the point now, is it?* Adults choose for children until the children are old
enough to choose for themselves – and even then it's from a necessarily
limited range of options. How would you feel about choosing between
sandwiches containing one of the following:

–   Dog turds
–   Human faeces
–   Cat poop

That's how I feel sometimes, when I look at the skinny, beguiling,
hypersexual white and pink vacuous jewelled princesses on offer for
girls. The choice is a fallacy. Each is a flavour of shit sandwich; which
particular flavour is fairly unimportant. Focusing on the 'choice' isn't
focusing on the right thing.

Of course, some children (of all flavours) love princesses. Princesses in
themselves are not necessarily harmful. Tiny ironing boards are not necessarily harmful (although I have to question the weirdness of the
designer who came up with them). The narrowness of the range of
choices, and the way they represent our gendered expectations, along
with the concomitant effect on children's interests and ideas about 'their'
territory can be extremely harmful, though. If I had it to do over again,
I think I'd treat the tiny ironing board more like the box of matches: not
until you understand the implications of playing with it, darling.

Kids like weird things. Do boys 'like' dinosaurs more than girls do?
I'm not sure how you measure that. We know that in some circumstances (younger years) children like things we nudge them towards –
and in others (gaining independence) it's about rebelling from those
cues altogether. But as we've discussed, if the baseline is really narrow – if

they've only ever seen certain things as toys 'for them' in the first place –
then it's not really 'choice' and it's not really 'rebellion'. There are only
so many times you can receive the message 'dinosaurs are for boys' in
60,000 different ways before you internalise it. And before you know
it, you're telling girls they can't play dinosaurs with you. (And then
you're a palaeontologist mansplaining women's own research areas to
them at conferences). And the segregation of playthings so often mir-
rors the segregation of children themselves, too.

> 'Preferences' for gendertyped toys and same-gender playmates
> begin to emerge around 2 years of age. The entrenchment of gen-
> der stereotypes and prejudice at such an early and formative stage
> of development has implications for children's identities, aspira-
> tions, and achievements.[9]

These 'preferences' are about fitting into a social order, about self-
categorisation to adjust to arbitrary boundaries placed on children by
adults. I lost count of the times my daughters were told to 'play nicely
with the other girls'. What is 'nicely'? Why should they play with 'other
girls'? Why are we perpetuating this compliance model for girls from
such a young age? Some parents explain that they think boys are rougher
and more aggressive, and they want to 'protect' their girls from them.

The most important thing to focus on, in my view: Are we raising
boys who think aggression is their only mode of self-expression, or the
only way of fitting in with 'boyness'?

'We're trying to teach boys and girls that you can be anything you
want to be, but yet we're still forcing an identity on a child', said one of
the volunteers in the gender-swap baby experiment in *No More Boys and
Girls*, wide-eyed. 'This isn't harmless stuff'. That avalanche of pink is
drowning our girls' ambitions and making meek-eyed princesses out of
powerful potential scientists, politicians and executives.

We may need to immunise against other people. Arguably the most
important job of good parenting and good teaching is giving young
people a set of tools by which to understand and navigate the world
they must live in. By understanding gendered toys and hobbies as a
marketing strategy, a traffic system to contain and filter them, children
can find their way around without them, too. Other people will give
children things, and sometimes those things will not be good for them.
Sometimes (like an ancient children's book that's overtly racist, or 'The

Big Boy's Book of Stickers' or a teddy bear with eyelashes), we can just file them in the bin, like adults. Other times we can explain how they might be problematic.

But tiny ones can't yet understand this in the same way. We need a good range of toys. We need to counteract the gendered toys with non-gendered toys and non-gendered ways of interacting with them. We need to point out the sad untruths of the gender discrimination in clear terms.

'That's a picture of two boys playing with a fire engine, but girls like fire engines too. Women can be firefighters, too'.

'All these dolls are for all the children to play with. Everyone can have fun with the dolls'.

'Those calculators are pink because someone thought it was a good way to market them to girls and women. But of course anyone can use any coloured calculator; they all work the same.'

In one study, just showing young children a counter-stereotypical image of a child playing with a toy had an impact on their choice of playmate and their ideas of gender flexibility.[9] We need more scripts, and we need to break the tired, tatty ones that are creating such boring and clichéd ideas of gender for all of us.

Later, the conversation can be more nuanced, the encouragement more subtle. I have met many adults who have had a life rich with unusual hobbies because someone, somewhere inspired them at school or at home with a metalworking taster day, an eye-opening science lesson, a birdwatching discussion or a weightlifting video clip, and none of this stuff should be at all related to gender. If you are a secondary school teacher, this isn't just for primary or early years. I heard of one teacher who gave out fluffy pink pens to boys who forgot theirs in the hope of shaming them; another confiscated a football from some boys and wouldn't give it back to a girl because she thought it wasn't hers (it was.).

As an example: my daughters enjoy playing video games. As I write this, they are playing a virtual reality game called *Creed: Rise to Glory* in which you are a pro boxer against an opponent (it's really just PE dressed up to look more fun). All my life, I have always thought of boxing as coded male, not for me, aggressive and stupid. I wouldn't have bought this game, nor would I have encouraged my daughters to try it (luckily, my partner did both of those things).

But – the game is fun and we all enjoy it.

But – hearing my eldest release her aggression this way makes me reflect on female strength in a powerful way.

But – over a cup of tea, my youngest has just asked me to take her to boxing lessons.

Gender could have so easily got in the way of this stuff, even for me, even in 2019, and it takes a force of will to makes sure it doesn't. But my children will grow up knowing that boxing isn't a place where they aren't welcome, and they will fight (I hope with words unless fists are appropriate) anyone who tells them so. That's worth something, and maybe it generalises too.

Now/later

Now: Audit your toys, your classroom equipment and what is available for your students to use as tools. Are they, or could they be seen as, gendered? (For example, calculators coloured blue and pink; toy cars and trucks; dress-up costumes; pens and pencils.) Have a conversation with students about this, and see what their perceptions are.

Later: Think about the clubs your school runs, the hobbies and extra-curricular stuff. Who goes to them, and why? Do you have a football club that's explicitly for boys, or a craft club that seems to only attract girls? Ask students what kinds of clubs they go to (or would go to if they were available), and why.

Graham says

Towards the end of *No More Boys and Girls* the class members are given a paper bag to take home, and in each bag is a toy. The production team carefully chose for the girls toys normally (and normatively) associated with boys, such as a robot car kit or a marble run, while the boys were given more creative toys, such as a craft bundle or puppet sewing kit. The packaging was taken away from the toys, and the children played with them at home and came in the next day to talk about them. Wise beyond her years, Lily hit the nail on the head when she talked about the robot car that she received: 'Boys buy that stuff because of what the outside package looks like – they make it look more girly or more boyish, don't they?' to a chorus of approvals from her peers. It would seem that children will enjoy a toy regardless of whether it is 'aligned' with their gender if manufacturers decide not to aim the packaging of their toys at boys or girls. This is slowly starting to happen, and great campaigns from the likes of 'Let Toys be Toys' has had an impact, but if you look in toy stores or catalogues, there is still a parted sea of gendered toys and games.

So what can we do in school? We have the opportunity to give our children the chance to play with a range of toys without packaging and without the fear of their thinking it's not for them – so let's do it! We introduced tangram puzzles to help with spatial awareness because many 'boys' toys' (like Lego and Meccano) are aimed at improving these skills, and many 'girls' toys' (such as crafts, dolls and play houses) are aimed at creativity or imaginative play. The children loved them, and with a little practice girls were soon able to complete the puzzles at least as quickly as the boys. This really helped me understand: Unless we give children the opportunities to use toys that help with spatial awareness, especially the girls, then how are they going to get better at it? On the flipside, it is crucial to allow our boys to experience imaginative role play, to play with dolls and to be creative. And it must be possible for them to have these choices without fear of consequences.

As a parent, teacher or caregiver, make your children aware of what the manufacturers do, and encourage them to look at catalogues (online or real) and analyse who is playing with what and the language used. Get children to write letters to the retailers or start a campaign asking for change. Another nice activity is to get children to design gender-neutral packaging for a toy. How can we make it appeal to boys *and* girls? This brings out some important assumptions and ideas to talk about.

Tl;dr

Toys are often horribly gender divided, and it's difficult to opt out. Let schools and classrooms be the place where we overtly question this, where we encourage a tremendous variety and range of play from all pupils. Let's throw away the really harmful stuff without regret, and let's go back to enjoying play ourselves without interacting with things in a gendered way.

References

1. Ulrich, I., & Ezan, P. (2016). Boys and dolls; girls and cars: Children's reactions to incongruent images in a retailer's catalogue. *International Journal of Retail and Distribution Management, 44*(10), 1047–1063.
2. Betteley, C. (2017). *Toys over the years.* Retrieved from https://www.bbc.com/news/uk-wales-40455985
3. Retailers. (2013). Retrieved April 20, 2019, from Let Toys Be Toys website: http://lettoysbetoys.org.uk/retailers/
4. McKay, F. (2018). *Raising children without gender stereotypes.* Retrieved April 20, 2019, from Let Toys Be Toys website: http://lettoysbetoys.org.uk/raising-children-without-gender-stereotypes/
5. Weale, S. (2016). Gendered toys could deter girls from career in engineering, report says. *The Guardian.* Retrieved from https://www.theguardian.com/lifeandstyle/2016/dec/08/gendered-toys-deter-girls-from-career-engineering-technology
6. Bates, L. (2015). *Everyday Sexism* (Paperback edition). Londonn New York, Sydney: Simon & Schuster.
7. NAEYC. *What the research says: Impact of specific toys on play.* (n.d.). Retrieved April 20, 2019, from https://www.naeyc.org/resources/topics/play/specific-toys-play
8. Schulte, B. (2018). *How different are men and women, really?* Retrieved April 20, 2019, from *Slate Magazine* website: https://slate.com/human-interest/2018/02/an-interview-with-angela-saini-author-of.html
9. Spinner, L., Cameron, L., & Calogero, R. (2018). Peer toy play as a gateway to children's gender flexibility: The effect of (counter) stereotypic portrayals of peers in children's magazines. *Sex Roles, 79*(5–6), 314–328. https://doi.org/10.1007/s11199-017-0883-3

Expert view: let toys be toys

Jess Day

- 'Girls are nurses and boys are doctors'. Rachel, age 5
- 'My daughter refused to get on a blue carousel horse when she was 5, stating "that one is for boys"! One of my son's classmates refused to use my daughter's scooter during a playdate as it was pink.' Ruth
- 'The catalogues make it look like caring toys are not for boys'. Charlie, 7
- 'My son was too embarrassed to get off at the "girls" floor in Hamleys because it is all in pink, despite there being something he wanted there'. Jo
- 'I know that's the girls' section because of all the pictures of girls ... Mr. Frosty is for boys, because there are boys in the advert'. Ted, age 4
- 'My daughter (4) said she can't become a vet, only a nurse, because she's a girl'. Rita
- 'My daughter just wanted to be a princess, and when I asked her about being an astronaut, a doctor – anything science related – she said that was for boys only'. Fran
- '[My sister] can play with this too. Look, there's a picture of a girl on the box'. Matthew, 4
- 'The colour of things is very significant – often children would play with anything unless it was pink – in which case the boys wouldn't touch it and, sometimes, the girls would be quite proprietorial about it ...'. Teacher

In 2017 toy catalogues, boys were four times as likely as girls to be shown playing with cars, and girls were 12 times as likely as boys to be shown playing with baby dolls.[1]

The Boys Reading Commission report found that boys' under-achievement in reading is associated with 'Male gender identities which do not value learning and reading as a mark of success'.

Toys are marketed in a more gendered way now than 50 years ago. In the Sears catalogue adverts from 1975, less than 2% of toys were explicitly marketed to either boys or girls.[2]

In 2012, half the UK toy stores reviewed by *Let Toys Be Toys* labelled toys 'for boys' or 'for girls' through store signage, or even labels on packaging.[3] A 2012 study found that all toys sold on the Disney Store's US website were explicitly categorised as being 'for boys' or 'for girls'. There was no 'for boys and girls' option, even though a handful of toys could be found on both lists. (The disney.co.uk site dropped 'gender' as a navigation category for toys in 2016.)[4]

A 2011 review on the 'Rambling Brick' Lego blogger site put the proportion of feminine minifigures in Lego sets at just 11%, although there's been significant improvement since.[5]

Studies show that children think boys are academically inferior to girls, and they believe that adults think so too.[6]

When infant school children were asked to draw a firefighter, a surgeon and a fighter pilot, they drew 61 pictures of men and 5 of women.[7]

'Men are doctors, women are nurses', announced my daughter, much to the surprise and amusement of everyone around the table. Given that most of the GPs at our local surgery are women, and the majority of doctors she's met in her short life have been women, she clearly isn't basing this on direct life experience.

You don't have to look far, though, to see where children pick up the idea that there are 'pink jobs' and 'blue jobs'. No nurse has worn a dress, cape and cap for decades, but the stereotype is alive and well in the toy catalogues.

It would be easy, from an adult point of view, to shrug off the importance of toys and toy marketing. But toys loom enormously large in children's worlds, and play is central to how they learn about and interpret the world. Billions are spent on developing, packaging, merchandising and marketing toys, and our children are the targets. These marketing messages form a highly influential part of the drip, drip, drip of gendered messaging, telling children that boys and girls can't like, or do, the same things.

Children are gender detectives, eager to solve the puzzle of what it means to be a boy or a girl, a distinction that the adults around them seem to make such a fuss about. Toy marketing gives them heaps of nice simple instructions about 'how to be a boy/girl', which they'll often then use to police one other. 'That's not for boys!'

About *Let Toys Be Toys*

Let Toys Be Toys is a campaign asking the toy and publishing industries to stop limiting children's interests by promoting some toys and books as suitable only for girls and others as only for boys. This campaign was launched in 2012 to challenge the labelling of toy shelves as 'boys' toys' and 'girls' toys', and we've largely achieved that goal in the United Kingdom. Fifteen UK retailers have changed their merchandising, and we didn't find any explicit boys/girls signage when we surveyed shops in 2016 – not bad for an online campaign run by volunteers and squeezed in around our work and family lives.

In 2014 we launched a similar campaign to see an end to book titles that indicate whether a book is intended 'for girls' or 'for boys', and 11 publishers, including Usborne and Random House group, have committed to stop titling books in this way in future.

The *boys* and *girls* signs may be gone from toy stores, but taking the gender labelling off products is just the start; marketing sends signals in myriad ways, including through language, colour, imagery and positioning. We suggest that it conveys implicit rules about what boys and girls are meant to like, and to be like. So we continue to work with the toy industry, and with parents and educators, to challenge limiting stereotypes. We want children to choose their interests for themselves and to feel free to enjoy the full range of play experiences.

Play matters

A sign that makes a child feel bad about their choice of toys is just plain mean, but there's much more to why we are campaigning. If we want to challenge the inequalities we see in adult life, from violence against women and girls and the gender pay gap to the crisis in men's mental well-being or boys' underachievement in school, there's no more important place to start than what we tell our children about what it means to be a boy or a girl, a man or a woman.

Different play develops different skills, so a varied play 'diet' is vital. As a campaign, we argue that it really doesn't matter whether boys and girls tend to make different choices – there's no good argument for restricting a child's range of play or for making a child feel bad about enjoying the 'wrong' toys.

After all, any innate gender differences will be free to appear if children are genuinely offered equivalent opportunities and a free choice. Thus, whatever you think about the innate differences between boys and girls, offering, and encouraging, a wide range of play has no downside, opening up opportunities and benefiting everyone. Come on. Who's against more fun?

The human brain is shaped by experience – the skills we gain are the ones we practise. In the *No More Boys and Girls* programme, the girls' progress in maths and mental rotation tasks was marked, following regular practice with tangram puzzles, once they got the message that girls could be good at these things and there was nothing to hold them back.

When I spoke at a British Science Festival event recently, an audience member shared his own real-life example: He had taught people to drive for 30-odd years and said he'd noticed no difference at all in the driving abilities of young women and young men, except in the area of reverse manoeuvring, where men systematically outperformed women. He started asking his students whether they'd ever had a remote control car as a child, and he found that all the boys had, but almost none of the girls. So he went out and bought a remote control car, and he lent it to his female students to practise with between lessons, with immediate results. The gender difference was almost completely wiped out. We're good at what we practise, and girls and boys are offered different toys and encouraged to practise different things.

If boys are taken to the park to develop their spatial skills[8] and encouraged to compete and be active, while girls are encouraged to look nice, be careful,[9] understand their feelings, have empathy, regulate their emotions and help others to regulate theirs, it's not at all surprising that we see different patterns of skill in male and female adults.

As parents, it's incredibly difficult to break these patterns, even if we want to – after all, we've been socialised in the same way. Research shows[10] that parents tend to assume that boys are more physically adept than girls; they punish sons more harshly; they talk to them less than to daughters; they are certainly less likely to discuss emotions with boys – with the exception of anger, which they are more likely to discuss with boys than with girls; and they are also less likely to read to boys or take them to the library.

Toys and books marketed to girls are more focused on themes of beauty, imagination, caring, cooking and cleaning. They feature stories about princesses or romance and include more passive play. But of course girls also enjoy a wide variety of active play and interests that aren't reflected in these choices. Dressing up, fantasy and nurturing play are all a great part of that varied play diet, but a constant emphasis on appearance and people pleasing feeds anxiety and body image worries, impacting their self-confidence, and their mental and physical health, into adulthood.

We find that toys and books marketed to boys mainly have themes of action, adventure, science, space and transport and that they are missing themes that revolve around caring and creativity, though of course boys enjoy all kinds of imaginative and caring types of play. But when a father with a pushchair wouldn't draw a second glance in the street, why does anyone find it surprising for a boy to want to play with a dolly or a toy pram?

People are usually quick to see the ways that narrow stereotypes harm girls. But boys lose out just as much when we tell them certain things are not for them. The way our culture devalues 'feminine' things means it's often harder for us to recognize this type of deprivation. But the stereotype of a 'proper boy' as rough, active, not creative, not emotional (apart from anger) and unable to sit still or pay attention does real damage. We see it playing out in boys' underperformance in school and harming their mental health and relationships. Suicide is the leading cause of death among men under 50 in the United Kingdom.[11]

Embedded in a culture that values masculine traits, it's hard for adults to see what boys are missing out on. Children may be more clear-sighted: A group of pre-teen boys came up with this moving list of 'what I don't like about being a boy':

Not being able to be a mother
Not suppost to cry
Not allowed to be a cheerleader
Suppost to do all the work
Suppost to like violence
Suppost to play football
Boys smell bad
Having a automatic bad reputation
Grow hair everywhere[12]

Research by the Boys' Reading Commission[13] identified stereotypes of masculinity that don't value reading and education as a key factor in boys' underperformance in reading. (This makes supposedly 'boy friendly' curricula actively harmful, rather than helpful, if they reinforce stereotypes.) I've lost count of the number of times people have said in front of my son that 'boys don't really read, do they?' or have proclaimed that so-and-so is a 'typical boy' because he won't pay attention or sit down or he isn't interested in drawing a picture. Like the kindly lady at the book festival who apologised: 'Sorry, the theme today is Alice in Wonderland, which the boys don't like'. This was the first he'd heard of boys not liking it!

When boys get the idea that learning, reading, emotions, creativity and caring for others are 'for girls', and that the most important thing in the world is to demonstrate that they're not 'like a girl', they're missing out. But these misconceptions also reinforce the idea that anything associated with girls or women is inferior, normalising misogyny and sexism from an early age.

There's no escape

As a parent, you quickly learn that no matter what you want for your child, you can't ever fully opt out of gendered norms. Unless you're incredibly ruthless about refusing gifts, your home will soon be awash with highly gendered playthings. A few Christmases ago my kids were given two Lego sets. My daughter received 'Andrea's Nightclub Stage', complete with stage set and cocktail glass (?). For my son: the Lego City police stakeout set. They couldn't have got my kids more wrong. He found Lego City downright terrifying (full of crime and natural disasters) and would much rather have had a Lego Friends school or cupcake bakery. Meanwhile, his sister is still annoyed that *all* the Playmobil pirates have beards!

And children are paying close attention to the cues, to learn what they're 'allowed' to want. My kids have always been encouraged to play with whatever they like. It still took my son a whole year to pluck up the courage to ask for the Lego Friends High School, which he loved with a passion. I found out he wanted it only when he spotted, in a shop, that the set included a boy minidoll, and he felt that gave him permission.

It's not just the kids who are under pressure from marketing; adults too feel huge social pressure to conform to the 'norm'. The trend for larger 'whole class' parties means that an awful lot of toys are bought for children that the buyer knows absolutely nothing about beyond age and sex. And when people feel obliged to stick to the conventional script, the result is a lot of very stereotyped gifts. I can remember the contrast between my daughter's sixth birthday gifts from people who knew her (pirates and leopards, her passions at the time) and those who didn't really (every single item was pink.)

There's no reason to believe this is what consumers actually want. A recent survey of Australian parents found that 92% of parents of 0- to 3-year-olds felt that it was important that boys and girls be treated the same, and that 79% wanted to take action to challenge traditional gender stereotypes. Another international survey of parents found that a majority thought that children should be raised in as gender-neutral a way as possible to guard against stereotypes.

And parents often feel they have to 'play safe' themselves. My friend didn't buy the Peppa Pig 'girl' pants that her son wanted (there were only George pig pants 'for boys'), because she didn't want him to be teased at the childminder's. Research shows that dads in particular are anxious about their children stepping outside gender norms out of fear of what other people will think.

When children receive gifts according to their gender, not their interests, it tells them that gender is a good guide to their decision making, that it's more than what they really think or feel. There's absolutely no point in telling older girls, 'Hey, women can be engineers too', or in telling boys, 'Yes, it's ok to have emotions other than anger, and to talk about them', if we've spent their formative years telling them just the opposite.

If we want boys and girls to grow up knowing they can freely choose their interests, studies and future careers from the full range available, then we need to take every opportunity to emphasise what boys and girls have in common, instead of constantly harping on about and drawing attention to every possible difference.

So what can you do?

In the primary classroom

- Make sure there's a good range of toys available: Nurturing or home corner play is just as important as construction or vehicles.
- Think about whether there are cues that label certain toys or areas by gender – take care with colour and language.
- Reassure children that it's ok to choose whatever they like, and challenge it when children come up with gender 'rules'.

- Use toys and toy marketing as a way to get children to think about stereotypes and choices – there are lesson plans available on the *Let Toys Be Toys* website, along with more tips.

At home

- Offer a wide range of toys, clothes and colours. Encourage family and friends who kindly buy gifts to do the same. People are often very happy to be given suggestions.

- When giving gifts, ideally ask for guidance about the child's interests, but if that's not possible, try to avoid falling back on stereotyped assumptions about what a child will want.

- Reassure your child that they can like any colour or toy they like – there's no such thing as a 'boys' toy' or a 'girls' toy'.

- Once they're old enough to start noticing stereotypes, talk about them. Why do some people think X is 'for girls/boys'? Do you think that's right?

- Toy adverts represent girls and boys in very stereotyped ways. If your children watch commercial television, take time to watch the adverts with them and discuss the adverts. What are boys and girls shown playing with? What are they doing?

- Support retailers who market toys in an inclusive way to boys and girls. See www.lettoysbetoys.org.uk/toymark for a list of *Let Toys Be Toys* Toymark retailers.

References

1. *Most toy catalogues still play to stereotypes – New research.* (2017, December 6). Retrieved April 20, 2019, from Let Toys Be Toys website: http://lettoysbetoys.org.uk/toy-catalogues-2017/
2. Sweet, E. (2014, December 9). *Toys are more divided by gender now than they were 50 years ago.* Retrieved April 20, 2019, from *The Atlantic* website: https://www.theatlantic.com/business/archive/2014/12/toys-are-more-divided-by-gender-now-than-they-were-50-years-ago/383556/
3. *Let Toys Be Toys briefing and survey report.* (2012). Retrieved April 20 2019, from Let Toys Be Toys website: http://lettoysbetoys.org.uk/wp-content/uploads/2012/12/lettoysbetoys_briefing_and_survey_dec_2012.pdf

4. Spinner, L., Cameron, L., & Calogero, R. (2018). Peer toy play as a gateway to children's gender flexibility: The effect of (counter) stereotypic portrayals of peers in children's magazines. *Sex Roles, 79*(5–6), 314–328. https://doi.org/10.1007/s11199-017-0883-3
5. Ramblingbrick. (2017, October 31). *Minifigure gender distribution: 2017 update.* Retrieved April 20, 2019, from The Rambling Brick website: https://ramblingbrick.com/2017/10/31/minifigure-gender-distribution-2017-update/
6. *Negative stereotypes about boys hinder their academic achievement.* (2013) Retrieved April 20, 2019, from *ScienceDaily* website: https://www.sciencedaily.com/releases/2013/02/130212100554.htm
7. Redraw the Balance. (n.d.). Retrieved April 20, 2019, from MullenLowe Group UK website: https://www.mullenlowelondon.com/our-work/redraw-the-balance/
8. Study. *Parents are not taking kids outside to play, especially girls.* TIME.com. (2012). Retrieved April 20, 2019, from http://healthland.time.com/2012/04/03/why-are-parents-less-likely-to-take-little-girls-outside-to-play/
9. O'Neal, E., Plumert, J. M., & Peterson, C., Parent–child injury prevention conversations following a trip to the emergency department. *Journal of Pediatric Psychology, 41*(2), 256–264. https://doi.org/10.1093/jpepsy/jsv070
10. Asher, R. (2017). *Man up: How do boys become better men?* London: Vintage.
11. Mental Health Foundation. *Mental health statistics: Suicide.* (2016). Retrieved April 20, 2019, from https://www.mentalhealth.org.uk/statistics/mental-health-statistics-suicide
12. *Understanding boys, understanding girls.* (2012). Retrieved April 20, 2019, from https://higherunlearning.com/2012/05/02/understanding-boys-understanding-girls/
13. Boys' Reading Commission. (n.d.). Retrieved April 20, 2019, from National Literacy Trust website: http://literacytrust.org.uk/policy-and-campaigns/all-party-parliamentary-group-literacy/boys-reading-commission/

Sexism and sexual harassment

Male midwives – male caring is a joke – the business end – a bit weird – protection – only a compliment – school uniform as a wrapper – not illegal – a sexist time warp – policies out of drawers – you're a slut – genitals are not valuables – it's just Dave – I'm fine – Groundhog Sexism – collaborating with men – a can of worms – lifting the rock – maybe I'm the ghost – I have a value beyond this – a downright powerplay – there is no comeback – red flags

Stats

In 2015, there were fewer women leading FTSE firms in the United Kingdom than men called John.[1]

Only 14% of students who have experienced sexual harassment reported it to a teacher.[2]

About 66% of girls in the United Kingdom have experienced sexual attention or sexual or physical contact in a public place.[3]

One in eight large employers admits that sexual harassment in their companies goes unreported, according to a YouGov survey of 800 HR decision-makers about women's experiences at work.[4]

The issues

'I have always had some doubts about the motives of men who chose obstetrics as a career', begins a post on Mumsnet. 'Did they want to be able to tell women what to do, when the women aren't in a position to argue?' According to The Royal College of Midwives, in 2014 there were 103 men working in the field compared to 31,189 women, and this figure has been static for around ten years.[5] We don't even have a name for a 'coded male midwife' that isn't gendered – although, to be fair, the 'wife' part is supposed to refer to the woman in labour that one is attending, who presumably doesn't haven't to be married, or indeed in a heterosexual relationship or indeed in any relationship, to receive such care.

One man reports telling his friends his choice of profession and realizing that they expected a 'punch line': being male and caring for mothers and babies is literally a joke to some people.

An interview with an Australian man working in the sector: 'One of the things I found about being a male midwife is [people questioning] the motive as to why a guy would want to be a midwife', Mr. Jones said.

'Is there some sort of deviant behaviour – or is there some sort of femininity that's coming out in me as an individual?'[6]

Deviant behaviour. Femininity. This sounds like fear, turned to suspicion, and I suspect that it often turns to hatred, too. An online poll of 8600 women showed that an astonishing 46% of them would prefer a female midwife, as opposed to being happy with or not minding a male one.[7]

From an interview with a man in the sector: 'One father-to-be told [the male midwife] that he didn't want to "share his woman with me"'.[8] Discussions abound of 'the business end' of the bed during birth. 'I hated the idea of a strange man having to touch me and look "down there"', said one woman.

No one is disputing a person's right to feel comfortable when in labour or to be cared for by someone they trust. But the question is, what are all these women – and sometimes their male partners – afraid of?

Are they afraid of men touching them because men routinely touch them without their consent?

Are they afraid of letting men into one of the last traditionally 'female' spaces left in contemporary UK society?

Are they afraid of men's love, care and empathy?

Think about men as carers: midwives, nurses, nannies. Think of them wiping bottoms and giving hugs and holding hands and offering support and easing pain. How does that make you feel?

One of the reasons why the sexism feels so blatant in the example above is that it is inflicted on men, I think. I imagine that excluding *females* from things occurs so often that, like a screensaver, we fail to notice it.

In *No More Boys and Girls,* one of the (male) pupils says, with a noticeable smirk, 'Men are better because they're stronger, and they have the best jobs'. One of the girls says, 'If you thought of a boy as being a nurse, it sounds a bit weird – and it would look a bit weird as well'. What looks or sounds 'weird', of course, is relative to what you're used to. My brother's a dancer, so it's normal for me to conceive of male-ness and expressive, beautiful dance and strength all in one thought without any dissonance. One of my friends is a stay-at-home dad, so it barely registers any more. Sometimes you only need one example.

The producers of *No More Boys and Girls* brought in some special guests 'to show the children that there is an alternative to what they think is the inevitable path for men and women'. The result was powerful. Pupils got to see and hear and engage with non-gender-stereotypical role models: a ballet dancer, a mechanic, a magician, a makeup artist.

Can you imagine meeting a male childminder, a female software designer, a non-binary model? Can you picture non-gender-stereotypical people doing a variety of different jobs? Do you use a mix of pronouns when talking about careers?

Our children are still growing up with fixed and limiting ideas about what they can achieve, based on gendered norms. Sexism affects careers in two ways: the choices pupils make about their interests, their capabilities and what they choose to pursue; and the more insidious issue of sexism in the environment, which begins in school and usually persists in the professional domain. This might range from 'benevolent' (treating boys and girls differently, often in the guise of 'protection'; not picking up on gendered insults) to intentional and/or institutional sexism, often in the form of unchallenged sexual harassment.

What do we need to 'protect' people from?

What assumptions are we making about people on the basis of their gender?

What, exactly, is it about being a firefighter that women 'shouldn't do'?

What is it about certain jobs that feels gendered to us, and why?

We need to talk about sexual harassment

A 2018 House of Commons report: 'Sexual harassment can include verbal, non-verbal and physical acts – including sexual comments, taking 'up-skirt' photographs, or unwanted sexual touching. Unwanted sexual touching, wherein the target does not consent to the touching and the perpetrator does not reasonably believe they consent, constitutes sexual assault'.[9]

'Reports from both students and teachers reveal that sexual harassment is prevalent in schools. For many students, it is simply the norm'.[2]

Sexual harassment affects the lives of girls and women in so many ways. Their confidence. Their expectations. Their emotional state. Their safety, both perceived and real. They adopt strategies to take up less space, to try and minimise their bodies and their existence to avoid this unwanted attention.

From a young age, we receive the message that girls' and women's bodies do not belong to them, that they can be touched, handled, groped and grabbed by males with little comeback or possibility of consequence. On the bus, in the street, under the table, hands wander and eyes wink and smiles smirk and women put up with it.

An epidemic

From the same House of Commons report: 'Around the world harassment and the threat of harassment can have serious implications for girls' freedom, autonomy and perceived safety. In both the UK and internationally, evidence shows that harassment of girls and women in public places is widespread and profoundly affects their lives'.[3]

Let's think about that. There is a 'widespread' issue that is 'profoundly' affecting girls and women with 'serious' implications for their autonomy. It starts with comments, language and subtle differences in expectations – and it starts horrifically young. Why aren't we doing more about it?

In a moment, I'm going to share with you something that happened to me outside a primary school that illustrates exactly how young it starts for the boys as well as the girls.

So far, this is about pupils. But it obviously doesn't end there – a school environment that is sexist for pupils is likely to be sexist for teachers as well.

I've been asking teachers about their experiences at schools. It makes for grim reading. I have paraphrased and collected their comments here to protect their identities.

Teachers report being verbally abused by pupils with gendered insults like 'slut', 'whore' and 'bitch'. They report male students ogling them, touching them sexually, trying to kiss them, following them home, shouting at them in public, simulating sex near or on them and, in one case, masturbating over them. They report little support from colleagues and little idea about whom to inform or how to deal with these issues. They report extreme anger and frustration at trying to balance the sensitive needs of young people and their own need to feel safe. Worse, some teachers are also being sexually harassed by colleagues, who crack jokes at their expense, comment on their bodies, make them feel self-conscious and talk about or to them inappropriately.

I have had pupils draw pornographic sketches of me and them, and hand them in to me; and I have been the target of rape threats and physical/sexual intimidation.

I did not report these incidents, generally. That was after the first time I reported such behaviour and I was laughed at and told, 'You can't blame them, can you?'

Are you feeling uncomfortable yet? Not as uncomfortable as I was, pinned up against the wall by a 6-foot Year 11 student, shaking, as he told me, 'Next time you give me detention, I'm going to rape you', as his friends watched and laughed.

This might be a good time to take a breather. Have you experienced being sexually harassed or intimidated? How did you feel and what did you do?

I talk to women about this all the time, and the stories are nearly identical – being asked to sit on men's laps, touched and groped and stroked, followed home, asked to smile, leered at and harassed in the street or on the bus or in a cafe or in a parked car. It starts young. Your pupils of 5 or 6 will likely be experiencing it. They might not notice it until later. By the time they hit puberty, they might find it remarkable – that is, if anyone is listening. Later on, they might feel like it's normal. Plenty of teenage or adult women are so fucking tired of dealing with it that they don't know whom to turn to, and they have encountered some adults who laugh, some who are dismissive and some who tell them it's 'only a compliment'. If you have ever, ever said that to a woman, never mind a school-age girl, shame on you.

From a Plan UK report on street harassment:

> All of the girls we spoke to had stories of intimidating and unwanted behaviour, with many having witnessed and experienced harassment from a very young age – some as young as eight years old. This often happened when they were in uniform, which they felt made them a particular target.[3]

All the fuss that gets made about young girls being at risk, the requirement to protect them, the worries about them walking home on their own or in the dark. *That's because of men sexualising them.* (If it weren't, we'd feel the same about boys.) It's because men feel that they are entitled to treat girls like eye-candy, and they somehow see a school uniform as a particularly enticing wrapper.

'But there are policies! There must be laws that protect people?' you might be thinking. 'Why don't they report it, and make the perpetrators face the consequences?'

A story hit the news two years ago about a teacher who took 'upskirt' pictures of pupils. Andrew Corish admitted taking photographs and videos of pupils for sexual gratification but was told his actions did not break the law. In 2017. Let that sink in. The judge ruled that none of Corish's alleged victims 'were involved in a private act under the legal definition'.[10]

What you may keep under your skirt is private, but since it's not a 'private act', just about anyone can have a good old look at it and not be culpable under the voyeurism law. Charming.

One of the students at this teacher's school approached me and wanted her voice heard.

'This prick worked at my school when I was there. It was a running "joke" that he would always stare at our chests when we spoke to him. I was never taught by him, but I remember testing this theory out once on the stairs and sure enough, he just looked at my breasts while I was speaking. Keeping in mind even as sixth formers who were allowed to wear our own clothes, we weren't allowed to wear low-cut tops, so our dress was always pretty "modest". Apparently even some of the teachers were creeped out by this but didn't say anything. It was so normalised. This was more than 10 years ago. Then just recently, [this story] comes to light and I feel bad we never said anything while we were there. If we had, it could've been nipped in the bud and the poor girls may not have gone through such trauma. We knew he was dodgy and we just went along with it – that's "just how he was". What's even worse is, this man had twin daughters who attended our school. When male teachers in girls' schools with daughters – people who have double the responsibility to ensure the safety of women on a day-to-day basis – betray such trust, it makes one feel very unsafe. This has got to be stamped out and girls need to be told that no behaviour that makes them feel uncomfortable is okay'.

Do you know anyone who gets away with being lecherous or making sexually inappropriate comments or jokes because 'that's just how he is'?

I imagine you're as horrified as I am at this point.

The truth – that both teachers and pupils are subject to sexism, often extreme – is the starting point. Before we think about possible solutions, it's important to acknowledge that these people are *angry*. People who have been oppressed and unfairly treated might react with a range of emotions, from total indifference to fury. If you have been discriminated against – and often not just once, but over and over – then you may well shrug it off, but you may not. You may be white-hot angry about it, compounded by a lack of action in dealing with it. Thus you are stuck in a sexist time warp, a looped tape where you can't make it stop. You may want to fucking scream.

If this is you, I'm so, so, sorry this has happened to you. You have the space and the right to be angry. Claim it, if you need to. Process that anger and own it. You have been treated abominably. Go and have a cup of tea and a cry, or a shout or release in any other safe way. Throw this book at the wall or out the window, if you like, imagining it to be whoever behaved like such a grade-A cunt towards you (I bet my editor puts stars in there instead of letters, because men can call women cunts as much as they like, but God forbid we write the word down in a book, eh?).

What makes me particularly furious is the ends of these stories: so often the final footnote 'Nothing was done'. If you have worked in a school, you know that unpredictable and challenging events happen. From pupils vomiting on me to parents threatening me, I have had colourful and exciting times at work on many an occasion, but I was fully aware this might be likely when I trained to be a teacher. Pupils misbehaving, to a lesser or greater degree depending on the setting, is also a realistic expectation; even colleagues behaving less than perfectly is something that fails to surprise me anymore (and on a good day I can acknowledge that they are as human and fallible as I am). But without systems of rules in place, and people in a position to monitor and run those systems; without policies that live in the classrooms and corridors and playgrounds and not just in desk drawers, we are failing in our very basic duties to make schools safe for girls and women and non-binary people and everyone. We should be doing better.

Have you ever had a pupil or a staff member report sexism or sexual harassment to you? What did you do? How did you feel about it?

Catcalling: not a compliment

So many of the stories feature people being shouted at on the street or in public. Recently, the metaphorical distance between catcalling and schools was dramatically reduced for me when the following incident occurred near my local primary school.

I had just wandered over the road to my local shop, passing my local primary school. I could hear the pupils noisily enjoying their lunch outside because it was a warm day.

I heard 'HELLO!' and smiled to myself (I was facing the other way).

Then 'HELLO! OI!'

Then 'LOOK AT ME!'

Then 'WHAT'S YOUR NAME?'

Then 'I LOVE POTATOES' (I smiled again).

Then 'TALK TO ME!'

Then 'WHERE ARE YOU GOING?'

Then 'ARE YOU GAY?'

Then 'YOU'RE A SLUT!'

I stopped.

I fixed them with my glare. They were 10- to 11-year-old boys. I am a teacher. I had to walk away because I was shaking so much with anger that I thought I might be misunderstood if I yelled at them through the school fence.

I walked up the hill, thinking. This is how it starts. This is how it starts, and I won't be complicit in it.

I walked up to the school fence.

'Hello!' said one of the boys, cheerily.

'Call your teacher over', I said.

I was pissed off, and I was shaking, but I managed to say this:

'Just now, as I was walking past, some of these boys decided to shout things at me – increasingly hostile things, when they couldn't get my attention. I'd like them to understand why that isn't ok ever, but also why it isn't ok to do it to women, because boys grow into men, and they don't stop doing it. They do it to feel powerful, and to try and make the woman feel small'.

Why does anyone yell at anyone they don't know? Because they feel bigger than they are. Because they can. Because they feel they are entitled to.

> Girls spoke about the range of emotions they felt when they were harassed. They talked about being embarrassed and ashamed for having attention drawn to them, disoriented and confused about who was doing the harassing and why, angry but in fear of what might happen if the situation escalated, and helpless but feeling responsible for making sure they stayed safe.[3]

Victim blaming

It's so, so easy to suggest that the practice of 'playing along' to avoid confrontation is at fault here. That, or whether our clothes were 'provocative', or whether we were drunk or sweary or wearing lipstick or high heels or had a reputation or were in the wrong place at the wrong time. There's a name for that.

Victim blaming is the unsavoury practice of laying responsibility partially or wholly at the feet of the victim of something, to deflect responsibility. It's commonplace in sexual discrimination encounters and is woven into the fabric of gender relations, from men going down to the pub to avoid a nagging wife to office workers tutting about a woman 'making a fuss' about sexual harassment. In terms of public harassment, the victim-blaming argument that is most often made is that women should not wear provocative clothing, get drunk or be present in the streets after dark or alone, 'for their own protection'. A common analogy is often employed: You wouldn't go out at night without locking your doors and windows (even though burglary is wrong). This same principle applies to women and girls.

Ouch. Need I remind you that we are not houses to be pillaged? Let me hand over to someone who responded to this on an online forum with a forensic takedown of the argument:

'Comparing the unwanted abuse of a woman's body to property theft shows us just how deeply ingrained the notion of women's bodies as property is and perpetuates this idea. In very recent memory rape really was considered a property crime, against that person's "owner" (husband/father etc.). In some parts of the world it still is'.[11]

You cannot compare a woman just existing and going about her daily life with 'keeping valuables in plain sight'. Women are not jewels for the taking. We are not displaying ourselves irresponsibly, flouting our bodies in the face of some creeping and creepy thieves who cannot help themselves from sweeping us into their sacks, grinning and shrugging. This is not funny or benign or inevitable.

Think about the way you view girls' bodies. Do you feel protective? Uncomfortable about the very thought? Worried that it is both your job and not your issue to consider? How do you feel about young women walking home after dark, wearing clothes that might be seen as sexual, drinking? Have you ever victim-blamed someone?

As I have said before, one of the most difficult issues around sexism is that it can be difficult to prove, talk about or assess. 'Did that just happen?' we might think. 'Did it mean what I thought it meant? Did they intend it that way?' We want to give people the benefit of the doubt, especially if they are our colleagues or our friends, and sometimes for less defendable reasons, such as the amount of admin it's going to take to process. We may not like to label it 'sexism' or 'sexual harassment' because that stinks of process, smells like procedure, seems too formalised – when it's just Dave, it's just a bit of banter, he's just a different generation, she's just touchy. This leads to victims not being believed, not being able to take things seriously, doubting themselves, finding a whole world of conflict that continues to shred them away inside long after the incident has occurred. I think about this often. There isn't an easy solution. But I think one place to start is to put ourselves in the place of someone on the receiving end of it and consider it from their point of view, the position it puts them in both during and afterwards.

There are more ways to silence women than just to shut them up

There are more ways to silence women than just to shut them up. You can, instead, ensure that all they are talking about is men. Kameron Hurley said that.[12]

Once an incident occurs, there's a synapse of time and space. It takes the longest time to process. You go from being off-guard and friendly – because who can possibly be on their guard all the time? – to disbelief, horror, frustration, anger. By the time you get to anger, indecision floods in too. Did they really mean it? (Yes). Did you precipitate it somehow? (No.) Is it worth causing a scene over? Are your feelings more important than politeness or keeping the peace? If you just swallow it, can you avoid a confrontation or are they going to keep going?

Everyone looks at you. They try to take their cue from you. If you don't react strongly and decisively and explicitly, they think everything's ok. What if it's not ok? How do you telegraph a need for support? How do you ask without asking? How do you reconcile the narrative of 'strong tough feminist' with 'this is really the sort of situation I could use a hand with, guys' – and not because you can't handle it on your own but because you really shouldn't have to. Are those onlookers as frozen as you, or are they uncaring or unaware or unsympathetic? Trouble is, it all looks the same.

No big deal.

And now, you have a clear choice. You can make an issue, or you can shut up. You can cause trouble, promote your own agenda, elevate your own feelings beyond that of mere object, or you can swallow it and internalise it and take responsibility for creating and resolving this 'incident' all on your own, the way you like to do things, the way independent people do who try not to involve people in their business all the time or seek attention or drag everyone down with them do. Are you going to be the party pooper? The miserable feminist? The predictable victim? Are you going to take the responsibility of changing the whole tone of the day, the responsibility you never wanted and yet inevitably got saddled with anyway?

Now you have a giant problem. You didn't start the day expecting it. You don't need it or want it. But either way, you've got a problem. And you did not create that problem, however you choose to deal with it. It's a roadblock in front of whatever you want to do now, and you can't shut your eyes and wish it away. You have to deal with it.

If you choose confrontation and discussion and education, it's a huge thing. If you choose silence and self-blame and anger and shame, it's a huge thing. It's effort and time and emotion that you could have done without. In reality, you always choose both in some way.

And then, there's managing the emotions of everyone else around you. Your mouth opens and out slips 'I'm fine'. You worry that they're blaming themselves, too, and that you're not reassuring them enough, and that you're not being ok is somehow your choice and it's an utterly selfish one. Stop ruining everything for everyone else.

I'm the kind of person who likes to be relaxed, independent and friendly. At least, I was. I've had a tiny taste of sexism in my life (and probably no racism or classism or ableism), and even this has shaped me like a tree growing around a rock. I'm all corners, splinters and crazy vertices in some places. I'm more challenging, more confrontational, probably harder work. I want to explain to people that it's their responsibility to take and that I didn't want to be this person; but if it's a straight up choice between that and smiling while I get called 'sweetheart', or having my knee squeezed by an old man, or staying silent while my daughters get patronised, I will fight, and you fucking started it so you'd better be ready for battle.

Except nothing seems to change. One or two people that you know and love will listen carefully, will question gently and expose their thoughts to you, and you feel maybe you are making progress – but everyone else seems to make it your problem while you continue to feel that it is theirs. There is no right and wrong, just tiredness on all sides. Everyone seems entrenched. Where to go from here?

Lucinda McKnight calls this 'Groundhog Sexism'.

> Groundhog Sexism is not accidental. It keeps you stuck on the basics, justifying your existence, re-hashing the same old arguments and facts. It wastes your time and energy, instead of enabling society to become more equal.[13]

* * *

What needs to change

The Cambridge University project 'Collaborating with Men' investigated issues surrounding collaborating between genders at work, because, as they state in the project aims: '"fixing the women" alone will not be enough to support the careers of ambitious young women. The culture in the workplace needs to change. That needs the collaboration of men'.

They identified six types of bias that favour men and disadvantage women in the workplace:

- **Personality and role congruence bias:** men benefit from association between stereotypical male values and leadership
- **Performance evaluation bias:** double standards in the way men's and women's performance and potential are assessed
- **Ability bias:** men tend to be promoted based on potential, whereas women are promoted based on experience
- **Language bias:** men talk over or don't hear women
- **Benevolent sexism:** well-motivated men make decisions for women that may 'kill careers with kindness'
- **Networking bias:** men's networks sideline women

Do you recognise any of these biases? Have you experienced them in the workplace? What about in your school?

The issues surrounding women and girls are so often categorised as 'women's issues' that men distance themselves from them, and it is hard to get men involved in making change. Men in schools may feel uncomfortable discussing sexism, bias or discrimination because it is, inconveniently, built into school buildings, systems and processes – and because there is little incentive for them to do so without accepting the title of villain. It may feel like an 'us and them' culture (it often is, but women didn't make it that way). They may be frightened about speaking up for fear of 'mansplaining'. They may be leaders of the school but unqualified, through lack of firsthand experience of sexism, to strategically plan how to eliminate it. They may have lived a life where they were unaware of the issues and may also feel that tackling them is 'opening a can of worms', creating conflict and confrontation where it is not necessary to do so. I have sympathy with these feelings, but they are not an excuse.

Without the cooperation of men and boys, non-males risk two things: taking on the problems themselves to solve (not sustainable, never mind unfair) and fighting a bitter battle of the sexes in which misunderstandings create perceived agendas and lack of education surfaces as a frustrating 'blame culture'.

It begins with an understanding that right now, the world that men and boys inhabit is simply not the same world that women and girls do. Everything else follows from there. (It is also true that women and girls – and other non-men – do not have homogeneous experiences of the world, either. I am heavily generalising and I hope you will forgive me.)

If you think sexism doesn't happen in your school, you are wrong. (It probably just doesn't happen to you.) It happens almost everywhere, almost all the time. Much of it is difficult to detect and prove, but much isn't. The stories abound and are horrifying. I recently attended a workshop on workplace sexism that began with quiet, worried women listening, and ended with a roomful of them speaking, crying and narrating. Their stories poured forth.

Have you ever spoken about workplace sexism? Have you attended a formal session on it or had an informal discussion with colleagues? What was said?

Clearly, we need to lift the rock of institutions and look squarely underneath at the squirming mass of assumptions, expectations and inequality they are resting on. Where on earth to start?

If you read various schools' endless witterings on websites and policy documents and job adverts, you might think this job is done.

'WE ARE AN EQUAL RIGHTS SCHOOL'.

'In our school, everyone has a right to be safe'.

'We value respect and fairness'.

'Everyone succeeds here'.

These are not different schools from those featured in the stories above. The disconnect between words and deeds is enormous. The attitude of 'it doesn't happen here' is so entrenched that breaking it down is our first and biggest hurdle. I have been catcalled, leered at and sexualised by pupils and teachers, and I have seen girls harassed in some way at every single school where I have worked. We have to start from the truth, while also acknowledging that the nature of that truth may be plural, complex and multi-layered.

When I walk around with someone who is non-female, often this scenario occurs: We are usually deep in thought and chat (I love to walk and talk). We pass someone on the street who is male. They catch my eye or stare at my body. Something passes between us. Then they see the man beside me and are gone.

'What was that?' asks the person I am with, puzzled.

'What?' I ask. Sometimes I don't even see it, but I usually do, and I want to know what they saw.

'That guy ... that was weird', they say. 'What ... why ... that was creepy...'. They turn around, staring hard at the back of the man. They squint with confusion.

They're right. It's often really hard to articulate how it feels to be creeped on. It feels like being gaslit the entire time, because in these sorts of cases the perpetrator didn't *say* anything or *touch* anything (though sometimes they do), but something passed between us, nonetheless. Something uncomfortable for me. Something about ownership and power. I can't tell you what that man was thinking, but I can tell you what it feels like to me. It feels like they looked at my face or my body (or both) and appraised me. Often, it feels like they looked at the man beside me and saw ownership, claim and belonging. It's like everyone's playing Pac-Man and I'm a little bit of food to be gobbled up, and the man beside me is the ghost, and so off Pac-Man trundles, down a new path, looking for a new and entirely interchangeable bit of sustenance, because that one's taken. Or maybe I'm the ghost, because I don't seem to exist as a real person. Just a phantom shag, a potential liaison, the spectre of a speculation they might make, which might result in a windfall of gold, a jackpot, a point scored in the jolly old game of bedknobs and wombsticks.

This also touches on a really important issue: Women and girls frequently have to swat off sexual harassment with 'I have a boyfriend'. It's a staple. 'I have a boyfriend', we smile, wishing they would fuck off. And usually, they do. (Sometimes they say something charming like 'I don't care, that's your problem'.) The 'I have a boyfriend' response speaks to ownership again. Rather than saying 'No' and being listened to, 'I have a boyfriend' means 'I am taken' in a way that seems to have a different kind of power in the patriarchy. (Interestingly, 'I have girl-friend' often has unpredictable effects, from total disgust to further sexual stimulation. Ugh.) I'm passionately interested in getting to a point where we don't need to reply 'I have a boyfriend' but simply 'No thanks', and it has the same effect. (See also wearing fake wedding rings or the distasteful practice of assuming a homosexual identity. Wearing borrowed rainbows, if you will.)

Until we can challenge our ingrained views about bodies, touching and consent, and until we can challenge sexist 'banter' and reorganise workplaces and schools and public spaces on fairer grounds, we cannot move forward. Yet this will take patience and a willingness to engage with difficult and complicated issues, taking responsibility when appropriate, managing blame and finding a mutual way through.

Reframing the debate so that it's not about men versus non-men can help, although it's paradoxical because sometimes people have to return to that simplistic and combative view when threatened, and because we've got to start the conversation somewhere.

The strongest counterarguments and why they're wrong

- 'Being catcalled and noticed is just a compliment; chill out'.
- 'How do you know something is sexism? You can't prove it'.
- 'School doesn't affect the workplace as much as you think it does'.

What a compliment is (not). We live in a strange world. We often struggle to communicate, especially with strangers. We rely on tired scripts: 'Nice weather today!', 'How do you travel here?', 'What do you do?' When you first meet someone, you reach for what's available, as your brain overloads in processing how to categorise them. Often, that available thing is a surface feature: lipstick, glasses, blue hair, patterned tie. In the absence of a holistic picture of a person – a legitimate whole – we divide them into easily available, digestible chunks, and pick one with which to start.

What is a compliment? It's worth considering. 'Something nice about a person', perhaps?

Who gets to decide what's 'nice'?

For women and girls, beauty, clothing or hair is often the focus.

When you meet a female for the first time, do you compliment them? What do you comment on?

I am embarrassed by 'compliments' about my appearance, and I suspect I am not alone. It's complex. It's not that I don't want people to find me attractive or appreciate the effort I have put in with my appearance. It's not that I think I'm terribly ugly. It's more that so often it seems unearned and quite the wrong thing to focus on. The world places so much value on my face, my breasts, my body, and my womb. I am trying to shift this value to my mind, my words, my relationships, my ideas. Every time I meet someone and they start with the surface stuff, I'm having to rewind the tape again and start at the beginning. I am having to work extra hard to be funny, to be interesting, to wave a great big sign in their face saying 'HEY! I HAVE A VALUE BEYOND THIS'.

Lisa Bloom, in an article called 'How to Talk to Little Girls', writes, 'I always bite my tongue when I meet little girls, restraining myself from my first impulse, which is to tell them how darn cute/pretty/ beautiful/well-dressed/well-manicured/well-coiffed they are', because 'teaching girls that their appearance is the first thing you notice tells them that looks are more important than anything'. It's so automatic, so easy, to focus on the glittery shoes or the hair bow, and not think about the mind and values and thoughts and likes of the person underneath them. Bloom advocates asking them about their favourite book instead.[14]

There is an argument that the old man squeezing my knee under the dinner table is just communicating a compliment, that it's his linguistic equivalent of 'you're very beautiful'. Some women speak this language too; for them, that sort of thing makes them feel indifferent, or special or attractive. I'm not here to argue with those women. But the thing is, telling someone you find them attractive isn't unequivocally nice, as we may have been led to believe. Sometimes it's more about you than them.

'Some women like it' is commonly used in defence of all kinds of behaviour. Undoubtedly, some women do. Some women like being wolf-whistled at like a dog. Some women like being grabbed from behind by a stranger. They get to decide that. But that in no way means that it's ok to do that to any or all women, because you simply don't know. Stop it. The small chance that someone might enjoy it is far, far outweighed by the likelihood that someone will find it degrading, gross or threatening. It's for this reason that I don't swear (much, usually) around people I don't know, or address strangers as 'you old git', or hug people as a greeting. Some people do like it. But it's just basic good manners to find out first.

One last thing: If you are yelling your 'compliments' at women, that isn't a compliment. Shut your trap.

Someone telling a girl they want to have sex with her – without her consent or encouragement or even knowing that those things are hers to give – is not a compliment. That is like saying 'I'll hold you down while I have sex with you because you're so attractive I can't help myself' is a compliment. That's the same reasoning that suggests that being sent images of someone's penis, or sexual comments, from *strangers* is a compliment. It isn't. How can you know if they'll like it? (Of course, they might. But the key thing is *you can't possibly know*. This is the same as not caring.)

I'm quite a fan of sexy messaging, on the whole, and I know a great many people who are also into it. I'm not condemning flirting or sexy chat. But this sort of behaviour isn't that. It's one thing to message someone you know or at least have met a few times and have decided they might like it, and, if they don't like it, *noticing* and *stopping*. It's another thing entirely to just shout at someone regardless. That's intimidation. That's a powerplay. That's not even remotely close to complimenting someone. If you have ever shouted or directed a suggestive remark at a woman on the street, I can guarantee you right now that either she or other women around felt crappy and weird about it. Once again, shut your trap.

Proving, scrutinising and challenging sexism

Ralph Waldo Emerson once said that, philosophically speaking, we should be a transparent eyeball. (I like this image very much, although scientifically it makes little sense. I think nonsensical ideas still have things to teach us sometimes.) We must see, and see what we see. He was talking about a weird inner/outer vision thing where he advocated man (urgh) being at one with nature. I'm talking about an ability to notice what we notice, to be aware that things often take us unawares. Sexism is a lens by which we (mis-)understand the world, and as in any other context, we have to be able to see the lens, too.

Unless we set up a randomised controlled trial, sexism can be hard to see and prove. But sexist attitudes – gendered thinking – can also be pretty clear, and having a proper discussion about it where people are allowed to make mistakes and move forward is better than waiting for offensive behaviour to be exhibited. If society accepts and sometimes encourages sexism and gendered thinking, we can be pretty sure that almost all our pupils will have absorbed it on some level, and it is our job to gently explore it so they can start to make up their own minds. Starting with friendly and accessible staff training is crucial, because sexism is such an insidious way of thinking that we will all be guilty of it at one time or another. (As I write this, someone has just called me out on using sexist language on Twitter. There is no comeback. I did it, and I'm sorry, and I'll keep trying.) There is no reason why, like Graham on *No More Boys and Girls*, we can't involve students in this process too, asking them to help correct us if we get it wrong and to debate the finer points of gender discrimination when they (think they) see it. Grey areas are ok and an important part of shifting the culture. We don't need to blame, accuse and punish all the time, only in certain cases, and that's an important thing to figure out as a staff and as a school. Similarly, I realise that challenging every tiny thing – especially if there's a minority of you currently promoting discussion – isn't always achievable or desirable.

By way of example, here are two potential incidents I was involved in today.

The first was a conversation about tech support. A professional tech support person had been called to an event I was part of. He asked me what was needed, and because I hadn't called him, I asked someone on my team to come over and explain what was needed. She did. Then something happened. She wanted a member of our team to stay with him and check something. I was still standing there. She asked another person on our team, who is male and was mid-conversation a few feet away, to come over and talk to the other guy about the thing.

I know, I know. 'That wasn't sexist!' you're thinking. 'You and your agenda again! You're seeing invisible sexism splashed all over the place! Turn your sexism blacklight off, woman!'

There is really no way I could prove that the request was sexist save asking the person who made the request to comment (and even then, so easy to retro-justify). And in the bigger picture, it wasn't a particularly painful or dramatic incident. In fact, I did precisely nothing about it at the time. But I also did something else: I talked to the man. (Actually, on this occasion, he came to talk to me.) He had noticed it too.

He had felt weird about it. And it was potentially part of a larger pattern of behaviour that we had both noticed.

The second thing that happened was a conversation between me and an eminent academic in my field, whom I know reasonably well. There was an age gap as well as an experience gap, both quite considerable. It was dinner. There were drinks. Everyone was generally relaxed. We were talking shop, and I – being a person who likes to be bold, as a general rule – saw my moment.

'I wonder how you might feel about writing a paper with me on this topic', I asked. (In academia, this is the equivalent of inviting your most senior colleague to team-teach with you or collaborate on lesson planning. That is, it's quite scary and exposing if the colleague is much more expert, but it's ultimately likely to be great for professional development. Also, I'm really good at managing people, deadlines and copy-editing – not to mention social media – so I knew I could bring some things to the table here.)

He smiled at me.

'How could I turn down a proposal from a beautiful woman?' he said.

Oh, reader. I don't think I've felt so much delight turning to so much disgust, at least not since since the time my newborn was put on my chest fresh out of my womb and immediately grunted out black tarry poop all down my body.

Once again, I did nothing about this. I had a 'yes', right? And we were in public, and actually we'd had quite productive conversations about feminism before, and I might decide to circle back on this one another time, but honestly, I just wasn't ready for it. I was tired. I had been drinking. I was disarmed, as is so often the case, by being in a room full of friends and colleagues and two days of talking freely about the stuff I was passionate about. It is also worth noting that I was, and remain, pretty convinced that this man was not intentionally being creepy. I don't even think this was a situation I'd be worried to go further with in case he asked me for sexual favours or touched me inappropriately. You can't always tell, but I didn't get that sense *at all*. No, this was a man of a certain generation expressing his admiration for me, but in a way that I happened to find unpalatable and very gendered.

How to describe this mismatch? Imagine you've travelled to a place with a culture that is not familiar to you. You meet someone and they frown at you and then slap you smartly around the face.

Then they break into a smile, and someone explains that this is their custom for greeting people like you. 'Arghhhh', you think. 'But I find that intrusive and unpleasant. And wtf does *people like me* even mean?'

Schools set the scene for institutional structure

High expectations, policies and structures in schools allow our pupils to have a mental framework for relationships that they can use to compare future workplaces. If that model is skewed towards entitled boys, they are less likely to notice entitled men at work. If it is skewed towards 'protecting' fragile girls, they are more likely to accept women being passive and helpless at work. If we routinely question gendered thinking in schools, we raise pupils ready to make important changes in less than a generation. Yes, we can't do it all. Yes, there will still be issues at home and at work that our pupils will need to take on themselves – all we can do is give them tools, language and evidence-based thinking to help support them as they do this. We can only foreground gender discrimination and send the message that it matters, but that is a significant thing in itself in a world where this discrimination often does not consistently register. Just as we were taught to be aware of stranger danger, of the potential for fire in a box of matches or the risks associated with playing on train tracks, so we can help pupils understand that evidence of gendered thinking should raise red flags for them.

Now/later

Now: Does your school have a sexism or sexual harassment policy? Is there one for pupils, for teachers? Read it and consider what is said and what is unsaid. Could it be improved?

Later: Arrange or ask for sexism and gender discrimination training at your school. Try asking a professional organization, or start by having a simple open forum to ask, 'What might sexism look like in our school and what can we do about it?' Make sure that everyone has an opportunity to speak and that you have a plan for dealing with aggression, silencing or intimidation.

Graham says

I started by thinking, 'I'm not qualified to talk about this. I'm a man for a start, and we rarely experience sexism'. I honestly don't think I ever have – although I do walk around with my eyes closed at times.

However, from a very young age I knew I wanted to work with children. I wanted to be in a caring career. I think this stems from the fact that I used to help my mum look after my younger brother, who was often ill. My family said I had a good way with younger children and they encouraged me whenever possible to continue with this. When I left school, I did my NNEB (nursery nurse) course and was one lone male in a group of over 40 students, but I can't remember any sexist comments, from friends, family, anyone. I loved football (watching and playing), going out, music, dancing etc., but I also loved looking after children, learning to sew, cooking and showing a caring side. Did this make me any less of a man? I don't think so and I'm sure my friends and family didn't either, so I was very lucky: I was breaking stereotypes and I didn't even realise it.

There was one incident I remember. I was working in a primary school, and the school secretary was ill for a few weeks, and because I was able to use a computer (this was the 90s), I was asked to cover for the secretary.

One day I received a phone call asking to speak to the Head. Unfortunately, he was out at a meeting and I relayed this message to the caller (a man). 'So who are you?' he asked. I replied 'the secretary'.

'Well then I'm the Queen of Sheba', he haughtily replied before putting the phone down, obviously under the impression I was the Head – because the secretary could surely not be a male.

It is so important that the pupils in our schools see it as normal that men and women can pursue any career that they want. Because of so many strong messages, there are still many children who believe men and women are suited to certain jobs; you only have to do the 'draw a firefighter, mechanic, ballet dancer or makeup artist' test to see this. Show children that they can be whatever they want to be, through books, posters, videos and, if possible, through real-life examples (parents are often a great resource for this).

There was a recent Twitter campaign where a mum tweeted to the West Midland Fire Service that her 4-year-old daughter had come home wanting to be a boy so that she could be a 'fireman'. The Midland Fire Service responded by filming a short video of its male and female firefighters, showing that whatever your gender, you can be a firefighter. The story made local and international news and totally changed that young girl's view of what she could be.

But where did this girl's initial thoughts come from? I can't help thinking that this could have been easily addressed in school before it even made it to Twitter (although it *is* a great story) – by making sure the books we read to children show women fighting fires, taking charge and having great adventures, as well as men caring, dancing and showing emotion. The work that we have done and continue to do in our school has meant that there have been more girls playing football and more boys dancing. It has had such a positive impact that our girls' team is now the most successful on the island (the Isle of Wight), and almost 50 Key Stage 2 boys have recently taken part in a ballet show, opening at a theatre for the 'Ballet Works' touring ballet show. The boys also received a free workshop with the stars of the show; 11 were male and were amazing role models. I marvelled at such power, physicality and grace.

Tl;dr

Sexism - discrimination based on (perceived) gender - and sexual harassment start young and are perpetuated by our expectations and our reactions. The sorts of conversations that move things forwards can be painful and can feel like blaming, but we need to involve everyone to make progress. Women's and girls' bodies belong to them, and no one should get to tell them otherwise.

References

1. Fewer women leading FTSE firms than men called John. (2015). *The Guardian*. Retrieved April 20, 2019, from https://www.theguardian.com/business/2015/mar/06/johns-davids-and-ians-outnumber-female-chief-executives-in-ftse-100
2. *Sexism in schools.* (2015). Retrieved April 13, 2019, from NEU website: https://neu.org.uk/advice/sexism-schools

3. Southgate, J., & Russell, L. (2018). *Street harassment: It's not ok.* Plan International UK Research Report. Retrieved from https://plan-uk.org/file/plan-uk-street-harassment-reportpdf/download?token=CyKwYGSJ

4. *Workplace sexism survey shows "disturbing" gap in male and female perception.* (2017, September 8). Retrieved April 21, 2019, from Jump for Me website: http://jumpforme.eu/companies-gender/statistics-reports/2017/09/08/workplace-sexism-survey-shows-disturbing-gap-male-female-perception/

5. Kelly, J. (2017). *I'm a man and a midwife. Are you ok with that?* Retrieved from https://www.bbc.com/news/magazine-41426691

6. Scully, A. (2018). Midwife breaking down gender barriers says men need to bring their A-game every day. *ABC News.* Retrieved April 21, 2019, from ABC News website: https://www.abc.net.au/news/2018-07-12/midwife-breaks-gender-barriers-says-men-need-to-bring-a-game/9944964

7. BabyCentre UK. (n.d.). *How would you feel about having a male midwife?* Retrieved April 21, 2019, from https://www.babycentre.co.uk/o566258/how-would-you-feel-about-having-a-male-midwife

8. Delivering progress: The male midwife. (2018). *Positive News.* Retrieved April 21, 2019, from Positive News website: https://www.positive.news/society/delivering-progress-the-male-midwife/

9. Miller, M. et al. (2018). *Sexual Harassment of Women and Girls in Public Places.* House of Commons Women and Equalities Committee: UK Parliament.

10. Teacher who filmed up schoolgirls' skirts will not face prosecution as judge rules it's not illegal. (2017). *The Independent.* Retrieved April 21, 2019, from https://www.independent.co.uk/news/uk/home-news/teacher-andrew-corish-film-up-schoolgirls-skirts-no-prosecution-not-illegal-judge-rules-croydon-a8041806.html

11. *Comparing rape to property theft. Campaign reaction – Not ever.* (n.d.). Retrieved April 21, 2019, from http://www.notever.co.uk/have-your-say/campaign-reaction/comparing-rape-to-property-theft/

12. Hurley, K. (2016). *The Geek Feminist Revolution* (1st edition). New York, NY: Tor.

13. McKnight, L. (n.d.). *Groundhog sexism.* Retrieved April 21, 2019, from Groundhog Sexism website: https://groundhogsexism.wordpress.com/

14. Bloom, L. (2011). How to talk to little girls. *HuffPost.* Retrieved April 21, 2019, from https://www.huffpost.com/entry/how-to-talk-to-little-gir_b_882510?guccounter=1&guce_referrer_us=aHR0cHM6Ly93d3d3 3cuZ29vZ2xlLmNvbS8&guce_referrer_cs=8NZrN6a3krzLktSJ1TCrpA

Clothing
and uniform

A revolutionary algebra of clothing – monkeys running around –
the red sneaker effect – the edges of power – menswear scares
me – she hasn't realised she's butch – not fitting – a lovely big
roomy vagina – distracting – cover up or be blown up – girls
have the right to be sexual – starkly binary – a paradox –
pansexual – a minority – running free – per-formed – we
shouldn't confuse children

Stats

At least 120 schools in the United Kingdom now have a gender-neutral
school uniform policy, and primary schools are adopting the stance
faster than secondary schools.[1]

Until 2012, female beach volleyball athletes were required to wear
swimsuits – either a one-piece or a bikini with a maximum side width of
7 centimetres.[2]

The issues

Every morning, as I step off the train and head through the city that
I work in, I smile to myself. On a good day, when the timing is right,
I pass another commuter going in the opposite direction. We've never
spoken.

I like design of all kinds, but I'm not heavily into fashion. I've often
heard people say 'I'm *living* for this look' and thought: how

extravagant. But this person's clothing does that to me: it makes me hum and buzz and glow with life.

This person is not easy to miss. They're tall and stocky and muscular and bald and coded masculine in many ways. What makes them look incredible is the surprising and wonderful way they rock a skirt. Kilt-style, but not always tartan, and they sometimes style it with boots, necklaces, vests, long socks; sometimes all in black; sometimes with a splash of colour. They stomp it out on the pavement like they're in a Paris couture show, and my head turns and my mouth gapes and I think: *look what is possible*. It has prompted a revolutionary algebra of clothing for me and has completely changed my mind about what looks (and feels) good.

Fashion, and all art, is about dreaming of the impossible, and then just tethering it to the ground – just by a toenail, sometimes – but enough that (usually) it is still practical.

Surely, fashion has nothing to do with school uniforms, which are *all* about being practical, right? We don't want our pupils hobbled or restricted, after all.

Have you ever worn a skirt?

Tights?

High heels?

A tie?

If you haven't, can you try, in your head, to imagine it for a moment?

If you think boys *don't* wear skirts – well, you're just plain wrong. (Multiple examples abound: my friend Jez, the guy I work with, male models on TV.)

If you think boys *can't* wear skirts, you may be closer to the truth. In our contemporary society (in the United Kingdom, in 2019), there are still barriers suggesting what is considered 'normal', 'traditional' and 'acceptable'. But those barriers are fragile and fall apart under scrutiny. There is no seat of ultimate judgement, no Special Council of Workwear that convenes once a year and make the rules about professional attire; no fashion police who stop you in the street amid sirens and flashing lights and inform you that you have *broken the law*. We are all just monkeys running around with arbitrary scraps of cloth (and sometimes metal and wood and plastic) on us to keep the rain off. The bleeding edge of fashion is weird and wonderful. People wear tails (furry or formal) and expose their nipples and wear their hair vertically and explore violently impractical silhouettes. The truth is that anyone can wear anything, but of course there are consequences. Deviation has a social cost, and looking 'normal' is something we all covet: to fit in, to be accepted, to belong.

School uniforms are important. In this discussion, I am sidestepping the issue of whether a school uniform should exist at all – that's for you and your school and your local area and your country to debate. Instead, I am examining the school uniform through the lens of choice. What choices do we give pupils and what are the effects of those choices?

Clothes that fit

Have you ever seen a picture of Mark Zuckerburg? Famed for dressing unobtrusively in dark grey T-shirts and jeans, he went to an investors' meeting a few years back in a hoodie and was met with outrage. Why? Surely nothing could be more 'normal' than the sort of outfit found on millions of people in the Western world?

Because of context. Wall Street isn't your living room, and custom and culture dictate that a suit and tie (at least for men) are more 'befitting' of this environment. To 'befit' means to suit; not just as in 'looking good', but in the meaning of 'suitable'. All this language around what is appropriate and decent and proper comes from the French 'suit', which is about following and followers. To wear a suit is to follow, to become part of, to belong. And Zuckerburg wore something that belonged, but not in that context. He deviated – that is to say, he did not follow. (Maybe he led.) This is how clothing can constrain us – not just physically but socially as well. 'Normal' versus 'formal'. If we don't choose the 'right' thing to wear (and this is heavily gender-dependent, of course), we are judged accordingly. And badly, right?

Wrong. Have you ever heard of the 'red sneaker effect'? Researchers at Harvard[3] looked at compliance and deviance in clothing. They found that people who intentionally dressed 'differently' (within limits) had higher status, because it showed that the person was independent and in control. This worked only when it was obvious that they had done it on purpose, and when they still behaved within the normal social confines. The researchers termed this the 'red sneaker effect' because it was akin to wearing red sneakers to a professional business meeting (as opposed to something more violently deviant, like wearing a clown suit). This shows us that clothing is a power statement that we can control, too. And this is unsurprising – in my ten-year career as a teacher, the phrase 'Tuck your shirt in' became almost completely automatic; school pupils use minor deviations as a form of control, to (try to) demonstrate power and status and to protest against the conformity of a uniform.

Uniforms are about much, much more than clothing. The way that uniforms are dictated and manifest in a school is about the edges of power, about how frayed or hemmed they are. Often, it is about sexualising and revealing girls' bodies and about covering and enabling the bodies of boys.

Is your school uniform policy gendered? Does it explicitly use different sections to outline what boys and girls should wear? Does it allow for identities other than these two?

Womenswear and menswear

I've been watching Project Runway, a candidate-elimination-pick-a-winner show about fashion design. Among the favourite phrases of the judges ('easy', 'tailored', 'simple'), the word 'feminine' stands out. 'It's strong, but still feminine' is an interesting one, the implication being that 'strong' and 'feminine' are somehow opposites. 'You need to keep the silhouette feminine; otherwise she looks like a man', says one judge.

What does it mean, to wear clothes 'like a man' or to be wearing something 'feminine'?

Why do we need to keep our genders separate when it comes to clothing? What do people who do not identify as male or female 'get to' wear?

'I'm a womenswear designer', says one contestant. 'Menswear scares me; I don't know what to do with it'. Are women's and men's bodies so grossly different that a person can learn all the techniques of fashion design – tailoring, draping, sewing, fitting – but only apply them, strictly, to one gender?

Of course, this isn't about technique – it's about sticking to the rules. Designing menswear could be no different from designing womenswear – and we could accordingly call it *designing peopleswear* – if we threw out the rules about what each gender is expected to emphasise and to disguise, the emphasis on the shapes we make in public.

'You have a strong point of view, as a designer', says one of the judges. I think: how can a person have a strong point of view when they're just regurgitating other people's rules?

In October 2016, I spent a month wearing menswear and wrote several articles about it. Let's skip the articles for now and go straight to the comments:

'[S]he hasn't realized she's butch', says one commenter. 'She clearly feels more comfortable psychologically/emotionally/physically in menswear every day which is pretty much one of the main definitions of butchness. Her writing reveals that she's lived a life heavily insulated in heteronormativity. There is an entire queer movement going on that embraces diversity in gender expression that does not need to indicate anything about one's sexuality. There are many straight butch women in the world. I think what holds many straight butch women back from expressing their butchness is fear of losing male approval'.

For many of us, the critique of living a life 'heavily insulated in heteronormativity' is of course, true. I imagine I find this particularly cutting because the author of the comment has assumed I'm straight (I mention having a boyfriend in the piece, and almost everyone has bi-erased me in this way). But something they say is true here, and that's that there is an entire movement devoted to queering clothing and promoting self-expression, regardless of one's sexuality, and as a writer, maybe I didn't work hard enough to find out about it. Many of the lesbian women I spoke to about the article were frustrated with me, citing the idea that they've been wearing 'menswear' (particularly suits and ties, as I did) for years. They were bemused and often pissed off that because I dyed my hair blonde and wore some lipstick with it, people were suddenly (if momentarily) interested.

The writer of the comment makes one more point, though, and isn't it a killer! 'I think what holds many straight butch women back from expressing their butchness is fear of losing male approval'.

It is, I fear, time to talk about The Male Gaze.

Back to Project Runway. 'I think men design clothes that they want women to wear', says Sonjia Williams, one of the contestants from Season 10, dejectedly. I wrote at length about one of the hardest realisations to hit me when wearing 'men's' wear – that all my life, the more important the occasion, the more uncomfortable I was. That formal wear for women so often means trying desperately to focus attention on the bits you want and to divert it from the bits you don't. That I have spent half a lifetime fiddling, pulling down or up, fussing, checking, tweaking and tucking as I constantly prepare myself to meet the eyes of others in this world, feeling somehow that this body I have is inadequate. That I am squeezed into a model of 'woman' that I did not design and that somehow speaks for me and leaves me silent. That the clothing I am couched in does not fit, and that this means I am not fit to meet their precious eyes.

Whose eyes?

There is a wealth of academic literature devoted to the obvious presence of the male gaze/female objectification in film, literature, art and life. Women are brought up to be aware of themselves, to be seen and displayed, to be the object and not the bearer of the gaze and to foreground the pleasure of the male viewer. It is hard to see skirts as anything but part of this paradigm. I wear a variety of clothing, and in my experience, skirts are in no way as practical as trousers on almost every level. Skirts and dresses, fun and interesting as I find them to wear, are about glimpses (or leering eyefuls) of flesh, skimming or hugging curves, nipping in waists, splitting to reveal skin, riding up to present exciting shadows, subject to wind and whimsy and wandering hands. Skirts were designed for the male gaze, not the female wearer. In fact, so much of 'women's' clothing fits into this category. Until I wore 'mens' trousers, for example, I'd never stopped to notice the difference. It is enormous, and the exact things that are enormous are the space to move and the pockets. It's almost like men's trousers are designed for comfort and space rather than showing off their arses.

Pockets. Oh, pockets. There is very little that angers me so much as pockets.

Clothing designed for women: *no pockets, tiny pockets, impractical pockets, pretend pockets. Don't spoil the line, bulge anywhere or ruin the illusion. What are you complaining about? You've got a lovely big roomy vagina to store things in, silly.*

Clothing designed for men: *here, have some pockets. Have some more. Pop your hands in all the way to the wrist. Waggle them around and freely adjust your junk whenever you like. Pop your wallet, phone and keys in, and don't forget the business cards, you important chap.*

You're never fully dressed without a smile

I've been watching Wimbledon this week. Sometimes, just occasionally, and despite assurance from the world that the BBC is impartial and impassive (ha!), you get a shot of a beautiful young girl, a flash of flesh or an arresting female smiling coyly. Watch almost any live coverage of sports, especially in the summer, and you will see this clear as day – the little aside shots, the gentle slo-mos, the vox pops without any actual vox – are firmly focused on 'attractive' women. The male gaze is present, and it often presents as a camera pointed towards the audience.

So why should we care? Why is this important?

We need to talk further about sexualisation of girls in school uniform.

'I walked home from school on my own from years 7 to 11, wearing full school uniform: trousers, blazer, tie. Every day I would get whistled and shouted at by men from their cars. On several occasions, guys from my school thought it was fun to come up behind me and smack me on the behind', says one woman.

'Anytime I wore uniform in public, I would get comments from grown men about how "sexy" I looked', says another.

'Every day I walk home wearing my school uniform. It's common for me to be shouted at; most of the time, men toot their horns and say something along the lines of "oi oi", display crude gestures, sometimes sexual comments. I feel so exposed and uncomfortable'.

'The school dress code is extremely biased towards boys. They can basically be comfortable and wear what they like, whereas for us it's about not showing off too much skin in case we provoke reactions in boys. What does that tell us about our bodies?'

These stories almost always end with the girl turning to a teacher or parent for help, and being told their complaints are not important, their concerns are not justified or their bodies are too distracting.

Their bodies – the things their amazing, powerful minds are encased in, the things every human possesses and has possessed since humans began and the things we all of us, every single one, have in common – are distracting.

Distracting.

Watch any 'comedy' show from the 70s and you'd be hard pushed to go an hour without some reference to an old man perving over a saucy girl in school uniform. These days, we've mostly realised that sexualising girls in this way is damaging in so many ways, but the comments, the shouts, the leers and the gestures persist. The grabbing persists.

How are we still so obsessed with girls' skin and bodies?

In 2019, still, multiple news stories tell of students asked to cover up shoulders or midriffs at school, for photographs, on mufti days or when male teachers are present. Girls' bodies: the ultimate distraction.

Often, the policy is utterly gendered – boys are not being asked to conform to the same rules. Girls' skin seems to carry a secret powder, a silent power, a special dynamite that, when exposed to the flame of lust from the male gaze, might explode in all of our faces. Like dynamite, we have weaponised the skin of girls, and we have placed the blame for the resultant destruction – despite the fact that it usually harms *them* – squarely with the girls themselves. Cover up or be blown up.

What needs to change

If we want to stop telling pupils that boys and girls are so very different, almost everything that emphasises that difference needs to be got rid of.

In *No More Boys and Girls*, they even kept their coats in separate cupboards. 'We just have a boys' cupboard and a girls' cupboard', says Graham. 'I don't know why; it's always been the same'.

If we maintain different uniforms for boys and girls, we are telling them that they are different, that their bodies should be covered up differently and their physical needs are different enough to warrant this.

In 2017, a school made the headlines when it banned skirts from its uniform in an attempt to make school uniforms more gender-neutral for its pupils. This was particularly ironic, given that the school in question was the one that Piers Morgan (a UK media personality known for right-wing views) attended. I was asked to comment on this for BBC News, so I read Piers' criticism.

Piers commented:

> It's disappointing to see one of my old schools getting sucked into this gender neutrality nonsense, which is being driven by a tiny minority of people. Let boys be boys and girls be girls, and stop confusing them in this ridiculous way.[4]

The strongest counterarguments and why they're wrong

I wonder if we might take those criticisms seriously (it is hard to take Piers Morgan seriously, I know, but he actually makes some interesting points here) and explain why they are wrong.

- 'Gender neutrality is nonsense'.
- 'It is being driven by a minority of people'.
- 'We should let boys be boys and girls be girls'.
- 'We should stop confusing children about their gender'.

Gender neutrality is far from nonsense. In earlier chapters, we looked at how scientific ideas of biological sex have shifted as we have learned more about human biology and our understanding has progressed beyond 'It's just chromosomes!' Hundreds of years ago (at least in Europe), you might have said that it was pretty straightforward to identify a man or woman, or a boy or girl. Now, we know that people can have different signifiers of sex – genitals, chromosomes, physical characteristics – that may or may not be binary. That is, some men have periods; some people are born with both a penis and a vulva; some women don't have breasts. People are born, every single day, who are not straightforwardly biologically male or female, and people make changes to their appearance, their behaviour and their bodies that signify a wish to identify in a particular way.

More than that, we know that people can feel strongly that the gender that others assume them to be feels wrong to them (this feeling can be temporary or permanent), and it can make them deeply, wretchedly unhappy. Our world is so starkly binary that not fitting into its sharp categories, living on a knife edge of people staring and judging and whispering and denying and refusing, can consume you. From a scientific point of view, there is clear and compelling statistical evidence that neither biological sex nor sociocultural gender is binary[5] and that insistently categorising people in terms of (perceived) gender can be harmful.[6] So gender neutrality, as a proposed solution to some of these problems, is probably not 'nonsense'.

There seems to be an obvious answer, which is to have a neutral category, a safe zone, a place of freedom, creativity and exploration, and maybe to think about just using it for everyone in the future.

In the long term, lowering gender boundaries to the point where gender just isn't important anymore is a radical but very significant thought experiment. If you think about it, there are only a very tiny number of situations where gender is important. When applying for a passport? Nope. As a school pupil? Nope. When I need to use the toilet? More on that later. In terms of sexual attraction? Interesting. As a pansexual (attracted to all genders) woman, I really have no need to categorise a potential mate by gender, although I do understand that for other people that might be more important. Of course – again as a long-term goal – it might be interesting to start considering why some people are attracted only to certain genders, and whether it's about particular physical signifiers and other cultural ideas. These may start to break down over time so that almost everyone shifts towards a more pansexual model. If you can consider both gender and sexual attraction as fluid spectra, it makes more sense not to worry about these things. If you've always lived with them as a binary, this can be frightening and confusing – but why?

Have a think about a world with no gender, or a world that is gender-neutral. What would bother you about it? What would be its advantages? How might you navigate it differently?

What does 'a minority of people' mean?

Now, to give Morgan his due, this is actually a very interesting argument. If we consider the principles of democratic utilitarianism for a moment, the idea that a very small minority of people should drive significant changes to policy or sociocultural practice could be problematic, of course. However, there is much more to consider here than just the idea that this is a 'minority'. First, along with considering the size of the minority that's being affected, it's also pertinent to consider the strength of the effect.

If there were one child in each school class who was affected by a certain issue – for example, a nut allergy – but the potential impact was huge (for example, the allergy might result in death), then we would consider that much more seriously than we would if the impact were small.

In the same way, the fact that women might be considered a minority in some professional contexts doesn't stop us from changing the way we deal with complaints from women once we start to realise the magnitude of the effect that things like sexual harassment can have on them.

It is abundantly clear that the effect of our preoccupation with gender on people who are gender dysphoric, trans or gender questioning is enormous. People are committing suicide, being harassed, being physically assaulted and/or becoming seriously mentally ill (not as an effect of being LGBTQ+ or non-genderconforming, but as an effect of other people's failure to deal with this in an acceptable manner). If we pursue the argument that this is a minority of people, we also should consider the large effect size and the potential consequences of not making those changes.

It is also important to consider the possible negative effects on the majority that the argument of Morgan seems to imply. Here we are presented with a sure and easy trade-off: minority versus majority. Which would you choose?

However, this is a problem of framing. The suggestion that making changes that will benefit a minority will seriously disadvantage the majority is worth questioning. In particular, when considering this issue, I'd like to ask: Why might it disadvantage pupils who had never questioned their gender if a gender-neutral uniform policy were introduced?

That very much depends on the policy, of course. Keeping everything the same, but changing the label 'boys' to 'option 2' and the label 'girls' to 'option 1' has been the policy adopted by some schools. Others have just categorised all uniforms listed as acceptable and let pupils choose. An alternative – narrowing the options to just one – is also possible; this might feel more difficult, because there is less choice available. It might feel oppressive. I'm not sure anyone is arguing for that, beyond acknowledging the practical considerations inherent in it.

Might there be benefits for everyone if we considered the issues that the minority are bringing to the table here? More choice, more freedom, less constraint. But should we also consider why gendered uniform exists in the first place and mount a challenge to its boundaries? Why might that matter?

Because not all uniforms are equal. Uniforms intended for girls are tighter, more for show and less for flow. They are more restricting, with fewer pockets. They are less practical and offer a narrower range of (comfortable or non-exposing) movement. Shoes are less sturdy and more decorative. These 'choices' imply that girls are passive and for display only, not for adventure or movement. There is still such a strong association between femininity and skirts/dresses that just removing the gender from the choices won't fully address these issues, not yet. What is uniform for and what do these choices (constraints) say to our pupils about our expectations of them?

The final point to note is that almost everything is almost always driven, especially at first, by a minority of people. (Popularity, as we know, does not guarantee success or value.) For innovation to spread, it has to start somewhere.

WTF does 'let boys be boys and girls be girls' actually mean?

If you have not done so before, I hope by now you are starting to question *What is a girl?* and *What is a boy?*

If so, I imagine that 'let boys be boys and girls be girls' is an odd phrase to you. I imagine that it is starting to have a hollow ring to it, as it does for me. The idea that performing gender in one particular way is 'natural' is simply a myth. The way that boys and girls behave and dress is so very sociocultural. It's in many ways an imposition, and to question it is extremely important. Similarly, there is a clear argument that elements of what we might think of as boyhood and girlhood are undesirable, and as adults, parents and teachers, we are obviously here to correct those. It doesn't matter how much we like to encourage boys to be adventurous – if they dig about in the mud when we want them to be learning maths, we make it stop. It doesn't matter how much we want girls to be take pleasure in home-making – if they want to cook on the stove when they're too young, we tell them not to. It is our place as adults in the children's life to encourage freedom but also to restrain appropriately. Often, this is about keeping the child physically safe. Even more often, it is about imposing cultural and social boundaries. The idea that we should simply let boys' natural 'boyness' shine, and the same for girls, is fairly meaningless when you think about it.

If you consider the idea of gender as being per-formed – that is, as never fully formed, as temporary in some sense – then being a boy or being a girl is simply what boys are and do and girls are and do. That, for me, seems to fit with the verb 'let' so much better than constraining boys and girls into choices that we have already made for them. 'Let' the child be neither gender, nor both. 'Let' the boy learn to knit. 'Let' the girl climb trees. Even more than 'let' – encourage, support and help the child to examine the possibilities of their choices.

We absolutely should keep confusing children

As a teacher I have been constantly and rather unpleasantly surprised by the idea that we shouldn't confuse children. Teaching children about the world should very much, at times, be about confusion. The world is confusing. Every day things happen that baffle me: sometimes good, sometimes bad, sometimes both or neither or I just don't know. Not a single person, I can imagine, would argue that it is ok to teach children that they will always understand everything clearly. Nuance, uncertainty, ambiguity and difficulty are at the centre of what it is to understand the world as a human, and if we try to protect children from this, we are doing them a grave disservice. If we teach the black and white but never the grey, children find hard boundaries that are then painful to cross later. If we fail to teach children to question, to critically engage and to wonder, we are not teaching at all but are merely filling the pail. At the very extreme end, this is called indoctrination.

I was presenting at a conference recently, and my daughter was in attendance. With a group of teachers and researchers, we explored the paradox of 'fairness' in schools. At the end of the session, my daughter had something to say. 'I've realised that people were lying to us when they said the world was fair and to expect fairness', she said. 'All my teachers were probably trying to be nice and not confuse us, but it just made me expect a different world to the one I got'. She was angry, sad and – of course – confused.

What is certainly confusing to children is to bring them up uncritically to see binary gender as crucially important, as salient and as a defining characteristic of a human being. Inevitably, at some point the child will meet someone who offers (or will discover within themselves) the idea that this is just not true. Someone will step out of the stereotype. Someone will be different. And if we teach that this difference is a confusing deviation that we can't handle, what does that mean? Flexibility is lost in categorisation, procedure and constraint.

What if we approached this differently and started with the idea that gender is fluid and just not that big a deal? Then, later, that gender and sex are complex and potentially confusing but that's ok, and maybe not always the way the world will be. (Unless you are someone who feels an uncontrollable desire to define other people, to tell children 'who they are' and to ensure that they remain within those boundaries, which I fear Piers Morgan has demonstrated himself to be with his comment about letting boys be boys and girls be girls.)

> ## Now/later
>
> **Now:** Think about the clothes you wear, especially in a professional setting, and the freedom and constraints you have. How do you make clothing choices? How might you feel different wearing different clothes? Are there any rules, explicit or implicit, that frustrate you?
>
> **Later:** Read your school's uniform policy. Does it mention gender? Are there different options for girls and boys? Are non-binary or trans pupils recognised? Consider contributing to updating the policy if updating is warranted.

Graham says

In isolation, a baby hat saying 'future footballer's wife' or a T-shirt in the girls' section proclaiming 'I'm too pretty to do maths' or even a boy's T-shirt emblazoned with 'little terror' on may not make much of a difference. You might think: *Why bother? It's not hurting anyone.* But the sum of all such messages that children are already getting has an impact. This continuous drip, drip of messages for girls about looks, being princesses and pretty, and the messages for boys about being strong and powerful (or naughty) and taking over the world, all add their own pressure and decidedly influence how children perceive themselves and each other.

Gendered clothing is becoming obsolete, and thankfully, when it does appear (such as in the recent 'Boden' clothing faux pas), some vociferous Twitter campaigns have had the desired effect. The Boden catalogue featured explicitly gendered messages: to girls, 'Girls, new clothes are in sight. Fill your pockets (and wardrobes) with flowers and race this way' and to boys, 'Boys start every adventure with a bike (or a pair of very fast legs), fellow mischief-makers, and clothes that can keep up'.[7] After much reaction on Twitter, Boden apologised, suggesting that they will 'stop asking Don Draper to write our copy'.

There are hundreds of examples of messages like the above on the internet. Why not talk to your pupils about it and ask how they feel about the messages? What messages would they like to see there instead?

Get them to design their own gender-neutral range of clothing. What do they notice about the colours and range?

Not long after the documentary *No More Boys and Girls* aired, during the summer holidays one of the parents from my class contacted me. She was having terrible trouble getting any new shoes for her son because every shoe shop they went into, he would look around and ask to see the manager before announcing, 'I'm not buying any shoes from this shop; they aren't gender-neutral'.

Our pupils now are our future adults. If we could get them all thinking as this pupil was, it would surely put pressure on clothes manufacturers to rethink gender stereotypical clothing, and maybe – just maybe – in the future it would not be an issue.

Tl;dr

Gendered clothing can be restricting in more ways than one. A binary gendered school uniform policy reinforces binary notions of gender and tells pupils of different genders that they are strongly different. We all need access to high-quality pockets and to practical, comfortable clothing as a default – other choices are then ours to make, as freely as possible. The choices that are available to us have all kinds of implications that might restrict that freedom, and thinking about this is important.

References

1. Ross, A. (2017). At least 120 schools adopt gender-neutral uniforms, charity says. *The Guardian*. Retrieved from https://www.theguardian.com/education/2017/may/15/120-schools-adopt-gender-neutral-uniforms-charity-says
2. *Skimpy difference: Women's athletic uniforms vs. men's.* (2016). Retrieved April 21, 2019, from indystar website: https://www.indystar.com/story/sports/2016/11/05/skimpy-difference-womens-athletic-uniforms-vs-mens/91405172/
3. Bellezza, S., Gino, F., & Keinan, A. (2014). *The Red Sneakers Effect: Inferring Status and Competence from Signals of Nonconformity*. Retrieved from https://www.hbs.edu/faculty/Pages/item.aspx?num=45809

4. Watt, H. (2017). Secondary school makes uniform gender neutral. *The Guardian*. Retrieved from https://www.theguardian.com/education/2017/sep/06/secondary-school-makes-uniform-gender-neutral

5. Kralick, A. (2018). *We finally understand that gender isn't binary. Sex isn't, either.* Retrieved April 21, 2019, from *Slate Magazine* website: https://slate.com/technology/2018/11/sex-binary-gender-neither-exist.html

6. Anatomy does not determine gender, experts say. (2018). *The New York Times*. Retrieved April 21, 2019, from https://www.nytimes.com/2018/10/22/health/transgender-trump-biology.html

7. *Children's clothing company Boden apologises for gender stereotyping message.* (2019). Retrieved April 21, 2019, from Metro website: https://metro.co.uk/2019/02/04/childrens-clothing-company-boden-apologises-for-gender-sterotyping-message-8438973/

Expert view: gendered clothing

Francesca Cambridge Mallen

Being a gender-conscious parent is a long, uphill battle. Despite picking the most ubiquitous pair of school trainers I could find, my daughter can't squeeze her foot past the open laces. On our return trip to the clothing shop, she races off to the nearest colourful offering she can see, the inevitable GIRL sign towering overhead. 'Girls shoes are just cut slimmer – it's the fashion!' smile the staff at the shop when I compare a similar but visibly wider pair lifted from the boys' section. Even basic school shoes for young children seem to embody the prevailing girls versus boys clothing culture in cut, shape, motif and messaging – girls sit still, adorned; boys run and jump and go on adventures.

The rise of trend-led school shoes, including wedges, heels and ballet flats, should alarm even those with a basic understanding of podiatry, stereotyping girls as style-focused rather than active. Comfort should be key, yet children's choices in clothing and shoes are being limited by gender-coded designs and displays, built on traditional ideas about what it means to be male or female. If we are to strive for a more equal society, equality for our children should be of paramount concern. A European Commission report that looked at equality between women and men made this point over ten years ago, concluding that 'action to combat gender-based stereotypes must start at a very young age'.[1] After all, we can and should all work towards fixing a bias that is socially, and not biologically, determined.

UK high-street sizing guides are, almost without exception, the same for girls and boys up until puberty, and yet the cut is radically different depending on which section you head for – meaning, in practice, that the garments are not the same size at all. A study of children in 2011[2] found children's body sizes have increased in height, chest, waist and hips since 1990, with only marginal differences between the sexes. However, a customer buying a plain white T-shirt[3] from both the girls' section and the boys' section will end up with entirely different products.

Perplexed parents have taken to social media to share photos of girls' and boys' clothes side by side to illustrate the practice of cutting inches off girls' tops and T-shirts, from both the length and the waist. When shoppers asked Lands' End why their girls' shorts were cut so much shorter than those for boys, they were told, 'Cartwheels seem to be easier in short shorts',[4] leading many parents to wonder if the company had ever met a child. According to an experienced childrenswear buyer for one of the UK's largest retailers (who wished to remain anonymous), 'Cuts of t-shirts and tops will be influenced by what the big sellers in womenswear are – so you're likely to see lower cut necklines and slimmer fitting styles for girls'.[5]

Urging retailers to be more consistent and upfront about sizing is one solution, but school uniform is also facing its own 'fashionising of childhood',[6] carrying implications from the sexualisation of females to toxic ideas about maleness. Technological terms like 'airtred soles'[7] with dinosaur treads are pitched in opposition to 'sensitive soles' with flowers (so popular a signal for 'girl' that some parents in the United States use Girly Glue to stick blooms to their newborn's heads).[8]

Pink clothes sell up to three times more than any other colour on the market,[5] and as a parent I can see why. When my daughter was young, I didn't question the choice; I just assumed that as a girl, she would prefer pink, and with all things pink came a tsunami of princesses, unicorns and flowers. By age 4, my oldest daughter could articulate not only that space science was a subject for boys, but that only boys were good at it. I realised with shock that my child was not immune to the daily drip-fed messaging that girls and boys were expected to behave, think and feel differently.

Gender-coding is big business, and by maximising a trend that demands what is acceptable for children to wear based on their sex, retailers benefit just segmenting the market as well as from creating new markets that didn't exist before. We can see this not just in the colour of clothing, but also in the very specific themes, motifs and slogans pitched to either sex based on outdated ideas about men and women in society.

The UK childrenswear sector will reach £6.2 billion in 2018,[9] but responsibility not to 'unduly stereotype'[10] within this lucrative sector, with a nod from the UK government, rests is articulated in a voluntary code of practice only. If we are not playing a part in tackling this issue, we are complicit in its reach and longevity. Young boys are told from the get-go, with a litany of design and motifs, that the sciences, construction and maths are a man's domain. Only 24% of the current STEM industries' workforce are women,[11] and we aren't going to improve on that figure until we start to question, and challenge, generalisations about women and girls. The drip-fed messaging that girls and boys are inherently different, from interests to aspirations to abilities, not only feeds undesirably *into* the classroom but also, to some extent, comes *out of* it.

In 2015 *Let Clothes Be Clothes*[12] (the parent-led group I founded and head up) led a campaign to highlight the exclusion of girls from science-themed clothing. Over 30 items of STEM-relevant clothing on sale in the boyswear department at Marks & Spencer (a large UK retailer) stood in sharp contrast to precisely zero such items in the section of clothing for girls. *Make sexism in the design and marketing of children's clothing extinct* (otherwise known as *#DinosaursForAll*[13]) attracted worldwide attention and cross-party political support against growing concern that negative messages were impacting the aspirations and career choices of girls.

In the last Girl Guiding Attitudes Survey, 68% of 7- to 10-year olds could identify products targeted as either for girls or for boys. The survey goes on to state, 'Some young women said the use of gender stereotypes to sell clothes was so normal to them in their everyday life [that] they did not always notice it'.[14]

But restrictions aren't just being imposed on girls; 'maleness' is likewise exploited by retailers through a litany of predatory teeth and claws, making dinosaurs a universal and beloved theme. Young boys have little choice but to go with the options already laid out for them, responding not just to wider societal expectations but also to fear of embracing anything unacceptable. Widespread use of gender coding has given rise to the belief that our clothing options are following a 'natural order', but there is no scientific basis to this assumption. Pink and blue actually performed a switcheroo after early trendsetters proclaimed blue a dainty colour and pink ideal for boys in 1918.[15] Their current fetishisation by marketers of toys and clothes (plus gendered cheese, pink or blue personal attack alarms, women's ear plugs emblazoned with 'sleep pretty in pink' and even gendered packets of fish food, based on who was doing the shopping) is unlikely to have any real longevity in its current form. Must we continue to ride the tide of other people's oddly gendered decisions on our own and our children's behalf, or can we do something about it?

Clothing is not merely for comfort. It is also part of a basic 'social signalling'[16] with dresses and skirts, in particular, heavily loaded with feminine attributes, in much the same way trousers were once considered exclusively masculine (and still are in some geographical and social areas). When schools prohibit girls from wearing trousers and shorts,[17] what are they actually telling those girls? As Human Rights lawyer Lord David Pannick QC states, 'At school, skirts for girls suggests a demeanour not required of boys',[18] implying that skirts, in a similar fashion to the trend for slip-on ballet flats, offer less practical room for movement, play and knee cover that seems required for boys.

Likewise, when we compliment girls on how they dress, we are choosing some pretty ugly stereotypes. As Grayson Perry puts it, 'Boys are rarely praised for how they look; they learn early that they are the ones doing the looking'.[19] A host on BBC Radio Merseyside told me that questioning this idea was 'stomach turning', believing it was the right of every girl to be complimented on their appearance. The idea that I didn't want my daughter to think her (only) value was in her appearance was completely lost on the presenter, who only narrowly fell short of calling me a bad parent live on air. I listed a number of other phrases, such as 'smart' and 'kind', but to no avail. Was I proposing a revolutionary idea?

Evidence suggests that girls as young as 7 are feeling pressure to place more value on their looks than on their abilities,[14] investing self-esteem and pocket money in 'dieting, grooming and shopping'[20], including clothing based on seasonal trends and footwear to match. Boys face similarly heavy gender expectations. Boyswear writhes in slogans like 'it wasn't me' and 'here comes trouble'. To 'be a man', apparently, means not only embracing and enjoying predator prints (such as teeth-baring sharks and dinosaurs) but also completely rejecting anything deemed feminine. This included the invisibility of popular female characters such as Rey, Skye and Wyldstyle in themed merchandise. The result is to straitjacket boys (pun intended) into an unhealthy ritual of male gender performance that encourages toughness over vulnerability at almost any cost and sees learning as not 'masculine' enough. Boys will be boys, after all. Exclusion rates are four times higher for boys[21] than for girls, and in adult males, the suicide rate is three times higher than that in females.[22] It is crucial for schools to consider what they can do to correct the toxic male stereotype.

'The female realm is simply given less value. Call a boy a sissy and it's an insult. Call a girl a tomboy and it's basically a promotion. Policing the clothing choices of small children is insane, as well as frankly weird,' Robert Webb in conversation with the author (2018).[23]

Many of the parents I've spoken with through our campaign struggle to counter the prevailing gender-policing of their boys, including those who simply want the choice of wearing a dress or a skirt. As one Mum colourfully put it, 'It won't make his penis drop off!'

What to do about school uniforms?

When researchers at Uppsala university[24] looked at gender-neutral pre-schools with a 'norm conscious' focus, they found that girls and boys were more likely to play together and make less stereotypical assumptions about gender in those schools. Uniform matters.

Girls banned from wearing trousers, boys banned from wearing shorts[25] and skirts banned outright in some secondary schools have blazed across UK headlines as if it's the coming of the apocalypse. Freelance journalist Ellie Mae O'Hagan, writing in *The Guardian*, came up with the most obvious solution, a call to all schools and governors to face gender stereotypes head-on with 'Don't ban skirts – let everybody wear them'.[26]

Whatever your feelings on the practicalities of skirts in the school-yard, having choice is key to a gender cool environment, not to mention telling boys that there is nothing degrading about wearing skirts. Gender-neutral, after all, should mean rethinking the clothes to which society has given a nominal gender. I spoke to singer Paloma Faith about her feelings on the phrase 'gender-neutral' and what it meant to her in practical terms. 'Children need comfortable clothing to learn, walk, crawl, run and climb, getting hands and knees dirty – together', she told me – and I think that 'together', is key. Physical restrictions, such as banning girls from wearing trousers and boys from wearing skirts, mirror some of the societal restrictions we are forcing on children. Ensuring girls and boys are dressed differently does not reflect equality and will not encourage children to see each other as equal. As a campaign group, Let Clothes Be Clothes has been focused on raising awareness about how this issue connects with some of the major inequalities in society, but real change will happen only when we take a stand together and call out stereotyping when we see it.

References

1. Report from the Commission to the Council, the European Parliament, the European Economic and Social Committee and the Committee of the Regions. (2008). Equality between women and men.
2. National Childrenswear Survey on bodyshape. (2011). Retrieved April 21, 2019, from https://www2.aston.ac.uk/news/releases/2011/april/childrens-body-shape
3. Complaint by Tonje Kleven Lung via Levi's Facebook page (18 June 2018).
4. Complaint by Lucie Burns to Lands' End UK via email correspondence (7 June 2018).
5. *Introductions: Childrenswear buyer.* (2018). Retrieved April 21, 2019, from SONSHINE website: https://sonshinemagazine.com/magazine/introductions-childrenswear-buyer
6. Pragma Papers: *Market snapshot UK, baby & children's market.* (2017). Retrieved April 21, 2019, from Pragma website: https://www.pragmauk.com/s/Pragma-Baby-Kids-white-paper-2017.pdf
7. Tesco and Mothercare called out for "sexist" marketing of children's clothes. (2017). *The Independent.* Retrieved April 21, 2019, from https://www.independent.co.uk/life-style/tesco-mothercare-sexist-marketing-childrens-let-clothes-be-airtred-boy-shoes-girls-a7881291.html
8. *Girly Glue, It's never too early to be girlie.* (2018). https://girlieglue.com/
9. *Market value of the children's apparel and footwear industry in the UK from 2017 to 2021.* (2018). Statista Statistic's Portal. Retrieved April 21, 2019, from Statista website: https://www.statista.com/statistics/800020/children-s-clothing-and-footwear-market-forecast-united-kingdom-uk/
10. British Retail Consortium. (2011). *Responsible retailing: BRC childrenswear guidelines.* Retrieved April 21, 2019, from http://www.byebuychildhood.org/sites/default/files/documents/Responsible_Childrenswear_Retailing.pdf
11. Wise Campaign. *Women in STEM workforce.* (2017). Retrieved April 21, 2019, from https://www.wisecampaign.org.uk/statistics-category/workforce/
12. *Let Clothes Be Clothes.* (n.d.). Retrieved April 21, 2019, from https://www.letclothesbeclothes.co.uk/
13. *Make sexism in the design and marketing of children's clothing extinct.* (2015). Retrieved April 21, 2019, from Change.org website: https://www.change.org/p/marks-and-spencer-make-sexism-in-the-design-and-marketing-of-children-s-clothing-extinct

14. Girl Guiding UK. *Girl's attitudes survey*. (2017). Retrieved April 21, 2019, from Girl Guiding website: https://www.girlguiding.org.uk/globalassets/docs-and-resources/research-and-campaigns/girls-attitudes-survey-2017.pdf
15. Henley, J. (2009, December 12). The power of pink. *The Guardian*. Retrieved April 21, 2019, from https://www.theguardian.com/theguardian/2009/dec/12/pinkstinks-the-power-of-pink
16. Entwistle, J. (2000). *The Fashioned Body: Fashion, Dress, and Modern Social Theory*. Cambridge, MA: Polity.
17. *Trousers for All*. (n.d.). Retrieved April 21, 2019, from Trousers for All website: https://trousersforall.co.uk
18. Pannick, D. (1999). Girls – why shouldn't they wear the trousers? *The Times*. Retrieved April 21 from https://drive.google.com/file/d/0Bz45kcU-Ek7CUDJNNVREeUdqMlk/view?usp=sharing&usp=embed_facebook
19. Perry, G. (2017). *The Descent of Man*. Germany: Penguin.
20. Walter, N. (2015). *Living Dolls: The Return of Sexism*. London: Virago.
21. *Exclusion of pupils*. (2011). Retrieved April 21, 2019, from politics.co.uk website: http://www.politics.co.uk/reference/exclusion-of-pupils
22. *Suicide facts and figures*. (2017). Retrieved April 21, 2019, from Samaritans website: https://www.samaritans.org/about-samaritans/research-policy/suicide-facts-and-figures/
23. *Good morning Britain*. Piers Morgan interview with Cheryl Rickman for *Let Clothes Be Clothes*. (2017). Retrieved from https://www.youtube.com/watch?v=5eUBgyxBQ04
24. Hedberg, T. (2017). *Children at Swedish "Gender-Neutral" Preschools Are Less Likely to Gender-Stereotype*. Sweden: Uppsala University. Retrieved April 21, 2019, from https://www.uu.se/en/research/news/article/?id=8848&typ=artikel
25. Morris, S. (2017). Teenage boys wear skirts to school to protest against "no shorts" policy. *The Guardian*. Retrieved from https://www.theguardian.com/education/2017/jun/22/teenage-boys-wear-skirts-to-school-protest-no-shorts-uniform-policy
26. O'Hagan, E. M. (2018). Don't ban skirts in school. Let everybody wear them. *The Guardian*. Retrieved from https://www.theguardian.com/commentisfree/2018/jul/03/ban-skirts-in-school-gender-stereotypes

Language and the media

Sweetpea – out of Adam's rib – feminine equivalent – postpeople – I'm bored of men – feminism ruins your life – Bechdel – men running around – where are all the women directors? – a virtuous cycle – perving – S'ralun – Yacht Club Swing – that's Mrs. Arscott – ambivalent accomplishments – the ultimate insult – the smell of the canteen –made and remade – a good egg – powerful words – Ma'am – did she put up a fight? – crusted cat turds – accommodations

Stats

Sixty-four percent of teachers in mixed-sex secondary schools hear sexist language in school on at least a weekly basis. Over a quarter of teachers (29%) report that sexist language is a daily occurrence.[1]

In UK theatre, female customers account for 65% of ticket revenue, but only 39% of actors, 36% of directors and 28% of writers of plays performed are women.[2]

The issues

In *No More Boys and Girls*,[3] one of the first things Javid notices in Graham's classroom is the way he uses 'love' for girls and 'mate' for boys, sometimes switching to 'sweet pea' and 'fella', respectively.

'Wherever they look, I want children to be faced with things that highlight their similarities, and not their differences', begins Dr. Javid in

No More Boys and Girls. He starts by putting up signs that say, 'boys are strong' and 'girls are strong'; 'boys are sensitive' and 'girls are sensitive'. He highlights that he believes the way to change the views of the children in the class is via 'lots of small messages, the sum of which is greater than their parts'. Javid asks a group of children, 'What if Mr. Andre called you all "sweet pea"?' The boys respond vehemently, 'No!' 'It's so weird'. It's all too easy to laugh this off as not mattering – but this stuff sinks in. He talks to Graham about this gendered language.

'It's hard. It's ingrained', says Graham.

What are your classroom routines, rituals and repetitions?

Are any of them gendered?

'Language is one of the most powerful means through which sexism and gender discrimination are perpetrated and reproduced', suggests research.[4]

> Both male and female students report the common use of language which associates negative characteristics with being female – 'you throw like a girl', 'don't be a pussy' – and more positive characteristics with being male – 'man-up'. This language is more likely to be targeted at male students, while female students are more likely to be subjected to gendered sexual name-calling – such as 'slut', 'slag' and 'whore'.[1]
>
> The contention that language is a powerful tool of sexism and racism is based on a theory that suggests that the language you think in structures the way you think. It reiterates the social patterns of our culture and thereby perpetuates cultural norms.[5]

Language can be a tool of real power, used with intent to routinely humiliate, degrade and shrink people down to size: the size of the space you want them to occupy. Alternatively, our intentions may not align with the way that language is received, and that is a huge problem. You might call me 'sweetheart' because you like me; I might receive the word by feeling patronised and diminished. Who bears the responsibility there?

> Language subtly reproduces the societal asymmetries of status and power in favor of men, which are attached to the corresponding social roles. Grammatical and syntactical rules are built in [such] a way that feminine terms usually derive from the corresponding masculine form.[4]

In many ways, 'feminising' language comes out of 'neutral/masculine' language like Eve supposedly came out of Adam's rib. Until we stop and think about it, it might make sense.

Except that non-men are not a subset of men. Mary Beard, in *Women and Power*: 'You can't easily fit women into a structure that is already coded as male; you have to change the structure'.[6] Even the word 'man' is often argued to be representative of all humans; a strong refutation of this is given by Devlin: 'Human. Just two letters more…. I am well aware that the word 'man' can mean 'human' – but not to me, it doesn't. To me it means 'not me'.[7] Here is the binary again, the othering of non-males through language. Using the 'generic masculine'. This is the principle of *invisibility*.

> The second sexist practice denounced by feminists, lexical asymmetry, does not hide women's presence in the world but produces comparable results, assuming that women are inferior to men. To use terms such as 'man and wife', to refer to adult females as 'girls' or to emphasize the importance of women's marital status with 'Miss' and 'Mrs', are all examples of this habit.[8]

This is the principle of *feminine equivalent*. It suggests that 'male' is the default, and that for clarity we should change the word when representing females, to reflect that. Logically, we have two problems here: one, that the male = default; and the other, that women need to be differentiated at all. Remember James Acaster's principle of racism, 'Is it relevant?' I would argue that, so often, differentiation between male and female is not relevant.

For example, the person who delivers my post presents as female. I have never yet had such a thing occur in my life; my first reaction was surprise and interest. My second was a dawning realisation that the term to describe their job was strongly gendered. In English, this word is 'postman' or, very occasionally, 'postie'. How, now, to describe them in speech? We had a discussion about it. 'Postwoman' follows the principle of *feminine equivalent* above, suggesting we need a different word because the person is (and I have presumed this) female. The undertones – that being female has somehow 'disrupted' the natural order – do not sit well with me. It is also, quite simply, not relevant. I would bet some money that this person spends a great deal of their time dodging comments about their (perceived) gender – most of them well-meaning, all of them pointlessly irrelevant.

The solution to this problem would appear to be a new word: post-person. Job done. But the conflict that ensues when you try to use a new or neutral word is interesting (try it).

How do you refer to people who deliver post, or fight fires, or police the streets, or take care of passengers on flights, or act on stage? Have you ever had a classroom discussion about gendered job titles?

Sexist battles are fought on domestic fronts

I'm quite difficult to live with, at times (surprise: of course, everyone is). One of the things I find myself doing often is getting frustrated with TV programmes or films.

The other day, I said, 'I'm tired of watching men do things. Men talking, men running, men solving, men driving, men fighting; that's like 90% of every film ever made. Women pop up to make tea and to ask emotional questions that further the storyline and to be a sexual temptation/distraction, but that's it. I'm so bored of *men*!'

The man I was talking to did not take the bait (he knew that this was not about him. I quite like him). The problem with concerning yourself with sexism, as many more eloquent than I have remarked, is that it ruins your (everyday) life. Many people speak of feminism like the red pill in *The Matrix*, or like scales falling from one's eyes on the road to Damascus, or (my favourite) like simultaneously the best and the worst thing that has ever happened to them. It colours *everything*. Like a stray ink cartridge in your washing machine, nothing will escape its influence. But without a feminist lens to make sense of the world, it can just feel like men are powerful, women are weak and nothing will ever change. I don't want to live in that world, even if the alternative can be hard at times.

Have you heard of the *Bechdel Test* – asking whether a film has at least two named women characters who talk to each other about something other than men (it's a low bar)? Applying the Bechdel Test, I realised most films don't even get close. And this is a minimum criterion; passing it does not guarantee that the film itself won't have sexist or homophobic or racist stereotyping, or lazy and inconsiderate gender role perpetuation. Nor is it a guarantee that any of the women will feel and look anything like believable, relatable characters. Oh, my kingdom for believable, relatable characters! For LGBTQ+ characters in whom their sexuality isn't a *character quirk* but just *is*!

Most TV and film bothers me. On a good day, it's hilariously predictable. On a bad day, it's frustratingly painful. Sometimes there are so many good-looking young hero-type men in a film (hint: more than one) that I can't actually tell the difference. (I am also terrible with faces). This makes following the storyline almost impossible. Sometimes the beginning of the film is half an hour of men with literally not a non-man in sight, and I have to turn it off. Sometimes a woman appears but speaks to the man in such a fawning, sycophantic way that I want to scream. Now, before I see a film, I ask someone, 'Is it just men running around doing shit and women running around after them'?

Who is writing and directing these films?

Considering the 2,591 films released between 2005 and 2014 in the United Kingdom, one report found that 13.6% of working film directors were women. They also found that 'the more senior a role, the less chance it is held by a woman, and, by extension, the less chance a woman has of being hired for it. Female representation in key creative roles and among film crews, like the percentage of female directors, has also stagnated during the last decade. Across the whole of the industry there has been no meaningful trend towards greater representation of women or any real improvement in their career prospects'.[9]

All this, despite the fact that 'UK film students, like the UK population as a whole, are broadly 50% male and 50% female. Similarly, entrants into the film industry are 49% female'.[9]

What has this got to do with education? First, the 'vicious cycle' and 'virtuous cycle' models that could actually effect change do not apply only to the film industry. Thinking about my own area, mathematics, it is clear that images and representations of mathematicians are highly aligned with masculinity (for example, see Heather Mendick's excellent 2006 book *Masculinities in Mathematics*[10]), and better representation of women and other marginalised groups would help to break the cycle of who is promoted, hired and given a platform.

Second, the film industry is extra-important because it's one of the key cultural influences that act on children and adults outside (and sometimes inside) schools. Films are entertainment. They are gobbled up by consumers young and old, and with them the sexist ingredients that might have been thoughtlessly tossed in to bulk them out. Sexism is not fibre, people. It's poison. Stop paying for it.

Theatre, darling

I love amateur dramatics (for reals, not hysterical emotional outbursts). But I have a problem. When I act in shows, I am only ever asked to portray women. I am also always 'supposed' to get changed in 'female' changing areas. For a pansexual person, that's a bit weird (assuming the reason is to ensure that I don't perv on people who don't want me to perv on them). Despite an interesting history of subversion, theatre is highly gendered. We presuppose, on the whole, that audiences want to see men playing men, and women playing women, and despite the fact that great acting is in fact the whole point, we often find the crossing of arbitrary gender boundaries to be a transgression of the fourth wall. Why is that?

What happens in casting for plays at your school? Is gender an important consideration?

Boys and girls

I'm watching the BBC series *The Apprentice*. 'Boys' team', snarls S'ralun, 'Over 'ere. Girls, you stand over there'. There are, at last count, some 14 fully grown adults in the room, all of whom who profess to be businesspeople – entrepreneurs who run their own enterprises, manage their own staff and take responsibility for turnover and clients and accounts and premises and all kinds of things.

Not boys.

Not girls.

Adults.

Why are they content to be infantilised by language like this? Why does no one stop the speaker and declare, 'Actually mate, bit awkward, but I'm thirty-six with two children and I'm not sure what you're getting at ....'

Because that's the entire point. This is about power, and keeping people in their place, and both the separation by gender (watch what happens as people start to 'cross the divide' after a few episodes) and the infantilising language are an important part of it.

Have you been called a 'boy' or a 'girl' recently? How about a 'lass' or a 'madam'? By whom? Did it bother you?

Why should it matter?

I love swing music. One of my playlists includes a live 1938 recorded version of the Fats Waller hit *Yacht Club Swing* (enjoy that earworm – you'll be humming it for days). Fats Waller was one of the greats of the swing era, a much-celebrated black musician. At the end, this exchange is preserved in full:

> 'Well Fats, I'd just like to come in with an official word here, **boy**'.
> 'What's that sir'?
> 'Well, you know, I just had to tell the folks that this music is com-ing from the new Yacht Club, over here on West 52nd Street, just off the Great White Way, and it's the old Admiral himself, Fats Waller and his orchestra'.
> 'Yes, that's…'
> (cuts him off) 'Now how's that, **boy**'?
> 'Oh man, that's a killer diller from Manila Mr Miller'
> 'Yeah, **boy**, and that … that tune you just played, that Yacht Club Swing, is very apropos, huh?'
> 'A … wha … apra who?'
> 'Very apropos, **boy**!'

The (mis)use of the word *boy* here, drawn out in a New York drawl, makes me feel physically sick. This short piece of dialogue has always made me uncomfortable, because even before I knew much about the use of the term 'boy' in the civil rights movement, I could hear, loud and clear, the patronising, demeaning tone of the way the word was used. It is about keeping a man – a brilliant, creative, inspirational man – down. It is about telling him he is less than you and less than other listeners. It is about making sure he knows his place, doesn't get ideas above his station. If you feel you can, listen to the recording and see if you hear it too.

As early as 1787, the slogan 'Am I not a man and a brother?' was used as part of the anti-slavery movement, echoed by Sojourner Truth's iconic 'Ain't I a Woman?' speech on women's rights in 1851. Later, in the 1960s civil rights struggle, posters and placards declaring 'I am a man' were displayed. This was in response to that term 'boy' being used in just such a racist, demeaning, and pejorative way.

More recently, a case that considers this question has been running since 2002. A federal appeals court in Atlanta, Georgia, struck down a $1.3 million award to an employee of Tyson Foods, after a black employee asked for a promotion. His manager instead brought in two white outsiders, saying that the money-losing plant needed new blood. A conversation was had in which the manager used the term 'boy'. The employee sued, saying that the manager's use of 'boy' to him was racist.

The NAACP Legal Defense and Educational Fund issued a response: 'It is widely recognized that the use of the term "boy" to describe an African-American man is deeply offensive and reflects discriminatory intent. Judge Clemon, for example, has said that when used to describe an adult African American man, "boy" is akin to the n-word'.[11] The NAACP describe the term as a 'racial slur' in this context.

It's not just males. 'For black women, gender and racial discrimination can collide in a single experience—like being called "girl"'.[12] Stories of women of colour being called 'girl' abound. Individual at whom the term is directed in this manner report it as 'degrading', often not knowing how to respond or freezing in the moment.

I see fully grown women being referred to as *girls* so often in my professional sphere that my response – 'I think you mean "woman"' – has become something of a running joke. I hope it runs. I hope it spreads like a common cold so we think much more deeply about the consequences of using 'boy' and 'girl' to adults; I hope we stop minimising them in this way.

What needs to change

Jessica Valenti: 'The worst thing you can call a girl is a girl. The worst thing you can call a guy is a girl. Being a woman is the ultimate insult. Now tell me that's not royally fucked up'.[13]

As teachers, our talk is crucial. Pupils may hear our talk as much as they hear that of their parents. The way we talk to them and about them, and to and about our colleagues, pervades a school as surely as the smell of the canteen. Our linguistic foibles may be fondly remembered by pupils (remember that teacher who couldn't say 'statistics', or who pronounced 'graphs' weirdly?) but they are also a window to our thoughts and values. They matter.

What do you call your class, collectively?

'Ladies and gentlemen'?

'Folks'?

'Boys and girls'?

'Guys'?

Every time we draw attention to gender in this way, it has an effect – for example, the stereotype threat effect suggests that it contributes to females underperforming in maths. True story. 'Priming' students by asking them to consider aspects of their identity that may be negatively (or positively) linked to mathematical stereotypes can have a measurable effect on performance that conform to and perpetuate stereotyping.[14] The American Psychological Association (APA) states that 'negative stereotypes raise inhibiting doubts and high-pressure anxieties in a test-taker's mind .... [E]ven passing reminders that someone belongs to one group or another, such as a group stereotyped as inferior in academics, can wreak havoc with test performance'.[15] There is a strong argument here that we should give up using 'boys and girls' and 'ladies and gentlemen' and, furthermore, start to include pupils, especially non-binary and trans pupils, differently.

> One of the biggest challenges people face when addressing or talking about trans individuals is the use of pronouns. What to use: he, him, his, she, her, hers, they, their, theirs? ... [B]egin by asking what pronoun that person prefers to use. Asking shows a level of respect and comfort.[16]

Gosh, imagine if we started each new class like this.

> 'Annabelle? Do you have any nicknames you prefer?'
> 'Yes, I prefer Annie'.
> 'Ok, no problem. And which pronouns do you prefer?'
> 'They/their, please'.
> 'OK, sure. Thanks, Annie. Everyone else, make a note of that too please, and try to respect their wishes. If we mess up, we 'fess up, but let's do our best'.

We could do this equally well with a quietly circulated list, or electronically or in some other way that shows we care and know it's important. It's not just that a minority of people would then feel respected and included – it's that we would all get a chance to reconsider our pronouns and, by extension, our relationship with gender. We would all get the opportunity to remember that someone's gender, like so many other things, shouldn't just be imposed on them by the viewer. It would normalise asking, listening and responding to someone's needs, and all of this work is important for everyone.

As I wrote this, I received an email from a colleague at the University of Cambridge, and they had specified their preferred pronouns in their email signature. Those times, they are a changin', and what a delight and a joy to be at the forefront of the movement towards a greater respect and dignity for gender expression for everyone! If you run a classroom, a lecture hall, a seminar room or a conference, you can make this small change too. If you are cisgendered, even better – you are modelling the sort of consideration towards those who aren't that marks you out as a good egg, and you are making things easier for our trans and non-binary friends and colleagues in the long run.

It goes without saying, I hope, that certain words just don't belong (casually, uncritically) in a school. Actually, maybe it doesn't go without saying, for two reasons: the first being that if you're anything like me, it may not sit well with you to make anything, especially words, taboo. But there's no way round this one. For me there are some words that are so often used as hate speech, discriminatory and cruel, far too much to be ok in a school setting. The second reason is that this stuff changes. It's complex. There have been multiple arguments made, for example, for the members of certain oppressed groups using and reclaiming for their own use words that, when used on them by others, aren't at all acceptable. I know of a variety of examples of this among many communities, and I'm sure many more exist that I'm not aware of.

So how can we know intent? How can we unravel the belonging and not-belonging of individuals in groups that gender and sexuality and all the intersectional ideas might bring forth? How can we keep up with usage and trends? This seems to me to be the sort of thing that should happen at staff meetings and at those fun September all-staff briefings, as well as in smaller and more intimate conversations between staff and their peers and occasionally students. Some words have power – not inherently, but because of historical and cultural and sexist and racist overtones that linger. We need to educate ourselves about what these words might be and to think about how we might mediate the relationships of our pupils with them without increasing their store of power tenfold. That's a particularly tricky paradox.

I don't have all the answers here, and I am highly suspicious of anyone who does. For example, my children have been freely swearing at home from about age 7 (when they first came home with these new words in their mouths like dogs with delicious and forbidden dripping pondy-tasting sticks). We decided that we would have a household where swear words were used with freedom, humour and sometimes frustration, and that has been mostly a joy. But what of the rebelling child who uses a gendered slur? What of the whispered racial put-downs that feel qualitatively different and very much *not* something I want to make space for in the airwaves of my home? Your school and classroom culture is your domain, and you don't need me to tell you that language plays a crucial part in that.

Titles

The existence of two traditional titles for women (Miss and Mrs), in contrast with the one for men (Mr), reflects the importance society puts on women's marital status.

We still, in most schools, use this system. Male teachers get 'Mr' or 'Sir'. Female teachers get 'Mrs' or 'Miss', often fairly haphazardly (I was a generic 'Miss' while married at one school and a rather pompous 'Ma'am' at another while unmarried). The name (and subsequent status) change of a female teacher can cause quite the stir. There was, after my divorce, simply no option for 'Ms' (which sounds very similar to 'Miss' in any case), and explaining it endlessly to pupils when staff didn't abide by it was somewhat wearing. What about women in same-sex marriages or civil partnerships? Proudly married homosexual men? What can we do about this?

The title 'Mx' has been suggested as a neutral equivalent to 'Mr'. (You pronounce this in the same way you might pronounce 'Ms', but with an 'x' on the end – saying 'mix' or 'mux' is fine, too). What would it take to change your school to using such a system? What might be lost, and what gained?

The strongest counterarguments and why they're wrong

- 'TV shows, film and theatre shouldn't be about gender – they're just entertainment'.
- 'Policing language is just political correctness gone MAD!'.
- 'I like my gendered pronouns, thanks'.

Entertainment and education have an intersection

Have you ever shown a film, or part of a film, in class? (No, not like that – I don't want to debate end-of-term Christmas films.) Did you check it first? What did you look for?

In schools, we filter 'entertainment' all the time – we want to avoid showing images and ideas that are not age-appropriate (whatever that may mean). Right now, it is recommended viewing for children to watch films with princesses who get drugged and wait to be kissed while unconscious, but not ok for them to watch films with characters discussing men having sex with men or drag queens. The systems in place fail, all the time, and they are old and outdated. Every story educates in some way, and we want to purposively choose the ones that we feel might fit with our lesson or our message.

Do you consider sexism when you decide what to show pupils? Do you invite them to look for it, to criticise it, to consider it?

There used to be a time when people mostly believed it didn't matter at all if entertainment was racist, sexist or homophobic. There are still many arguments about whether these things are justified if they are ironic, if they are true to a particular period in history or if they are funny. Schools are natural battlegrounds for these ideas, because we can't (and shouldn't) wash and clean everything that we show to pupils; we need to expose them to some germs so they can develop immunity. The key, to some extent, is to control when and how much, and to explore responses sensitively. To do this, we may have to step outside our own uncomplicated enjoyment of things – to realise that *Grease* might have great, catchy tunes, but to ask whether a woman 'put up a fight' has implications that we might want to talk about.

Policing language happens in schools anyway.

No schools allow pupils to say whatever they want to whomever they want. Every school has systems for administration and for names and titles, definitions of abuse and processes for dealing with hate speech. Updating those is important work. Figuring out the boundaries of jokes and 'banter' (urgh) is crucial to the culture of the school, and it so often happens on the margins, when teachers are tired and pupils are high on comedy and no one wants a confrontation.

On the other hand, the words we use are hard to police, and regulating them can feel like silencing. Is it ok to ask people not to voice what they are thinking? Are we drawing unwarranted inferences about intention, or encouraging people to take offence at language?

'Our social relations contribute to the linguistic meaning of words. This is why political language criticism implies neither the cruel intentions of a particular person nor the expression of conversational partner's sensitivity in the first place'.[17]

Asking people to use different words may change their thinking – or at least prompt some rethinking – but that is most certainly not a guarantee. The words may be a symptom of hatred, fear or intent to dehumanise others. Alternatively children may just be emulating adult speech without much understanding. Either way, exploring the thoughts (or lack of them) underneath the words, rather than just banning them, would be advisable – even though it might also expose some ugly prejudices. But they were always there, like the crusted cat turds flattened out on the lawn that only got exposed when you mowed it.

Changing language is a proxy for cultural or social change. In many ways, this is a problem, because what we are actually doing is attempting to coerce people into changing their performative words, and not their beliefs. But what is the alternative?

Guess what? You get to choose your pronouns

As so often happens when we are considering others and encouraging empathy, we are creating new options for everyone.

> Pronouns function as high frequency reminders of how we perceive each other's identities, without us ever having to come right out and say it. Unlike most gendered words in English, we use pronouns in virtually every conversation. Their use is so common, even automatic, that they also seem to imply something about what we think at a deep level'.[18]

Sometimes we just don't (think we) think about things until we do.

The way we communicate with one another (verbally and non-verbally) both betrays and affects our relationships with them. Recently, while having a discussion about inclusion of preferred pronouns on conference materials, someone I know responded with frustration. 'Can't I just ask the ones who look like they might be a different gender?' they asked.

Well, no. Because what we're talking about is a tiny revolution. It's the fledgling tender beginnings of the idea that someone's identity is not what you impose on them. It's about the human kindness of understanding that people may have made thousands upon thousands of accommodations for you – to keep you comfortable and socially relaxed – and maybe, just maybe, it might be right to make some of those accommodations for them. For a generation of people who have truly believed you can know someone's gender by looking at them, this might feel huge. For many of my children's generation, I suspect it's a much more integrated way of knowing someone, and it's high time our institutions, rules and policies caught up.

> For a person who is transgender or non-binary, sharing pronouns can be a bit riskier. If someone is transitioning at work and only a few people know about it, sharing pronouns may out them before they're ready ... That's why we ask cisgender people to lead the change by sharing pronouns. It normalizes the process, has little risk, and actually makes for a safer environment for everyone.[19]

(More on this in the next chapter, where we discuss in more detail issues related to being trans).

Now/later

Now: Spend a lesson, or a day, thinking about your own language as you teach. Try and make a note of any gendered language you use. Reflect on why and how you use language in this way.

Add your preferred pronouns to your email signature, your Twitter handle or your LinkedIn account (or all of them).

Later: Have a look at the physical landscape of your school environment and the linguistic landscape of formal talk (such as assemblies) with an eye for gender. Do people routinely use 'boys and girls/ladies and gentlemen'? How are teachers addressed? What changes might make a difference?

Graham says

'Men are only 38% of NHS 'Talking Therapy' referrals yet 78% of deaths by suicide are male'.[20]

Now why is this? Why is it that seems that women can talk about their problems more than men? I think I have a simple answer to this, but not such a simple solution. In the same way as we (quite wrongly) expect our girls to be caring and sweet and to grow up wanting a family and to have children, we expect our boys to be strong and provide for others, and if they show any sort of emotion it is seen as a weakness, or they are told to 'man up' or 'boys don't cry'. None of this is right, or helpful. So what happens when a boy/man cannot live up to these expectations?

During the documentary there was a simple diagnostic test carried out by the team. They gave each pupil an emotion word and asked them to suggest words linked with that emotion. The girls were great at this, the boys generally were not.

What's the problem? You may be thinking, 'Just give the boys the necessary vocabulary and that will solve that!' Unfortunately, it isn't that simple, and of all the discoveries from the documentary, this has been the hardest problem to address. The expectations of being the best, wanting to be first, having to win, and the fact that losing or showing emotion is seen as a weakness, are so ingrained in so many boys (and men) that when they *don't* win or they *do* feel strong emotion, it often manifests itself in anger. Robert Webb talks about this in his brilliant book *How Not to Be a Boy*, where he suggests that all too often, whatever emotion boys are feeling ultimately it comes out as anger, so feeling ashamed becomes anger; sadness becomes anger; uncertainty becomes anger – and even feeling afraid becomes anger. Unless we can give our boys the emotional literacy skills and space to talk about their emotions in a safe environment without fear of judgement, then we are unlikely to have generations of men that are able to do it.

We have had some success by looking at books such as *10,000 Dresses*, *The Flower* or *My Princess Boy* and talking about emotions and empathy, but this needs to start much younger, in pre-school or EYFS (early years foundation stage) at the latest, and it needs to continue as part of PSHE (personal, social and health education) throughout schooling, including in secondary. Ultimately, we want our children to grow up independent, strong and confident; to pursue their own destiny, whatever that may be; to show compassion, caring and respect and to be able to express emotions freely – in short, to be great humans.

With regards to film and TV, and particularly in terms of female representation, there seems to have been a small shift. We now have our first female Dr. Who; we have had some brilliant female leads in films such as *Wonder Woman* and *Captain Marvel* and in the latest *Star Wars* films. With more recent Disney animations, we have had Merida from *Brave*, Elsa from *Frozen* and of course the wonderful *Moana*. There is emphatically still a long way to go, but it's a start, and it is good to see the major movie studios showing awareness of the problem. Keira Knightley recently went public about her feelings about many of the older Disney films depicting females as poor role models (basically waiting for men to save them) or making poor choices, to the point where Knightley has purportedly forbidden her daughters to watch them. I can understand her views, and I agree that as role models they are sometimes pretty poor, but I would still let my children watch them and then talk about what they have seen. The sorts of questions I would ask:

Are the choices made the right ones?

What did you think of the female and male characters in the story and how they were portrayed?

What would you do differently?

I don't think we want to shield our children from stereotypes in entertainment media – and I'm not even sure we could. But certainly we want to make our children and our pupils aware of them so that these young readers and viewers will to be able to spot them, learn from them and react to them thoughtfully.

Tl;dr

Our language matters, and our habits and patterns may be having unintended consequences on those around us. However, there are issues inherent in policing language and media when actually what we are trying to do is engage with and challenge beliefs. Film and theatre have some pretty tired gender stories. Are we talking about them or just swallowing them like sweets?

References

1. *Sexism in schools.* (2017). Retrieved April 13, 2019, from NEU website: https://neu.org.uk/advice/sexism-schools
2. Purple Seven. (2015). *Gender in theatre.* Retrieved from http://purpleseven.com/media.ashx/gender-thought-leadership.pdf
3. *No More Boys and Girls.* (2017). Outline Productions/British Broadcasting Corporation. Broadcast August 2017, BBC 2.
4. Menegatti, M., & Rubini, M. (2017). Gender bias and sexism in language. *Oxford Research Encyclopedia of Communication.* https://doi.org/10.1093/acrefore/9780190228613.013.470
5. Facebook, S. P. (2017). *The psychology of freedom: How sexist language harms women.* Retrieved April 21, 2019, from Libertarianism.org website: https://www.libertarianism.org/columns/psychology-freedom-how-sexist-language-harms-women
6. Beard, M. (2017). *Women & Power: A Manifesto.* London, England: Profile.
7. Devlin, K. (2018). *Turned On: Science, Sex and Robots.* London, England: Bloomsbury Sigma.
8. Darr, B. (2016). *Do they use "them"?: Gender-neutral pronoun usage among queer and non-queer college students* (University of Tennessee Honors Thesis Projects.). Retrieved from https://trace.tennessee.edu/cgi/viewcontent.cgi?referer=https://www.google.com/&httpsredir=1&article=3001&context=utk_chanhonoproj
9. Follows, S., & Kreager, A. (2016). *Cut out of the picture.* 139. Retrieved 21 April 2019 from https://d29dqxe14uxvcr.cloudfront.net/uploads%2F1461930983739-erk37ak82v20lnpl-0dacf96122678073f64e99c9b75e90bf%2FCut+Out+of+The+Picture+-+Report.pdf
10. Mendick, H. (2006). *Masculinities in Mathematics.* Maidenhead, Berkshire: Open University.
11. *Hithon v. Tyson Foods, Inc.* (n.d.). Retrieved April 21, 2019, from NAACP Legal Defense and Educational Fund website: https://www.naacpldf.org/case-issue/hithon-v-tyson-foods-inc/
12. *Black women on being called "girl" in the workplace.* WUSF News. (n.d.). Retrieved April 21, 2017, from https://wusfnews.wusf.usf.edu/post/black-women-being-called-girl-workplace
13. Valenti, J. (2014). *Full Frontal Feminism: A Young Woman's Guide to Why Feminism Matters* (2nd edition). Berkeley, CA: Seal.
14. Steele, C. M., Spencer, S. J., & Aronson, J. (2002). Contending with group image: The psychology of stereotype and social identity threat. In *Advances in Experimental Social Psychology* (Vol. 34, pp. 379–440). Academic Press. https://doi.org/10.1016/S0065-2601(02)80009-0
15. Lorenzo, C., de (n.d.). Science says being told you're "bad at math" can lead to this kind of anxiety. Retrieved April 21, 2019, from Bustle website: https://www.bustle.com/p/what-is-math-anxiety-a-new-study-says-that-racial-gender-bias-around-math-ability-has-mental-health-consequences-13142529

16. Teich, N. M. (2012). *Transgender 101: A Simple Guide to a Complex Issue.* New York, NY: Columbia University.
17. *Is there such a thing as politically correct language?* (n.d.). Retrieved April 22, 2019, from https://www.unibas.ch/en/Research/Uni-Nova/Uni-Nova-130/Uni-Nova-130-Essay.html
18. Zimman, L. (2016, August 29). *Trans pronoun FAQ,* Part 1. Retrieved April 22, 2019, from Trans Talk website: https://medium.com/trans-talk/trans-pronoun-faq-part-1-e96b5d10d425
19. Masure, M. (2018, August 10). *Why I put pronouns on my email signature (and LinkedIn profile) and you should too.* Retrieved April 22, 2019, from Medium website: https://medium.com/gender-inclusivit/why-i-put-pronouns-on-my-email-signature-and-linkedin-profile-and-you-should-too-d3dc942c8743
20. Office for National Statistics. (2016). *Suicides in the UK.* Retrieved April 22, 2019, from https://www.ons.gov.uk/peoplepopulationandcommunity/birthsdeathsandmarriages/deaths/bulletins/suicidesintheunitedkingdom/2016registrations

Trans people, trans issues

An umbrella term – genitals on the table – very angry – life and death – macho men in heels – the 'you-ness' of you – the context is the problem – fitting in – I couldn't prove I was a girl – whiffs, groans and splashes – walls – period chats – Basher McRamshank – constant cultural messages – sterilised – emotional support for a poop – a nappy of the mind – nakedness is so interesting – stuck in their skinny jeans – #stallsforeveryone – they just need to pee – holy heteronormativity – how to woman – powerless and infantilised – Baby Shark on a fidget spinner – empathetic and feminist

Stats

Around 1% of the population might identify as trans, including people who identify as non-binary. That would mean there are about 600,000 trans and non-binary people in Britain, out of a population of over 60 million.[1]

In the previous year, one-third of transgender people reported a negative healthcare experience, such as verbal harassment, refusal of treatment or the need to teach their doctors about transgender care.[2]

Twenty-nine percent of [trans] respondents felt that their gender identity was not validated as genuine, instead being treated as a symptom of mental ill health.[3]

Some 40% of trans people have attempted suicide, almost nine times the rate for the general population.[2]

The issues

What does 'trans' mean? 'The umbrella term 'trans' refers to a wide range of people who find (or have found) that their personal experience of gender is different from how gender is conventionally constructed. Therefore, those who would typically be considered trans include trans men (those assigned female at birth but who identify as male), trans women (those assigned male at birth but who identify as female), those who use alternative labels (e.g., 'bigender', 'androgyne', 'polygender') to describe their gender identity and those who do not define their gender at all.'[3]

From a resource for young people: 'Trans is an umbrella term. It includes cross-dressers, transgender and transsexual people as well as anyone else who is in any way gender variant. Before we start it's important to understand that sex is between the legs and gender is between the ears. Sex is male, female and intersex, and has to do with your chromosomes, genitalia, hormones, etc. Gender is man, woman, boy, girl, androgynous (gender-neutral), and has to do with your internal sense of self and how you choose to express yourself'.[4]

Is gender identity innate in some way? Is assigning sex at birth problematic? Is the whole notion of being trans full of contradictions and difficulties that are hard to navigate without upsetting somebody? You bet (to the last one, at least). Should we steer away from talking about being trans on that basis? I believe absolutely not.

Genitals on the table: I am not trans. (That is a terrible joke in terrible taste, not least because my trans friends tell me they are so tired of people being so very weirdly interested in their genitals.) I have never really dealt with, personally, any of the issues surrounding gender identity in any way that has left me on the margins, threatened or mentally ill. This chapter, therefore, has been a particularly sensitive undertaking as I have spoken to trans people and read their stories and debates and considered the issues very much from the outside in. I will never understand first-hand some things about being trans.

One of the major issues around being trans is the lack of dialogue and discourse, particularly in schools. Once again, we find that 'deviance' from 'norms' gets equated with all kinds of sexualising, very weird assumptions, and fear. This is also in part due to the paradox inherent in feeling like your gender identity is 'wrong' or 'mismatched' – if there is no such thing as a fixed gender identity boundary, then why would it matter anyway? Why can't Alex just be Alex, male or female, both or neither?

Because, I would respectfully suggest, we are not there yet.

Have you ever met anyone for whom their gender is not immediately obvious? How long have you gone without knowing someone's gender? How did it make you feel?

What does it means to be trans? Can we 'diagnose' being trans? How could or should we react to our children or our pupils questioning their gender?

Is it possible that, like identifying with other LGBTQ+ labels, being trans is sometimes about being part of a community and feeling marginalised, in addition to the core issue of feeling misgendered in some way?

Many people are very angry in our world about the mere existence of trans people. Some argue that if you haven't lived X years as a woman, with periods or oppression or other disadvantages, you have no 'right' to claim that identity now. Others insist that a vulva, vagina, ovaries or womb (and the concomitant issues with sex, pregnancy or contraception) should dictate one's 'womanhood'. In the sections below, I treat this issue just as I have the issues discussed in all the other chapters – with the caveat that I am aware that this, of all issues in the book, may be the most sensitive, divisive and painful.

> People who are not transgender – meaning whose gender identity does match up with their birth sex – often naturally accept the gender binary system as a given.... But for trans people living in a culture where the gender binary rules all, it is a daily battle.[5]

The problem is that gender segregation also patently exists for exclusion. If you happen to be trans (literally, moving across genders), then you are hitting those barriers, hard. You are tripping over something which may have been invisible to cisgendered people for their whole lives. It's easy to see why people don't get it sometimes.

But make no mistake: This is life and death. One study of young people found that forty-eight percent of trans+ young people (under the age of 26) have attempted suicide at least once. This compares to around 26% of cisgender young people.[6]

All parents with gender-variant children express these fears, over and over again:

Will my child make friends? Who will love my child? Will my child suffer as the victim of hate crimes? Will my child suffer sexual violence? Will my child commit suicide? Will my child be murdered? These fears can be absolutely debilitating.[5]

What happens to our children who don't feel comfortable with the way society genders them? It breaks my heart to say that the answer, often, is: awful, terrible, unnecessary things.

We are not 'born' with a gender, in the sense that we are not born with the constraints and expectations of gender roles that later may come to define us. We grow up in a world that largely uses and defines only two categories of human and tells us which one we are, usually (though not exclusively) based on what's in our pants.

But what if that doesn't fit?

There are several important ways that in which even young children may reject their gender assigned at birth. Bathroom behaviour, including peeing standing up for girls; swimsuit aversion; type of clothing and especially underwear choices; and strong preferences for playing with toys of the 'other' gender. However, this does not necessarily mean the child is transgender; they may be gender non-conforming. What does this mean?

Gender non-conforming refers to behaviours or choices that fall outside what is considered 'normal' for the person's biological sex. This means, of course, that the term and the idea are defined by a 'normal' ideal of binary gender (and one that is dynamic and changing according to the culture and time you live in).

Your gender identity is the deep, internalised feeling you have about whether your sex assigned at birth feels 'right'. It largely can't be measured or made visible to others (although this is a matter of dispute); you have to ask the person. And gender identity is often clearly communicated as early as 2-4 years old.[7] If you have never reflected deeply on this, and your assigned sex at birth is the same as your gender identity (this is called being 'cis-gender'), consider this for a moment:

Imagine yourself in a different body, but with your mind unaltered (as if they can be separated!). What would change? How might you feel? Imagine this new you as a child, an adolescent, a teenager. What sorts of choices might you have made, and what kinds of behaviour might you have engaged in that you didn't at the time?

If this feels weird, that's perfectly ok – it *is* weird (almost all the best things are). Considering yourself in a different body, or gender role, is something we are not routinely encouraged to do, and if you haven't ever been gender non-conforming or experienced a mismatch in your gender identity, you might find it almost impossible. Your gender identity and sex might feel so closely aligned with the 'you-ness' of you that they are virtually inseparable.

But that's not true for everyone.

Why do people 'become' trans or gender questioning?

> Transgender identity is not the result of divorce, child abuse, disappointment at the sex of the child, or … an overbearing parent, a lenient parent, or an absentee parent. The studies that once implicated parenting in whether a person becomes transgender have all been widely disputed.[8]

Consider your own ideas about this. Is there a sense in which you feel that telling pupils about all the options around gender identity and fluidity (not to mention being gay, lesbian, bisexual, asexual, …) might cause them to take an 'unnatural' interest in them? That you might be suggesting it's something they should *do*, rather than *be*? That if you hadn't brought it up, it wouldn't be an issue? Does that feel logically consistent with the idea that these are protected identity characteristics that individuals, to a large extent, do not choose?

Have you ever had a conversation with pupils about being gender non-conforming or being trans? What did they say? How did you feel about it?

While it is true that parenting and teaching cannot 'cause' a child's gender identity, they can and do have one potent effect: to influence how supported a child feels about their own gender identity, and most particularly to make a real difference during a period of change and upheaval when they may be feeling confused, anxious or frightened about it.

As adults, one of our greatest responsibilities is to ensure that children in our care have time and space to be who they are (they cannot, indeed, be anything else). If they are disabled, we do not ask that they become non-disabled. If they are trans, then, we should not and cannot ask them to be otherwise. They should not be an inconvenience to us, a problem to be solved. They did not ask to have these issues thrust upon them, and they almost certainly don't want to keep confronting them daily with almost everyone they meet. (I imagine that's incredibly exhausting.) It's the context that's a problem, not them, and if we suggest otherwise, we are failing them in the most regrettable way.

You may be starting to see that same paradox emerging here once again.

For those of us for whom binary notions of gender are not only unhelpful but generally are not descriptive of how we feel, the idea of firmly rejecting one and becoming the other seems like it isn't necessary. If gender weren't a thing, wouldn't it be no big deal being a trans person? If we could all be more fluid, not expected to be pigeonholed, wouldn't that be a good thing? Yet why is there sometimes such a strong desire to enforce and cross the gender boundary among those who are gender non-conforming or transgender?

One way to consider this is as a way of 'fitting into' a pretty inflexible system that is in place already. 'Patricia Gagné and her colleagues (1997) examined the coming out process of trans people, who, according to their data, most often cling to the standards of the binary sex/gender system in order to have their gender identities and expressions be understandable'.[9] And that's crucial, because so much of trans experience is the opposite – it's about feeling out of place, being a problem. That makes me both angry and so, so sad, because it seems so unnecessary.

> Much of the literature written about this community is punitive in nature, or contains language that pathologizes the group as a whole. Words such as 'miserable', 'troubled', and reference to an individual's transgender identity as a 'problem' are common, and do not include differentiation between one's gender identity and ... mention of society's role in creating the distress within the individual.[10]

We need to talk about toilets and other gendered spaces

Much of the public debate around trans rights seems, rather oddly, to have focused on toilets. One trans person tells their story:

> I remember quite clearly the first time someone actually called the manager when I was in the girls' toilets...What was I supposed to do? I couldn't prove I was a girl, because I'm not a girl, but I didn't

think I looked enough like a boy either to be anywhere else. Where was I supposed to go if both options got me in trouble?[4]
Under current laws, trans people have a default right to use whichever single-sex area they choose, but can be turned away if doing so can be justified as proportionate.[11]

In schools, as in other public buildings, we often still have gendered toilets – except perhaps for toilets for those with accessibility needs, where necessity seems to be the smother of discrimination – and so trans pupils may feel that toilets are a particular site of worry or exclusion for them. This is because 'being' trans, as we have seen above, covers a wide variety of states, many of which won't be reflected in the outward appearance of the pupil (or indeed the teacher). This leaves us, as teachers, in a position where we may feel that female-only or male-only spaces are under threat, and we need to police them.

You know what's interesting? Speak to almost anyone in depth about their (public) toilet habits and you'll hear the same sorts of things: 'I just can't go when I know people are listening', 'I hate it when people try and talk to me in there', 'I just go as quickly as I can, I feel so uncomfortable with people looking'. Shit, piss, vomit and period, despite being (almost) universal humanisers, also function as degraders in contemporary Western society, and the particular rituals we convene around them act just like the rudimentary cubicle walls, shielding others from the whiffs, groans and splashes that we are terrified will betray us as *just like them.*

This is surprising, because public toilets can be the site of heartbreakingly lovely humanity – a lent tampon, a passed bouquet of toilet paper, the loving act of door-holding or bag-holding or coat-holding. None of these things give a (splashy ol') shit about gender (and in case you're wondering, I know some wonderful men who do indeed carry tampons for their daughters or partners). Far from requiring gender segregation, toilets would appear to be one of the most obvious places where we *don't* need it.

The other day, I was chatting to my friend, who is cis-male, and we were having a great and very deep conversation as we walked down a corridor. It was the kind of conversation where you forget where you physically are, because you're so enthusiastically considering the subject matter (it was about mathematics education, which is my research specialism). As we got to the end of the corridor, our destination – the toilets – appeared. I veered left, he right. We stopped talking and looked at one another, having the same thought in the same moment. *Why?* It seemed so weird. Nothing about what either of us was about to do – presumably pee (or maybe expel some other bodily waste)– was different. Nothing about it was shrouded in mystery. I didn't particularly care to see him pee, and most likely that worked the other way around too – and I'm not generally a fan of the weird-toilet-conversation thing either – but that wasn't the point. We'd spent the last 2 hours together, and at that moment, because our mutual bladders were full, society somehow had deemed that we should part company, please, immediately. In fact, I could hear him peeing through the not-so-sturdy wall between the toilets. The jet-engine levels of noise of the hand-driers made it obvious who had washed their hands. When I came out, we talked about my annoyingly heavy period. There was nothing about the wall between the two gendered spaces that changed the interaction materially – it was a metaphorical as well as a literal wall that forced our gender into saliency.

A moment's thought will reveal that our private toilets at home are overwhelmingly mixed-gender spaces. Many shops and restaurants have gender-neutral toilets. My university college has them. As I consider this issue, it seems to return to an argument more and more about individual privacy rather than gender – lockable cubicles for everyone and the removal of urinals seems to solve so many problems.

Changing rooms, changing genders

But what about changing rooms? What about safe spaces?

Caroline Criado Perez writes, persuasively, that women have not just felt, but *been*, unsafe in public spaces on a global scale for some time, and that their fears have so often been dismissed as 'irrational' that victim-blaming has been utterly baked into this debate. For women, it is clear that specifically public nudity, or near nudity, can be dangerous, and Perez argues that better public design is the solution, fuelled by good-quality collection and use of data.[12] But there are two issues with this in education, as I see it. Schools are not, on the whole, well-designed spaces, nor are they often awash with money for redesign, nor is the money they do have value-free, which means that building large individual cubicles for showering and changing in may be bottom of the list for both financial and political reasons. As with toilets, ensuring everyone feels safe and comfortable

175

can be expensive and divisive, and bringing trans people into this debate – I imagine quite unwillingly, at times – means the media have a particular angle that can be exploited endlessly. Should trans women and girls be 'allowed' in female-only changing rooms? How do we divide changing spaces if not by gender, and how can we ensure that gender-questioning young people feel safe without having to make irreversible choices?

Most of the public hype around these choices narrows the debate to suggesting that trans pupils are getting 'special treatment', ignoring the most pertinent issue: women and girls are often not safe in public spaces, especially when they are not fully clothed. Moreover, we are torn between wanting pupils to find nudity commonplace and unremarkable – encompassing all kinds of difference – and the manic fascination we have with other people's bodies evident in TV shows like *Naked Attraction*. Teachers and schools are under a very particular pressure to ensure sex is kept out of their buildings, their lessons and their references, unless state-mandated and approved. What better way to do that than to make sure boys and girls never see one another unclothed?

Except: it's all backwards.

In primary schools, often students change in a gender-neutral situation until someone somewhere decrees 'Puberty!' and separation occurs. 'Quite right', you may be thinking. But then what? Then we have inserted this idea *sex* into their gender interactions, effectively telling them that to see another of the 'opposite' sex without clothes on is to commit an offence. (Whereas, actually, offences happen all the time in schools, and they're so often not in the changing rooms, and they're so often not happening in the eyes and minds of pupils, but with their words and hands, but that's another chapter entirely.)

While I do agree with Criado Perez that good environmental design, based on the needs of those who require protection, is something that needs way more attention than it gets at present, I can't agree that this is a solution. The problem isn't just that females (and others) aren't feeling or being safe because they haven't got anywhere to retreat to. The problem is that they *have* to retreat to somewhere in the first place. Corralling pupils by gender doesn't teach them anything expect that they need protection from other genders – and maybe sometimes they do, but how in the hell else do we break this cycle if not by addressing it head-on?

And trans people are the victims here too. Majorities of trans pupils are bullied, victimised, harassed or even physically assaulted when trying to use gendered spaces.[13] A focus on redesigning the spaces suggests there's nothing we can do about this, or about the sexual harassment or bullying that happens when pupils take their clothes off. Really?

If the primary purpose of schooling is education, why on earth are we not teaching our young people how to behave in the public spaces they will be using for the rest of their lives? We spend *hours* on assembly etiquette, correct uniform, pleases and thank yous. How is it possible that we can't give the same focus to bare skin and what it does(n't) mean? How can we be letting trans or gender-questioning pupils struggle with these issues on their own?

Gender-neutral spaces are problematic. But many of the reasons *why* they are problematic begin at school, and if we believe that heteronormatively separating pupils by gender when they hit puberty is better than explicitly teaching them to get undressed and to pee and poo in spaces with other humans in a sensitive and thoughtful way, there seems no end to this cycle. I've talked about the theatre in previous chapters; when I am placed in changing rooms with other women, it becomes so obvious to me, as a queer woman, that it is my specific behaviour as an individual, not whom I'm attracted to, that is the salient issue. That behaviour (respecting privacy, being careful of others' bodies, helping and supporting when invited to do so, accepting others' bodies as they are) is not a gendered behaviour for me, and I believe that, with guidance, it need not be for our pupils either.

Names and pronouns

I've mentioned pronouns in earlier chapters. Often, we seem to worry about the weirdest stuff (see above). If a student at your school wants to use different pronouns, there should be space for them to do so. Asking everyone their pronouns and modelling the practice of informing others what pronouns you yourself prefer also send a powerful message that this is more than just an inconvenience, and that everyone has the right to consider these issues – they're not just 'for' trans people, just as period chats aren't just 'for' females.

Asking people what nicknames they have, along with which pronouns they prefer (within reason – it is probably ok to veto 'Basher McRamshank', at the beginning of the year) can subvert all the scary 'legal name vs register name' stuff that might feel more formal. Try to raise no eyebrows if Amelia would rather be called Andy or Ian Ella. Find them later, quietly, and ask them if they'd like to discuss it further. Students might jump on the bandwagon and poke fun at this practice a few times, but the joke's on them if you resolutely take them at their word and treat transphobic behaviour as seriously as you would any other transgression of that type. 'Why exactly is it funny that Alex want to use a "girl's" name', Charlie?' Usually, it's because for these giggling pupils, being 'misgendered' – usually feminised – is the worst thing they can imagine. Good. Now you know, you can begin to tackle it. Just remember that's your job, not Alex's.

What needs to change

Put simply: We are consistently failing to accept and protect, never mind embrace, people with trans identities.

> Being trans isn't just about dressing in a certain way or changing one's body, it's also about the need we all have to have our identities affirmed by other people. When trans people are misgendered, it's just another instance of the constant cultural message that trans identities are not real, not important, not worthy of respect the way cisgender identities are.'[14]

Legally, the Equality Act protects people's right to use the bathroom according to the identity they choose to have organisations accept and respect their gender. But often, these issues are still being debated as if they weren't settled.

Sometimes it gets particularly sinister.

In 2019 the *Economist* tweeted, 'Should transgender people be sterilised before they are recognised?' Paris Lees responded as follows: 'The fact that a publication that is respected around the world now thinks that its acceptable – in any context – to ask if members of a minority should be sterilised reveals how low public discourse has sunk in the UK and the unprecedented atmosphere of hostility towards trans people'.[15]

Another important point to note is that 'often, trans people's experiences have been subsumed within studies of lesbian, gay, bisexual and trans (LGBT) people. The notion of a collectivised experience among

LGBT people serves to conflate and consequently overlook the distinct needs and issues of trans people who, within this context, form a small minority within a minority'.[3]

The strongest counterarguments and why they're wrong

- 'We need to protect gendered spaces like toilets – otherwise anything could happen'.
- 'It's obvious – women have periods, breasts, ovaries and wombs and are defined by them alone'.
- 'People who are trans have not experienced life as that gender, may have benefited from undue privilege or may not have faced gender oppression in the same way'.
- 'This is just a trend, a fad, a phase – young children should not be 'allowed' to be trans'.

Those toilets again If you have been used to gender-segregated toilets all your life, you may be forgiven for sleepwalking around public spaces and accepting that that's just what people do.

Except no one really has.

Does your toilet at home have a gender identity label on the door? Thought not.

In my bathroom at home, all sorts of shenanigans go on. For example, I enjoy taking a bath with an audience, much like I imagine Regency-period royalty used to. (I don't mean they mutely watch and clap; I mean my children and partner routinely come in and chat with me and play weird bath games, and we talk about bodies and make potions and other fun stuff. I highly recommend it). In my house, bathroom time is often a more-than-one-person activity. My children are older now, but bathtime together used to be one of their favourite things.

Using the toilet is also not a strictly private activity – it can be (there is a lock on the door, and we all use it at times) but often we will have chats while weeing, or I'll have an inquisitive visitor watching me deal with periods, or one of my children might request emotional support for a poop (I find this both adorable and odd). I don't routinely close the door. Parents of young children might recognise this one. But this doesn't just happen at home; in public spaces, my two daughters and I regularly go for a wee companionably in the same toilet, particularly if there's a queue. As they get older, I have been thinking: I honestly don't know what I'd do if one of them were coded male. I like peeing together. I also like that I'm not worrying about where they are. I don't think that I'd feel ashamed or worried about my body around a son (although of course, he might); I'd feel ashamed or worried that we had to constantly split up to pee in public.

The idea that peeing and pooping and perioding is private is fairly specific to the space and time we live in, and, as we have seen above, it is not a rule that makes sense to everyone. The idea that toilet practices should *always* be private, therefore, just isn't demonstrably true. Even in the current system, we have a particularly odd legacy solution to male urination – the urinal. I have never yet met a man who likes this, and I've met plenty who actively loathe it. It's the sort of thing that gets more bizarre the more you think about it. Even toilet stalls are notoriously not soundproof. Talk about your issues with public toilet space – how you have a nervous bladder or an anxious sphincter in these environments – and people will nod enthusiastically in agreement. Public toilet space, segregated as it is, is often not a private or comfortable place *for anyone* at present. Rather than blaming trans people or the tiny minority who use toilets unwisely, uncharitably or unlawfully, perhaps we could start with that.

And then we come to parenting challenges in these sorts of spaces. All too often, we still have 'male' and 'female and baby change' options (my local swimming pool, bafflingly, has 'Male and Disabled' or 'Female and Family'). Do dads not exist in civic planning, or do they just not ever have cause or opportunity to change nappies in the minds of those considering toilet options? (I'm enjoying the idea of 'changing a nappy in the mind', or indeed *of* the mind. Filth.) I refuse to believe fathers don't work in places where these decisions are made. Why, then, are we sending these strongest of signals that childcare space is only for mothers? Why aren't we doing better?

Parents with children whose gender is different from their own may also recognise the challenge of 'When is it time to separate in public toilet space?' that I alluded to earlier. For 2- and 3-year-olds, it's easy. They come in with you. Ages 4 and 5 might also not be a problem, but when is it weird? What arbitrary boundaries we draw. 'Girl' children must not see strangers' penises emitting a stream of urine, although adult men pretty much *have* to see them unless a stall is free. 'Boy' children can't be *near* where women are expelling urine. What in the name of biology are we so afraid of?

Bodies, that's what. Swimming changing rooms are similarly fraught at times. If, like me, you've hissed 'Don't stare!' at your children more times than you can count, you might recognise the underlying parental terror that your child might be looking at *other people naked*. Why? I realise those people might not be crazy about it, but nakedness is so very interesting. Partly, of course, because we're taught from such a young age that we're not supposed to be looking at it.

I can only draw two conclusions here. One is that we feel we should 'protect' children from bodily functions and nudity. This is frankly hilarious. That is pretty much all there is to small children, apart from the occasional lull when they are eating or asleep. I've been pooed on, peed on and puked on, and I've had every single part of my body (and theirs) inspected in great detail by my children. Bodies are our first sense that we are different, autonomous and separate to other people, and therefore fascinating. My other conclusion that we are teaching children that gender separation is, at these times, necessary for some other reason. I'd like to question this, robustly, specifically when talking about getting changed or going to the loo.

If you think that getting your genitals out is uniformly sexy, we have a problem. Nudity is not foreplay. Plenty of times people get their bits out (getting changed, breastfeeding, toileting, changing sanitary protection, changing medical equipment, washing) and they're emphatically not doing so to do you a sexy naked dance; they're just stuck in their skinny jeans, or changing a catheter. Know the difference. If in doubt, assume not-sexy-nudity until someone is gyrating in your face and whispering, 'Shall we make the beast with two backs?' in your ear. Done.

Toilet stalls are much like toilet walls. Sometimes there is literally no difference. It's all just a societal metaphor for binary gender difference. Let's just have #stallsforeveryone.

Invisibility of 'other' genders causes all sorts of issues later on. Like the conviction that women are 'enigmatic, beautiful creatures' or penises are terrifying slimed eels of procreation. We could all stand to see and talk about nakedness and difference a little more. This goes tenfold for people who are further from the 'norm', who have been placed on the margins. If we all knew at least one trans person, disabled person or non-binary person, and had popped to the loo with them before, I'm not sure we'd even be having this debate. Are you really arguing against someone's right to release their bladder 3 metres nearer or farther away from you? They *just need to pee.*

It's like when there's a huge queue for the loos and you see a parent with a little one saying, 'I HAVE TO GO NOW IT'S COMING OUT QUICK IT'S COMING OUT' – you just let them through. No one in that situation argues the point – 'Actually, we've all been queuing for a while now, and it's not fair' – they just step aside. This is nothing to do with infantilising trans people but everything to do with politeness and humanity. *They just need to poop.* I have no idea why anyone cares what gender they are or which door they go through. It absolutely baffles me.

Similarly, gender segregation does not guarantee privacy, safety or freedom from harassment. I have been harassed by men before, but never in the many gender-neutral toilets I frequent. Gender-segregated toilets aren't the solution to arseholes who harass – the solution is that they need to stop harassing people.

Think about traditionally gender segregated spaces. Would you be comfortable getting your body out in front of 'other' genders? Can you articulate why?

Holy heteronormativity, batperson. Have you ever thought changing rooms and toilets should be gender-segregated to stop people of 'opposite' sexes from being sexy with one another? If you think that segregating genders is about preventing people from ogling one another, or (accidentally?) having sex while other people release their buttholes all around them, you are somewhat disrespecting and definitely erasing the hundreds of thousands of people who exist in the world who aren't heterosexual. If you enjoy having sex in toilets, who am I (or indeed my noxious bodily odours) to stand in your way, but let's not pretend that separating people gender will stop it. If, as I suspect, toilet sex is mostly about necessity, it's happening anyway. I have managed for a couple of decades quite successfully not to sexualise other women in these sorts of spaces, and other queer people report similar. It's almost like people not wanting to be sexualised is something we respect and comply with. Weird!

Actually, no one really knows what it is to 'be' a woman

I have a friend who has had a double mastectomy. Is she is a woman? My relative was born female but no longer has a uterus. Is she a woman? Today someone mistook me for a man and called me 'Sir'. Am I still a woman?

What does it mean to be a woman, or a girl? How do you decide?

'Being a woman means …' sentences echo throughout thinkpieces, op-eds and articles all over the internet and print. For so many people, it seems that they have written down their first thought and gone no further. 'Being a woman means being womanly, strong and confident and trying to live up to the world's standards', says one. 'Being a woman means being feminine and emotional', says another. The problem here is that we are back to those old gender stereotypes, roles and expectations. Biological and psychological gender differences – however positive – feel restrictive and retrograde. Why can't I be a feminine and emotional man? Do non-women not ever feel like they have to 'live up to the world's standards'? Why the exclusion?

I know it might be really convenient for you, and for the world, if we could pin gender down like a penis on a donkey. I know it's hard to articulate what our shared understanding of being 'female' or 'male' means, because there's such an iceberg of collective assumptions underneath it that we have all been performing on top of nearly all our lives. But it seems pretty clear to me that these things are meaningful only on an individual level, and that they absolutely should be questioned even then. I cannot, and should not, tell you how to woman.

Gender privilege, gender oppression One of the things you are likely to take for granted in your life is 'cultural safety' – that is, the provision of services that appropriately recognise diversity. For some trans people, they so often don't get this.

> Questions were overly irrelevant, prying and sexual. My first doctor asked about masturbation repeatedly, which made me feel uncomfortable … [and] I feel utterly powerless and infantilised in my dealings with [the doctors], entirely at the mercy of their restrictive, unpredictable, arrogant and incompetent service.[3]

'Some trans people felt that clinical sessions ran counter to the preservation of their dignity and human rights', says the same research report.

Have you ever felt that a routine medical appointment left you 'powerless and infantilised'?

For some trans people, the tiring work of having to hyperperform their gender in order to 'pass', the worry of managing other people's reactions, and the inability of various systems to deal with their 'gender transgressions' can be overwhelming and frustrating. The debate about whether someone has been advantaged or oppressed by different gender privileges 'before they were trans' seems to miss two important points: one, that they are usually at a severe disadvantage *now;* and two, that 'before they were trans' is pretty hard to define. Many people who define themselves as trans have been dealing with gender nonconformity nearly all their life. The image of a man who wakes up one morning, pops on a dress and goes off to enjoy all the benefits of female toilets after a few decades of male privilege seems an odd way to see it.

Discussion of privilege is almost always contentious and difficult. It is hard, as I write this, to swallow the fact that I have had plenty of advantages in my life that others haven't – and done far, far less with said life by some measurement – because people are so darn self-centred and desperate to believe they've endured unique hardship. (Of course, some of them have.) I think we need to talk more about this stuff. But I also think the debate about pre- and post-gender change privilege for trans people is focusing on the wrong things, especially while we still live in a world where trans people are overwhelmingly not safe and not in possession of some of their basic rights.

A wealthy, white guy in the TV show *Mad Men* muses at one point: 'you know, I used to jump off mountains. It never occurred to me that I had an invisible parachute'.

What is your school policy on trans pupils? How do you protect their rights and safety?

How do we respond to children who are gender nonconforming?

Schools are full of fads, and of despairing teachers getting irritated by them (or wildly enthusiastic teachers performing Baby Shark on a fidget spinner while flossing). In many ways, gender nonconformity is a fad – in the sense that many children explore these boundaries when prompted to do so by observing peers or adults around them doing so. It's also true to say that for the majority of pre-pubertal children, gender dysphoria does not 'persist' into adolescence; it persists for around 15% of them.[16] If you think people are 'trying' gender nonconformity because it's more visible, you might be right.

So what?

Do you think that questioning gender identities, constructs and expression (for everyone) is harmful? Dangerous? A waste of time?

In the same research paper, we see 'without pressure to conform, children may not be dysphoric'. An environment where gender boundaries are not rigidly upheld makes for safer gender nonconforming pupils – and for more empathetic and feminist pupils all round. That sounds like the sort of classroom I'd want to be in.

If a pupil presents to you as gender questioning or nonconforming, it is important to remember that gender variations are not disorders. Such a pupil is not ill or abnormal. What to do? Expert advice suggests that you need neither discourage nor encourage gender-related behaviour or expression. No one needs to socially or biologically transition or make key decisions in a hurry if the environment is supportive and gender-neutral. Talk to parents in the same way you would about any pastoral issue. Then, if pupils and parents feel they would like to make changes, be accepting and supportive, and ensure other pupils and teachers behave similarly.

Now/later

Read some stories or vignettes about trans people's experiences, and reflect on the differences or similarities with your own life. How have you been privileged? How might your life be different if you were trans?

Investigate your school's policy on trans students, and consider whether it focuses on protecting and supporting the child or those around them. Consider contributing to its rewriting if necessary. If you have trans students at your school, invite them to give you their views or to speak to the whole school if they feel comfortable doing so. Invite a trans speaker for school assembly.

Graham says

When Lucy suggested the titles for the chapters of our book, it was this one that I approached with the most trepidation; it's not that I don't think it is important (very much the opposite) – but I just feel so underqualified to talk with any authority about it. That is what scares me. The Department for Education want us to talk to our children about being trans and what it means, but where do we start? As an educator, there are some subjects that I feel less qualified to teach (such as art or history), but if I need to know something about either, I search for it on the internet or ask somebody on Twitter. Similarly, if we are going to teach our children about gender identity, we need to do it correctly. Just as I wouldn't want to teach them incorrect historical facts, I don't want to use the wrong term or paradigm when talking about gender identity.

I know of teachers in schools who have arranged for speakers to come in and talk to pupils about gender identity, only for there to be such a backlash from parents that speakers have been cancelled. However, we need to be strong, to have the courage of our convictions and (despite the backlash) invite speakers to our school, talk to children about gender identity and be open and honest. If we don't, what message does this send – not only to our children but also to the trans community? It is hard to fight generations of prejudice, and people are often scared of what they don't understand.

Tl;dr

Being trans may comprise many ways of feeling in the 'wrong' gender and crossing gender boundaries. Examining gender nonconformity, far from being a trivial fad, can benefit everyone. A gender-neutral classroom, and freedom from any pressure to perform gender, can allow pupils to feel supported while they figure out how they feel about their gender in their own time.

References

1. *The truth about trans.* (2018). Retrieved April 21, 2019, from Stonewall website: https://www.stonewall.org.uk/truth-about-trans
2. James, S. E., Herman, J. L., Rankin, S., Keisling, M., Mottet, L., & Anafi, M. (2016). *The Report of the 2015 U.S. Transgender Survey.* Washington, DC: National Center for Transgender Equality.

3. Ellis, S. J., Bailey, L., & McNeil, J. (2015). Trans people's experiences of mental health and gender identity services: A UK study. *Journal of Gay & Lesbian Mental Health, 19*(1), 4–20. https://doi.org/10.1080/19359705.2014.960990

4. *A guide for young trans people in the UK.* (n.d.). 28. Retrieved April 21, 2019, from https://www.mermaidsuk.org.uk/assets/media/17-15-02-A-Guide-For-Young-People.pdf

5. Teich, N. M. (2012). *Transgender 101: A Simple Guide to a Complex Issue.* New York, NY: Columbia University Press.

6. Nodin, N. (2015). *LGB&T mental health – Risk and resilience explored.* Retrieved from RaRE Research Report website: http://www.queerfutures.co.uk/wp-content/uploads/2015/04/RARE_Research_Report_PACE_2015.pdf

7. *Is three too young for children to know they're a different gender? Transgender researchers disagree.* (2018). Retrieved April 22, 2019, from KQED website: https://www.kqed.org/futureofyou/440851/can-you-really-know-that-a-3-year-old-is-transgender

8. Brill, S. A., & Pepper, R. (2008). *The Transgender Child.* San Francisco, CA: Cleis Press.

9. Wyss, S. E. (2004). 'This was my hell': The violence experienced by gender non-conforming youth in US high schools. *International Journal of Qualitative Studies in Education, 17*(5), 709–730. https://doi.org/10.1080/0951839042000253676

10. Burgess, C. (1999). Internal and external stress factors associated with the identity development of transgendered youth. *Journal of Gay & Lesbian Social Services, 10*(3–4), 35–47. https://doi.org/10.1300/J041v10n03_03

11. Transgender people can continue to be denied access to some women-only spaces, government says. *The Independent.* (2018). Retrieved April 22, 2019, from https://www.independent.co.uk/news/uk/politics/transgender-people-no-right-single-sex-spaces-government-penny-mordaunt-toilets-changing-rooms-a8414771.html

12. Criado Perez, C. (2019). *Invisible Women: Exposing Data Bias in a World Designed for Men.* London, England: Chatto & Windus.

13. Gash, A. (n.d.). *Explainer: Why transgender students need "safe" bathrooms.* Retrieved May 12, 2019, from The Conversation website: http://theconversation.com/explainer-why-transgender-students-need-safe-bathrooms-50831

14. Zimman, L. (2016, August 29). *Trans pronoun FAQ, Part 1.* Retrieved April 22, 2019, from Trans Talk website: https://medium.com/trans-talk/trans-pronoun-faq-part-1-e96b5d10d425

15. Paris Lees, personal communication, March 2019. Tweet 20/03/19

16. Drescher, J., & Byne, W. (2012). Gender dysphoric/gender variant (GD/GV) children and adolescents: Summarizing what we know and what we have yet to learn. *Journal of Homosexuality, 59*(3):501–510.

Expert view: trans pupils and the early years

Deborah Price

Discussions and stories about gender, often featuring people who are trans, are all over the news at the moment, and that conversation has filtered down to early years (also called nursery or pre-school). It seems like a new thing because the public spotlight is focused on it at the moment, but in fact young children have always discussed gender as they have tried to make sense of what it means to be a boy or a girl.

Any day in any nursery class, we can hear children talking to each other and exploring what is the same and what is different between them: 'You can't do that because you're a girl'; 'Boys don't like to play with that'. What is important is not the conversations that children are having, but the way we respond to them (as teachers and as parents). That response is the single most important thing we can do to support a young trans person – and I would also say it is the most important thing we can do to support *any* child. It is this response that I hope has changed over the years from being limiting or dismissive to being more supportive and exploratory. I'll say it again – this is a good and useful thing not just for children who might be trans or questioning their gender, but for everyone.

Why is that? In the early years we are not just supporting and look-ing after the children in our care; we are also supporting and nurturing the young person and adult that they will become. Sometimes we have a good sense of who they are and will be, and sometimes we have no idea, but our encouragement of their exploration ensures that they have a full range of options open to them and do not feel that anything is closed.

About 25 years ago I was a pre-school inspector, and I remember trying to persuade one manager to stop lining the children up in lines of boys and girls. She was really resisting me and was arguing that the children didn't always know whether they were boys or girls and that this activity would help them. I turned to a little boy who was standing next to me (and quietly picking his nose).

'Are you a boy or a girl'? I asked him.

He was a bit taken aback but pondered my question thoughtfully.

'Well, I know I'm not a girl so I think I must be a boy', he said.

I like to think that this pre-school (and many others I visited) went on to 'line children up' in different ways after that. It did make me reflect on how children understand their gender and what they think about it.

These conversations in early years range wider than just being boys and girls and extend to explorations of difference in general: 'I wear glasses'; 'I have darker skin'; 'You have long hair' and these differences cover race, gender, personality, ability and disability – everything that makes us special, unique, and different and the same. It's important to put any discussion of early years and trans pupils into this context of a wider and more general discussion of difference.

It's also important to be aware that discussions about sexuality are not about sex. Sexuality and sex are not the same, and this false notion has historically stopped people from having these important discussions. 'These are little children', I often hear from practitioners. 'Can't we just keep them little innocent children and let them play'? Well, yes, you can if you ignore the myriad ways that children are constantly taking in messages about sexuality and gender from society, their family, other children and the wider media around them. We can – and absolutely should – talk to young children about sexuality way ahead of any interest in sex.

Discussions with young children about being trans are not about medical intervention, which is what often worries people. In the early years, such discussions consist of talking about what it means to be a girl or a boy, or neither or both, and how the child feels about that. These feelings might change from day to day, and in these early years a child may be definite that they feel like a boy or a girl or may change their mind – and, of course, this is ok.

In reality, what it means to be a boy or a girl goes beyond medical definitions and is shaped by society. What it meant to be a girl when I was growing up in the early sixties is different from what it means now in many respects (although, depressingly, some aspects of what it means are the same). It's important not to panic or overreact but to see gender discussions in the context of a child finding their place in the world and exploring what it means to be comfortable in their own skin.

From the moment that a child is born (and even before), people are making assumptions about gender. 'Look at him kicking his feet, he's such a bruiser, bound to be a footballer' and 'Look at her flirting, she's going to be a heartbreaker'. This might feel harmless and normal, but in fact it is causing problems: It is we ourselves who won't let children be themselves, and it is we who inflict gender stereotypes on newborns in order to shape them into replicas of the way we think men and women should be and behave.

That might sound harsh. You might be thinking, 'Is it really that serious?'

I would encourage you to turn your 'gender audit' on and really notice the representations of men and women that children see and hear around them. Think about how rigid and confining those representations can be. A good place to start is the Twitter account 'Gender Diary' or the book that accompanies it, where two parents (male and female) kept a record of the ways in which their children were gendered by other people and the effects they saw.

By having open and honest discussions with children about gender from early years, we can help them define themselves in a manner that reflects who they want to be – a very important and basic way for humans to be happy. Our support and help can be a beacon of light in a world that might be trying to close that self-exploration down. I always talk to early years practitioners in trans awareness sessions about being that hope-inspiring person in a child's life. Discussing their early years with young adult trans people, I hear a lot of negative comments about the teachers and education professionals in their lives. I ask my trainees if they want to be remembered in that way, or if they want to be remembered as that one person who let the young trans person be who they wanted to be.

Sexuality and sexualities

My people – soft and pretty – proto-relationships – orgies all of the time – not all boys fancy all girls – blanket dick pics – shameful secret Love Egg – get off – sex with snakes – men find it sexy – feathered multi-coloured rainbow – minority stress – saying the unsaid – frustratingly inconsistent – nuclear-type sexual rocket fuel – dominant garlicky flavour – wormy little inconsistencies – genital caves – every 7 seconds – anything up my bum – knocking on doors – Well-Informed Prophylactic – convinced I was an oxbow lake – not a cause for panic

Stats

Only 13% of LGBT+ young people have learned about healthy same-sex relationships.[1]

In an analysis of national survey results from 2006 to 2008, the percentage reporting their sexual identity as bisexual is between **1%** and **3%** of males and between **2%** and **5%** of females.[2]

The issues

I'm talking to a dear friend, female-presenting, in their fifties. They are telling me that they think they might be gay.

I smile, happy that they have felt able to confide in me, hopefully knowing that I won't judge them or be weird with them (or assume they fancy me). But something feels odd. They pause for a beat and tells me they haven't ever had sex. I ask them if they are attracted to women.

'I don't think so', they say.

I'm confused.

'So ... why do you think you might be gay?' I say hesitantly. I don't want to override their feelings, or tell them what they ought to be, but it seems strange.

'They feel like my people'. They smile.

I think about this person often. I think about that idea that some people feel drawn towards the LGBTQ+ community not (just) because of their sexual preferences, but because they feel that they will be welcome there, that there is a community that will accept them, because they are 'different'.

We are always looking to belong, to be seen and understood, to be accepted, to find our tribe.

How do we do that? Is it important to hang out with people who like the same things we do? What about fancying the same type of people we do?

Identity werk

As a bisexual (finds both genders attractive – depends on a binary) or pansexual (finds all genders attractive – a better fit for me) woman, I am not confined to finding one gender attractive. It wasn't always this way. I grew up without really questioning my sexuality, because I had internalised some deeply held ideas about gender. These were:

One man and one woman make a relationship.

Romance is to be desired and achieved at all costs. Romance is the thing.

I am soft and pretty; I want a man that is hard and in control to complete me.

Why would I find women attractive when I *am* one? That would be egotistical.

It took me years of work to undo this – years in which I had to re-examine each of these ideas individually. I had always thought that finding women attractive wasn't the real me, somehow – it was just a quirk, a phase, a flight of fancy. That it was something for 'others' – the sorts of people who wore dungarees or who had cropped hair or hairy armpits. I'm quite a feminine-looking female – in the sense that I happen to have a body with curves and choose to have longish hair and wear makeup, for example – and my narrative for what a homosexual woman 'looked like' just didn't have enough space for someone like me in it. Besides, I thought, I like men. I didn't even have a word for that, growing up, so naturally, I thought it wasn't even a thing. Pick a side!

This is one good reason why we need a beautifully diverse range of role models for children. Doing this sort of identity work is hard. If I had seen a person – maybe just the one – with whom I felt I could identify, who had talked about being bisexual in the most matter-of-fact way, maybe I could have been saved some heartache and soul-searching and just understood a little more.

Let's return briefly to the idea that if we teach children about something, they will do it (more). Would better information about being bisexual have changed what I did as a teen? Most likely. Would it have encouraged me to *be more bisexual?* I reckon. (Although what does that even mean, exactly?)

Why is that a problem?

It's because we have a deep-rooted and entirely wrong idea that children and teens exploring homosexuality, as well as other issues around gender and identity, is wrong. It's deviant. It's dangerous and subversive. I think it's time to really question that.

What would 10-year-old me, or 12-year-old me, have done differently?

I think this is really important: *Talking about sexuality isn't about forcing sexuality on children.* At age 10, I wasn't really interested in sex or touching other people. Letting me know that finding girls attractive as well as boys was a thing that wouldn't have made me go and have sex with girls, any more than telling a full person there's leftovers doesn't make them eat it. But it would have helped me come to terms more easily with some inner thoughts and feelings that were starting to develop. It would have made me feel less alone. You remember being an adolescent, right? The feeling of aloneness is one of the most painful things.

Later, as I began to feel attracted to others, it would have helped me make sense of that in a different way. I might have had different relationships. Some of them might have been with girls. But if you're considering that and saying 'Ugh, lesbian relationships at 12 and 13!' then you're part of the problem. Children are having those heterosexual relationships all the time – not necessarily sexual ones, not necessarily even what we would call a relationship, but proto-relationships where they're imitating adults and finding boundaries and deliciously exploring this weird thing called attraction and seeing what it feels like, trying it on for size. This is normal and healthy. But the prevalent feeling is that this is acceptable only when they're hetero relationships – if they're anything else (and god forbid they're something even *more* 'different', like polyamorous), then we panic and think there's a problem. We are more tolerant of children's relationships with animals than we are with relationships between same-sex people, for goodness' sake.

This perhaps stems from a very deep-rooted and wholly wrong connection between non-heterosexuality and sexual deviance. There are some people in this world who truly believe that all homosexuals are paedophiles, that lesbians are trying to corrupt others into joining a cult and that all queer people are out there having orgies all of the time. (That seems ... unlikely. I have a job and everything. All the time? I'd never have finished this book). If I tell men upon first meeting them that I am bisexual, I can often see them thinking it means I'm much more likely to have sex with them, because they think it means I'm more sexually prolific. (Why? That makes no sense. If anything, I'm slightly more likely to have sex with the woman standing next to you, buddy. A friend of mine proposed that this may well be a rainbow-flavoured version of the Conjunction Fallacy,[3] which is a fascinating topic for a PhD dissertation if I ever heard one).

As usual, fear of difference plus ignorance leads to wildly illogical conclusions. There are even greater ramifications, too: This has a huge effect on people's feelings about homosexual parents, for example (they are often seen as second rate, deviant or in some bizarre way 'spreading' homosexuality). If you think this (and this is a very common bias), it's likely that this faulty assumption is leaking out to young people you are dealing with on a daily basis.

Think about a child in your family, or your own child, and consider your feelings about them having a boyfriend versus having a girlfriend. Are the two situations different? Do you have concerns? What are they?

Who fancies whom?

In other areas, we understand well that teens, more than at any other time in their lives, are constructing (and deconstructing and reconstructing) identity for themselves. If we don't allow them information or freedom to explore sexualities other that normative hetero ones, they'll probably find them anyway – but some will find them later, and more painfully, and with a sense of loss of self that is wholly unnecessary.

But, you may well ask, if boys and girls aren't neatly fitting together in yin-and-yang couples, how on earth can children negotiate the complicated land of *Who Fancies Whom*?

Like that isn't already a thing?

In case you need reminding, not all boys fancy all girls, and vice versa. Shock! This works for other kinds of non-hetero attraction too. So if I approach a guy to see if he likes me back, there is some probability he will not (or indeed, he may fancy me but may not be looking for what I am looking for at that point in my life). Similarly, if I approach a female, this probability may well be higher, or lower, but it's still not a dead cert (depending on where I am and how sexy I am looking, obviously). Guess what this teaches me? Not that everything is terrible and that no one fancies me – and not that men or women or others are a 'better bet' (attraction doesn't really work that way for me). It teaches me to look at other people attentively, to be sensitive for signals of attraction and to tread carefully and consider how appropriate or intense my attraction signals are to them.

In a world which works on the basis of consent (and ours, I hope, is headed in that direction), there is no incentive for me to want to be painfully rejected by another human; there is, however, incentive to manage the gathering of information about attraction in a way that considers the feelings of both parties. That's also known as listening to a person and tuning in to their body language. There is also no shame in having been politely rejected (more on that in the next few chapters). If we could start exploring those principles with children, we would be onto something huge.

Experiencing attraction and approaching other people we feel attracted to are inherently complicated. They are also full of feelings that involve guilt, obligation, status and self-worth. These are not trivial matters. They cannot be reduced to 'chat-up lines', dating profiles or sending out blanket dick pics (not portraits of darling little penises shyly hiding under blankets, but images of erections sent to multiple people in the hope that one of them bites. Or, er, licks?).

Figuring out whom you are attracted to (in many different ways) and whether they are attracted back is just the first step. What do you want from them, and is it the same thing they want from you? How do you feel about your own body and sexuality, and how can you communicate your desires and needs to another person, or multiple people, without being too demanding, seeming too weird or sexually harassing them? How can you be expected to find the sweet (G) spot of having a fun sexy time without exploring all kinds of stuff and considering attraction to all kinds of people?

The bell(end) of shame

I meet a variety of adults who have a serious amount of shame about their own sexuality – and often they're not the LGBT+ ones, perhaps because those people tend to have done a serious amount of identity work on their own needs and desires already. No, I talk to a great many heterosexual, heteronormative people who have married their first sexual partner, have been single for years or have been in a long-term relationship (or relationships) since they were young. Perhaps they have grown and matured as people but left their sexuality stuck in their late teens, with all the trauma and tongue-tied embarrassment that went with it. These people are telling their partners they don't masturbate or use porn, and feeling guilty when they do. They are fantasising about other people and then beating themselves up internally for doing so. They are harbouring secret desires that they fear would alienate them from their partner if revealed, so they are carrying these desires like a dreadful, shameful secret Love Egg with broken batteries within them. They are faking orgasms or sexual enjoyment because it feels awkward not to (and to admit this would be to derail a long-distance train they're not ready to get off yet. Which is ironic, because I'd really like them to be *actually* getting off, happily and free of shame.)

Here are some pertinent lyrics from 'The Buzzing from the Bathroom', one of the most beautiful and heartbreaking songs ever written (listen to the whole thing, sung by Michael McMillan, for full effect):

We used two different positions
Every other Sunday night
All her writhing, moaning, sighing
I thought I was doing it right
But as I drifted off to slumber
Thinking I had brought her joy
She would slink off to the bathroom
With that blasted plastic toy

How do you feel about your own sexuality? How do you feel about discussing your own sexual desires, interests and fantasies, and how do you communicate this with your sexual partner or partners?

How can we communicate to pupils important information and ideas about sex and sexualities in a shame-free way if we are so full of shame (and confusion) ourselves?

Cissing (trouser) snakes

I've just been in a primary school playground on a visit. My daughter (aged 10) was there with her best friends. 'Do you talk about important stuff?' I asked. 'Do you have good chats?' They all laughed and nodded.

'We talk about *inappropriate* stuff', they said. That wasn't their word. I sensed teacher speak.

'Like what?' I asked. My daughter gave her friends the universal 'Don't worry, she's cool' nod.

'Periods', one of them said. 'And having sex with snakes'. They erupted into laughter.

'My friend wants to know if she could have sex with a snake, and if so would she have a snake baby'.

Is this *inappropriate*? The stuff about periods, unquestionably not. If you were about to have pants full of blood and pain – at any chuffing moment – which would afflict you monthly for the next few decades, you might be asking questions about it too.

But sex with snakes and snake babies? How might we deal with this as a serious question, and where in the curriculum is there space for it? Although the idea may be inherently funny or indeed disgusting to you, encased in the shell of this question are the seeds of many interesting things. Biological questions about genetic material and ethical questions about consent, for example – neither of which I consider 'inappropriate' for 10-year-olds. It would be so easy to think 'Arghhhhh – sex with animals! I can't talk to kids about this!' – and I suspect so many adults have done this that these children now see anything having do to with 'the s-word' (sex not snake) as completely off limits. I can't be sure, but I'm fairly confident that said child wasn't planning on performing such an act – it wasn't about that. It was the same thing we do as adults when we fantasise about taboo acts, a childish precursor to tentacle porn: it was a questioning of all kinds of boundaries. It was a positioning of our self and our sexuality, tentatively, in a new domain. Kids who can do that without shame, I would hypothesise, turn into adults who can the same, and I am fully supportive of this kind of questioning. No snakes need be harmed in the making of a confidently sexual (or indeed happily asexual) human.

Non-hetero-sexualities

When you think of homosexuality, what comes to mind? How do your thoughts differ when you consider gay men versus lesbian women?

Let's talk about homosexuality, bisexuality and pansexuality. A friend sent me an article based on a piece of 'research': A new study that purports to reveal the origins of lesbianism is claiming that same-sex relationships in women exist only because they turn men on.

This 'scientific study' comes to the conclusion that 'lesbian and bisexual attraction all stems from male desire'.[4]

There are many, many unexamined and unhelpful ideas surrounding particular sexualities in our society. The conclusion that women have same-sex relationships because men find such relationships sexy was published in a mainstream journal, along with the idea that being attracted to other women has an evolutionary benefit for women because men like it. Guess how many homosexual women were part of the study? Um, none. This idea is pretty problematic for me.

Imagine that you are a homosexual woman. How might you feel about such a view? How might it affect your life?

Gayness in the eye of the beholder

It is so very tempting to meet someone and think – oh, they look (or act or sound) homosexual. The assumption – going back to my friend who found her tribe – is that there is a set of characteristics for men and a set for women that reflect homosexuality. That *we can tell* before they tell us. Yesterday, wearing a full three-piece suit and tie, I opened a door (as is my wont) for someone about to reach it at the same time as I was. They were female in appearance. They paused. I thought I saw something like this thought race through their brain: '*Why is she doing that? Is she lesbian? Is that a come-on? How should I respond?*' (For info, I just like opening doors for people, and I do it for everyone. No sexual compensation is required or expected.)

It's important to get past the idea that a tendency to touch people, campness or exuberance; or butchness, being intellectual or espousing feminism (or whatever else you use as proxies) are markers of someone's sexuality in any way. Just as for gender, we might see things that aren't there. Just as for gender, we need to start feeling comfortable with feeling uncomfortable. Do you need to know that the 11-year-old in your class is gay? What does that mean at 11, anyway?

Many, many LGBTQ+ people whom I meet profess a deep discomfort with the fabulous, glittered, feathered, multi-coloured rainbow of gayness that is supposed to represent them in some way. They are quiet or shy individuals who don't like Pride festivals or dancing 'til 4 a.m. with shiny greased dynamos. It speaks to society's restriction of 'queerness' to these arbitrarily palatable stereotypes that it would still insist on trying to constrain people in this way. Whom you fancy is about whom you fancy, and not anything else. (It is also subject to change over a lifetime.) Sometimes, I think we get preoccupied with the 'sexual identity' part of LGB individuals and lose sight of the fact that they are *individuals* first and foremost.

What needs to change

Can you think of a shape that looks like a star from one direction, a rectangle from another and a hexagon from another?

Neither could I, really, until I saw it (such a thing does indeed exist, and it's beautiful).[5] Then it made sense, in the same way that being pansexual only made sense to me after I realised it existed. Before that, I probably couldn't even have conceived of such a thing. That's because I didn't have broad, honest and LGBTQ-neutral sex and relationships education at school.

'Research indicates that being LGB or having a Trans identity is not in itself associated with mental distress and increased rates of mental illness, but that [the] negative impact of transphobic, homophobic and heterosexist cultural norms that spur the discrimination, bullying, marginalisation and stigmatisation of LGB&T people may be'.[6] This is often termed 'minority stress'. What does that mean?

We have created a world in which to have a different sexuality or gender from a very narrow norm is almost always to become stressed, ill or unhappy – through entirely preventable, persistent non-acceptance. If not actively trying to change it, then we are participating in and perpetuating this created, norm-obsessed environment, largely intolerant of this kind of difference, seeing it as deviance and morally judging it to be wrong. This intolerance is woven into the fabric of school culture in all but the most determinedly inclusive settings, and it disadvantages LGBT+ pupils so severely that it undoubtedly continues to affect not only their mental and physical health but also their achievement. This is a social justice issue, for sure.

If you still respond to expressions of sexuality, especially LGB sexuality, with disgust, or if you associate it with abnormality, it is time to think very, very carefully about the consequences of this and to re-educate yourself.

Here is Yuval Noah Harari, in their book *Sapiens:* 'How can we distinguish what is biologically determined from what people merely try to justify through biological myths? A good rule of thumb is "Biology enables, culture forbids" .... Biology enables men to enjoy sex with one another – some cultures forbid them to realise this possibility'.[7]

Invisibility and shadows

> The messages we give our classes through the curriculum are key to creating a whole-school approach to inclusion. We are literally *saying the unsaid*. It's the invisibility of LGBT+ people and issues that make children think there is something wrong with them.[8]

The Section 28 legislation, although repealed in 2000 in Scotland and 2003 in the rest of the UK, continues to cast a long and dark shadow. Many schools continue to be haunted by the imaginary spectres of 'promoting' homosexuality, and the question of when to explore ideas of sexuality with children refuses to go away. Some have 'dealt with' this issue by persistently ignoring it; for others, an appeal to 'innocence' suggests a rationale for waiting as long as possible, ideally until secondary school, to talk about anything that borders on 'sexual' or to do with 'sexualities'.

But they're wrong.

How old do you think children are when they notice difference?

How old are they when they begin to explore what it means to have a relationship with a significant other?

Arguably, we're hetero-forcing the latter on them at a very early age. I have seen countless parents and teachers of nursery-age children make jokes and comments about 'boyfriends' and 'girlfriends'. Children of different genders are being weirdly paired up by adults long before they know or care about attraction. But try to do this with children of the same gender – and for some, it takes on a very different hue.

'Ella played with Amelia all day today. They're like a little couple, so cute! They were holding hands for ages, and Amelia said she loved Ella'.

'Have you got a boyfriend, Gabriel? Is Henry your boyfriend'?,

Both of these for some reason feel more adult, more sexual than their heterosexual equivalents, but why?

Our standards of acceptability are frustratingly inconsistent, and we need to revise them.

We need to talk about asexuality

Asexuality is one of the least talked about, but most important, ideas in the world.

Imagine, for a second, what it might be like if you didn't experience sexual attraction. Or if you liked people but never felt the urge to have sex with them. How might the world be different? Would you feel you had to hide this characteristic?

'While estimates for the asexual proportion of the population are limited and may vary, the most widely cited figure is that we are roughly 1% of the population'.[9]

If, like me, you are raising or teaching teenagers, it may have dawned on you that our world appears to be run on some sort of nuclear-type sexual rocket fuel. As soon as you become aware of this magical intangible that drives social interaction, advertising and entertainment, it's hard to miss. Everything is about enticement, pursuit and satisfaction; the narrative model of sex has permeated so many structures that, like an insidious termite mound, it is often hard to disentangle from those structures themselves.

But if you're asexual, you might have a different inner story. The sexual *need-get-relax* arc might be utterly baffling to you, or you might get it but feel frustrated that you can't or won't take part in it; you might feel completely excluded.

Something to think about in depth: Not all significant relationships are currently, or are on their way to being, sexual. It's worth considering asexuality in more detail because analysing different types of attraction helps us reflect on our own (a)sexual behaviour and, crucially, how we teach and model it to others.

Research suggests that attraction can be split into parts: sexual, romantic, sensual and aesthetic.[10] This means that the 'pull' (or 'push') we feel when confronted with another human (or entity of any kind, for some people) might be a blend of all those, or just some of them. Sexual attraction feels like a kind of desire, the wanting to be sexual with another. Romantic attraction, on the other hand, is wanting to be emotionally involved with another or to have a relationship with them – and many people who identify as asexual say that they clearly feel this attraction. Sensual attraction is the part of being with someone that is touch-specific but not specifically sexual (although there may be a crossover for many people) – think hand-holding, stroking, hugging, kissing. Finally, aesthetic attraction is an appreciation for the way someone (or something) looks.

When we say, 'I like Charlie' or 'I find AJ attractive' or 'Ali is *lovely*!' we might be mixing up these types of attraction all together, or we might feel only one or some of them. Not a problem, you might say, except that we live in a society where sex dominates, and therefore sexual attraction is deemed to be the most powerful and potent force in attraction, often inseparable from the others. So if a pupil or friend says, 'I find AJ attractive', there is an (age-appropriate) assumption there that they want to have sex with AJ, or at the very least kiss and touch them sexually.

But what if they don't?

What if they think AJ is a beautiful human but don't want to have sex with them?

What if they would love to be in a relationship with AJ but don't feel comfortable touching them at all?

What if they want to sleep with AJ (in the sense of spoon, hug and nestle in with) but without any sexual contact?

What if they want to buy AJ dinner and watch them have sex with someone else?

What if they would like casual sex with AJ but don't want any emotional involvement?

How do these differing patterns of attraction fit into your ideas about human connection? Would you feel qualified or comfortable giving advice to pupils, friends or your children who asked about these issues?

Thinking about asexuality forces us to confront what relationships actually consist of – and all too often the dominant garlicky flavour of sexual attraction overpowers the subtlety of all the other delicious and delicate herbs present: communication, romanticism, touch, love – because that is largely how we demonstrate those things. Sex is the approved tool (ha ha) for expressing attraction. A relationship without sex may be seen as deficient or abnormal, just as we might perceive certain types of behaviour that we don't like or sanction as sexual deviance. But at least sexual deviance is (sometimes) discussed; it may be uncomfortable, but it's known, and we have reference points. Asexuality may be completely alien to us, despite a pretty high degree of prevalence and the fact that it raises significant issues about the nature of relationships – issues that we cannot and should not ignore when dealing with young people.

Here's a difficult question, for instance: Do you think that anyone 'deserves' sex?

In the example above, where one person might want to snuggle another one in a bed without sexual contact, how did you feel about that? How might those feelings change if one or both people slept naked, as many prefer to do?

No matter how feminist we feel in principle, there are biases and wormy little inconsistencies about life that fall out when we shake our principle tree hard enough. I'm imagining a consent-age teenager, specifically a female, telling me she slept in a bed with a male, and she was naked, but she didn't want sex with him, only to cuddle. It is very hard not to feel some vestige of a sentiment I know to be inconsistent with my principles here: *That's not fair on him. He deserves something. If you make him aroused in that manner, it's not ok to 'just' cuddle.*

But there are some seriously unquestioned assumptions here. Why do we assume the male wanted sex at all?

Why is cuddling seen as 'less than' having sexual intercourse here?

Why is nudity associated with sex so strongly?

All of these things are absolutely crucial to question, and the younger the better to some extent. If we grow up thinking that the only model for attraction is sexual, we are missing out on what a relationship is or could be, and we are failing to understand the point of view of those who identify as asexual and simply choose to be celibate, or place a high value on other types of attraction and interaction within a relationship.

Men need to be able to refuse sex

'All men are completely repressed. All men only want to have sex. There are no exceptions, all three billion men are like this' is one of my favourite lyrics from the ironic song *Let's Generalise about Men*, brought to you by the brilliant team of writers on the TV show *Crazy Ex-Girlfriend*.

Along with many dangerous and unhelpful stereotypes about gender, the prevalent one about men being sex-fiends and women being sexual party-poopers is particularly insidious. You don't have to look very far in the media to see men dreaming about women: having them, touching them, sexing them, enjoying them; and women denying them, refusing them, acting shocked or scandalised or just plain old fed up with being constantly asked to open up their genital caves as places of delight and refuge for all these wearisome penis creatures. Women, if the media are to be believed, are like hotel managers at the end of a long week and a 12-hour shift. They might have a small amount of room to put you in, but they're not even sure it's worth the paperwork.

Sighing, they might say, 'Go on then', but their heart's not really in it. They'd rather be elsewhere. They're just doing you a favour, and you'd better not forget it the next time the bins need emptying ....

This model of gendered sexuality has some really serious issues, as you can imagine. Unquestioned, it leads to some unhealthy behaviours, cycles and relationship frustrations that are often avoidable. For example, one thing I feel deeply, deeply sad about, when I consider the (horribly heteronormative) narrative of 'sexy man, reluctant woman', is the poor guys who don't want to actually have sex feeling they somehow *have* to. Dodgy claims like 'Men think about sex every seven seconds!' have a lot to answer for. (There is no research basis for this, and even when research does get performed, we're relying on people self-reporting after the fact, which is notoriously unreliable). More recent studies have uncovered a more interesting picture suggesting, for example, that the range among people of all genders is *huge* (different participants reported thinking about sex between 1 and 388 times a day).[11] These studies also revealed that there was a gender difference – the median number of times men thought about sex was 18.6, and for women it was 9.9 – but, because these researchers asked about other things as well, they found this difference was also replicated for food and sleep. So while it would be true to say this study found men thought about sex around twice as much as women, they thought about food and sleep much more, too. Does this mean men want sex 'more' or are more sexual? Not necessarily. What, for example, if women are doing more housework and emotional work and other types of work and have less time for all three of those things?

An expectation that all men want sex all the time – I'm sure you don't need me to tell you – is entirely unreasonable, as well as utterly unrealistic. It also feeds into a very dangerous idea that men cannot be raped or touched non-consensually, and this misconception isn't just a prevailing culture issue; the law in most countries reflects this, too. Rape is defined in UK law as 'A person (A) commits an offence if —

a.   he intentionally penetrates the vagina, anus or mouth of another person (B) with his penis,

b.   B does not consent to the penetration, and

c.   A does not reasonably believe that B consents'.[12]

This literally does not allow for rape of men by women, nor does it consider any other variants, including something that is not a penis. We have a legacy here to demolish, and it starts with better educating our pupils and children. Boys, just as much as girls and people of other genders, must have the freedom, the tools and the language with which to say no to any kind of sexual activity.

In the TV show *Peep Show*, rape of a man by a woman is explored in a particularly confrontational way. The show is filmed from the (alternating) first-person-perspective views of the two main characters, Mark and Jeremy. In this episode, Mark meets a woman and later wakes having sex with her. Because we see through his eyes, and because he says that he doesn't want it to happen and asks her to stop, it is crystal clear that the act is non-consensual. Later, Mark says: 'It wasn't rape, all right? It was just a minor sexual assault. She didn't force anything up my bum – that's why it's not rape'.

His discomfort with identifying this act as rape, and the possible consequences, is obvious. In the narrative, this is about 'ruining' a relationship with the woman's father, with whom he is hoping to get a job; it is also about his sense that he can't, or shouldn't, be raped, because he is male and she is female.

Women need to be free to enjoy sex

If there's something I'd like to shout from the rooftops in true Hollywood style, it's this: I'm not arguing about the fact that women should have 'better' sex. (Maybe they should, but that's not for me to determine. What is 'better', anyway? All the women's magazine's I've ever read seem to think it's more expensive paraphernalia, or a proliferation of weirdly automatic counting techniques. Don't read women's magazines.) This is about women and girls being allowed space to enjoy sex in a *shame-free fashion*.

My daughter is 13. We had a gentle chat about masturbation last year. This year, we got a little further into it – what it means, how people do it, when and where might be the best (and worst) places to do it. She asked me about myself. It stimulated a good discussion about privacy, reinvigorating our commitment to the family rule of knocking on doors (and waiting for a response).

Does that make you feel uncomfortable?

Do you feel like I'm encouraging her to do it?

Damn right, I am – when she's ready, and without shame or worry.

Plenty, though not all, of women's sexual issues stem from the fact that they don't know their own bodies well enough to know what they like and how to ask for it. People, in general, are poorly informed about women's masturbation. (Around half of those people are female.) For example, most people think women masturbate by vaginal penetration, when actually, only around 10%-20% of women do.[13] This means there's a load of women who 'think' women do something, and who actually like something else, and might feel weird or excluded by that. They also might have tried a great deal of vaginal penetration when they began to masturbate, trying to 'fit' the model of what sexual stimulation is supposed to be. That makes me sad.

This is also an area that is blatantly sexist, in my view. Talk to parents of teenage boys, and they'll tell you that they expect (if not entirely like) their kids to masturbate. It's a powerful trope, seen as a rite of passage for young men to self-explore voraciously in this manner. What of young women touching themselves sexually?

An expert, Dr. Emily Nagoski, explains: 'Women masturbate in … different ways. They rub their clitorises with their hands … They press their vulvas against pillows, couches, chairs, and the bed. They spray their genitals with jets of water. They rock their pelvises and tighten their thigh and pelvic muscles …. Sometimes they even put their fingers inside their vaginas'.[14]

Regardless of what you may have learned from porn, the vast majority of women masturbate without vaginal penetration, most of the time. Plenty of women do use penetration – around 20% at least occasionally, and about 10% do so regularly[13] – and that's cool too. But the reality is not like the cultural narrative. The reality is way, way more multifaceted and interesting.

Ah yes, you might say, but only women. Girls – teens – should not be touching themselves in this graphic manner. We shouldn't be giving them information about it, because then they'll do it.

Actually, we *should* be giving them information about it because they *are* doing it (and often hiding it well).[15] We also should be giving them information so that when they feel like doing it, they'll feel ok about it. The information isn't the problem here. The problem is our level of discomfort with some basic facts and the unquestioned way we pass them on like a virus. Time for the Sexual Information Condom of Power! Time for the Well-Informed Prophylactic of Honest Sexual Discourse! Time for the Femidom of Feminist-Friendly Free Access to Sexual Research! (You get my drift.)

The strongest counterarguments and why they're wrong

- 'Anything other than monoheteronormative relationships count as sexual deviance and shouldn't be 'taught' in schools'.
- 'Sex is for adults only; talking to under-18s about sex will just make them do it'.
- 'Sex is dirty and shameful and has no place in schools at all'.

LGBT-inclusive sex and relationships education is good sex and relationships education. As I write this, there is a debate raging about 'teaching' homosexual relationships in schools. 'You can't teach my child about your disgusting sodomy!' rages one parent.

Here is a Twitter thread that took this apart with panache and humour.[16]

Paul Coleman: 'Homophobic parents are right to be worried about their children turning gay after lessons about LGBT awareness. I lived as a Tudor wench for 2 years following a history class'.

Dr. Sandra Leaton Gray: 'I did Benjamin Britten for music A level and now I live with a man'.

Nick Taylor: 'I spent a few weeks curled up near a river convinced I was an oxbow lake after being radicalised by a particularly inspiring geography teacher'.

Janet Lawn: 'After studying Viking history I built a longboat and pillaged Jorvik. The longboat is still on the drive because I don't live near a river'.

The research is clear: 'Young people find themselves in a shifting sexual landscape due to changing attitudes towards sexuality, greater variation in sexual behaviour and increased gender equality. School-based sex and relationship education (SRE) is seen as vital for navigating these changes'.[17] Let's make sure the boat we're navigating in isn't 17 years old and full of LGBTQ-shaped holes.

Children are exploring sexual ideas and sexual organs whether we like it or not. Children masturbate, or touch their sexual organs, all the time. A study of infants and children aged 4 months to 42 months showed that *all* the children who were observed had masturbated, usually multiple times per day.[18] Another study showed that almost all children had masturbated by age 2.[19]

'It is not unusual to see children try to pleasure themselves through physical exploration and masturbation .... Masturbation and sex play in children are not cause for panic; many children engage in these behaviors'.[20]

In a private, comfortable and consensual setting, children masturbating is healthy. I know, it feels weird to talk about it. But it's happening anyway.

More expert advice from SexInfo Online at the University of California: 'It is important for caregivers and parents to keep their reactions to children's consensual sexual activity and play positive. If a child is told that these activities are "bad", he or she may learn to associate sexual activity with feelings of guilt. Children may carry this guilt with them into adulthood, which can negatively impact their sexual lives'.[19]

There is an important balance to be found between parenting and schooling here, as well as obvious issues with finding boundaries. I can't (and shouldn't) tell you how to negotiate these, except with honesty and consideration, and by putting the child first. But let's, as always, start with the truth. We shouldn't sexualise children, but neither should we deny that (some) children (sometimes) already have sexual interest, ideas and urges. We can manage these helpfully and healthily, or we can blame, ignore and turtle-neck our way into all kinds of future problems *for the child themselves.* The fallout falls largely on them.

Sex is not a four-letter word

I mean, it isn't. Either literally or metaphorically. I rest my case.

There is robust, scientific evidence that when good quality SRE is taught by trained educators in schools young people are more likely to have their first sexual experience at an older age, to use contraception and to have fewer sexual partners.[21]

Apart from the 'fewer sexual partners' part – which emphatically isn't a measure of 'success' or 'failure' in sexual relationships – this is something we would do well to understand and embed in our practice of sex and relationships teaching.

Now/later

Now: Think about your relationship with your own sexuality: at age 10, age 15, age 20, beyond. How has it changed? What worries you or makes you uncomfortable about it? What feels good and healthy? What, or who, helped with that?

Later: Explore the way your school curriculum deals with sexualities and the way it presents LGB issues. Consider how you might feel if you were a homosexual parent. Would such parents be confident and proud to be part of your school's lessons on these issues? Would they feel adequately represented and visible?

Graham says

As a school we always teach sex education in the first few weeks of the new school year (September). I think the reasoning behind this is to associate sex education with classroom rules, and to lay down the foundations and expectations for the rest of the year. You can talk about consent and respecting one another and what that looks like in your class. I also think it helps your relationship with the children. If they can see you openly talking about penises and vaginas and the millions of other names that the children use for their body parts (one of my favourite parts of SRE is when children share these), then surely talking about fronted adverbials and improper fractions will be a doddle!

I recently saw a post shared on various social media sites about a boy on a bus who was with a girl whose period had started on the bus ride home (original author unknown). He quietly took her to one side and told her she had a stain on her trousers and gave her his sweater to tie around her waist to cover it. She was embarrassed at first but he reassured her – his experience of growing up with sisters had educated him well. This boy was rightly praised for his actions.

That brings me to teaching SRE in segregated classes. Do you teach girls about periods in one room, while boys are taught about wet dreams in another? How is this helping either get a better understanding of what happens to their bodies? If boys know about what happens to girls during their periods, then surely there will be greater empathy, and such well-educated boys will be equipped to offer assistance in a situation like the one above, regardless of whether they had sisters or not.

Does your school teach sex education with mixed classes or gendered? If the latter, why? And can you change it?

With the internet age and the changes in society that have come with it, I feel our children are growing up much quicker, but they are often getting an unrealistic view of sex, so we need to teach them that it is not all like what we see in the media – and real life sometimes suffers by comparison. Even if this takes us out of our own comfort zone as educators, it is important to remember that sometimes we are the only people in some children's lives who will discuss the issues raised in this chapter, and we owe it to them.

Tl;dr

We all grow up with different relationships with our own sexuality that need consideration, even (and maybe especially) heterosexual people. Sex isn't shameful. Educating pupils about all kinds of sexualities is important. It's worth it for us, as adults, to question our own feelings about all kinds of sexualities to make sure we have dealt with any disgust or shame that might get in the way of honest, informative and useful discourse with pupils.

References

1. The Independent. (2017). *LGBT+ issues could be taught in school sex education for the first time in history.* Retrieved April 22, 2019, from https://www.independent.co.uk/news/education/education-news/lgbt-issues-taught-schools-uk-first-time-sex-education-lessons-rse-government-change-a8118056.html
2. *Sex FAQs and statistics.* (n.d.). Retrieved April 22, 2019, from https://www.kinseyinstitute.org/research/faq.php

3. Jarvstad, A., & Hahn, U. (2011). Source reliability and the conjunction fallacy. *Cognitive Science, 35*(4), 682–711. https://doi.org/10.1111/j.1551-6709.2011.01170.x

4. The Independent. (2017). *Lesbian relationships only exist because men find it a turn-on, claims study.* Retrieved April 22, 2019, from https://www.independent.co.uk/life-style/lesbian-relationships-men-turn-on-same-sex-female-attraction-menelaos-apostolou-cyprus-university-a7766606.html

5. Hartburn, S. (2001, November 30). Many-to-many Shape Sorter. Retrieved April 22, 2019, from *The Aperiodical* website: https://aperiodical.com/2019/03/many-to-many-shape-sorter/

6. Nodin, N. (2015). *LGB&T mental health - Risk and resilience explored.* Retrieved April 22 from RaRE Research Report website: http://www.queerfutures.co.uk/wp-content/uploads/2015/04/RARE_Research_Report_PACE_2015.pdf

7. Harari, Y. N. (2015). *Sapiens: A Brief History of Humankind* (J. Purcell & H. Watzman, Trans.). London, England: Vintage Books.

8. Barnes, E., & Carlile, A. (2018). *How to Transform Your School into an LGBT+ Friendly Place: A Practical Guide for Nursery, Primary and Secondary Teachers.* London, England; Philadelphia, PA: Jessica Kingsley Publishers.

9. *The asexual visibility and education network.* asexuality.org. (n.d.). Retrieved April 22, 2019, from https://www.asexuality.org/

10. Byrne, D. (1969). Attitudes and attraction. In L. Berkowitz (Ed.), *Advances in Experimental Social Psychology* (Vol. 4, pp. 35–89). https://doi.org/10.1016/S0065-2601(08)60076-3

11. Smith, R. *How often do men think about sex?* (2013, June 10). Retrieved April 22, 2019, from The BMJ website: https://blogs.bmj.com/bmj/2013/06/10/richard-smith-how-often-do-men-think-about-sex/

12. *Sexual Offences Act.* (2003). Retrieved April 22, 2019, from http://www.legislation.gov.uk/ukpga/2003/42/2017-03-31?view=plain

13. Arter, J., Fu, T.-C., Herbenick, D., Sanders, S. A., & Dodge, B. (2018). Women's experiences with genital touching, sexual pleasure, and orgasm: Results from a U.S. probability sample of women ages 18 to 94. *Journal of Sex & Marital Therapy, 44*(2), 201–212. https://doi.org/10.1080/0092623X.2017.1346530

14. Nagoski, E. (2016). *What 60 years of research says about women's masturbation.* Retrieved April 22, 2019, from Medium website: https://medium.com/@enagoski/what-60-years-of-research-says-about-womens-masturbation-f3b842343454

15. Klass, P. (2018, December 18). Why is children's masturbation such a secret? *The New York Times.* Retrieved from https://www.nytimes.com/2018/12/10/well/family/why-is-childrens-masturbation-such-a-secret.html

16. Coleman, P. (2019, March 20). *Homophobic parents are right to be worried about their children turning gay after lessons about LGBT awareness. I lived as*

a Tudor wench for 2 years following a history class. [Tweet]. Retrieved April 22, 2019, from Twitter website: https://twitter.com/PColemanchester/status/1108438951629651970

17. Campbell, R., Denford, S., Hutten, R., Johnson, A., Owen, J., Pound, P., Shucksmith, J., Tanton, C. et al. (2017). What is best practice in sex and relationship education? A synthesis of evidence, including stakeholders' views. *BMJ Open, 7*(5), e014791. https://doi.org/10.1136/bmjopen-2016-014791

18. Ajlouni, H. K., Daoud, A. S., Ajlouni, S. F., & Ajlouni, K. M. (2010). Infantile and early childhood masturbation: Sex hormones and clinical profile. *Annals of Saudi Medicine, 30*(6), 471–474.

19. Unal, F. (2000). Predisposing factors in childhood masturbation in Turkey. *Eur J Pediatr, 159*, 338–342.

20. *Childhood sexuality.* SexInfo online. (n.d.). Retrieved April 22, 2019, from http://www.soc.ucsb.edu/sexinfo/article/childhood-sexuality

21. Department for Education. *Changes to the teaching of sex and relationship education and PSHE.* Online response submitted by the Royal College of Paediatrics and Child Health. (2018). Retrieved from https://www.rcpch.ac.uk/sites/default/files/2018-04/changes_to_the_teaching_of_sex_and_relationship_education_and_pshe_-_department_for_education.pdf

15 | Relationships and PSHE education

A shining beacon - keyrings with tiny babies' feet on – a pillow fight – protected characteristics – a dangerous toxin – it's not about being homophobic – tentative strategies – a newborn cranium – feelings pirates – a clear asymmetry – partner-swapping – disrespectful if beguiling – the hots for Idris Elba – responsible non-monogamy – more ethical – conceptual gravy – Ian Wright's special guy – arguing against cohesion

Stats

Sex and relationship education (SRE) is regarded as vital to improving young people's sexual health, but a third of schools in England lack good SRE, and government guidance is outdated.[1]

Half of respondents rated the SRE they received in school as either 'poor' or 'terrible'. Just 2% rated it as 'excellent' and 10% rated it as 'good'. Those respondents rating SRE quality as 'poor' are more likely to be non-cisgender, and those rating it 'fair' or better are more likely to be cisgender.[2]

The issues

If they're lucky, our pupils are going to live a life filled with relationships. They will be negotiating attachment, attraction, jealousy, envy, rejection, betrayal and forgiveness. For many of them, their bodies, brains and minds have already been scarred by trauma. (This is true of many more pupils than you might think. Around 14% of people asked in one study scored 4 or more – the maximum group – on the Adverse Childhood Experiences scale.)[3] The task of guiding them through sex and relationships education is both crucial and scary for us as educators. What if they ask a personal question? What if one of them comes out to us? What if our views disagree with those of their parents and this causes them conflict? How can we be respectful of religious and cultural practice but still deliver the curriculum thoughtfully?

Whatever the government does or doesn't mandate, and whatever is or isn't written on your school documents, you are teaching PSHE (personal, social and health education) and/or SRE (sex and relationships education) all the time. This is about your values, your words and your example. That one of the reasons why LGBTQ+ teachers have been encouraged to come out to pupils if they can, because the example of these teachers is a shining beacon to our pupils, who so often look up to them in ways they can't even begin to imagine. The visible representation of non-binary people and homosexual relationships to pupils can be in a textbook (I wish!) or it can be right in front of them, in their classroom and their assembly hall and their corridors. How powerful that can be.

Even if you are not an explicitly designated PSHE teacher, you are teaching it in all kinds of ways. This is simply not a situation where you can distance yourself from these issues or say they're for other people to deal with, such as teachers in your school who are gay, trans or bisexual. Careful and thoughtful examination of LGBTQ+ issues, relationship issues, love, sex and attraction is a responsibility of all of us.

I asked some friends and colleagues about their experiences of PSHE education at their school. One responded,

[M]y school was in a tiny village and we experienced HUGE amounts of shaming. The only real 'sex ed' we received was by an anti-abortion organisation who came in to give a presentation – they gave us key rings with tiny babies' feet on. The same school told my sister's year that being a lesbian would mean you would go to hell – unsurprisingly there was no material on LGBTQI+ relationships/identities. No info on mental health, consent and eating disorders (which were rife in my year) – or support to students. It was a small all girls private school – and it seems private schools get to teach whatever they want (or don't want)!

Here's another example:

'My SRE at secondary school consisted of nothing whatsoever. In primary school I watched an animated video of a heterosexual couple having a pillow fight.[2]

Others told me they had felt erased by a focus on heteronormative (male-female) relationships. Many, many people told me that they felt these lessons were peremptory and dismissive, designed to tick a box that released responsibility, or discharged uncomfortable questions without really addressing them.

A rising tide raises all expectations

Maybe, just maybe, we're at a point where the tides are changing.

The PSHE association: 'The national curriculum states that "all schools should make provision for personal, social, health and economic education (PSHE), drawing on good practice". PSHE education ... is part of Ofsted's remit to inspect. The relationships and health aspects of PSHE education will be compulsory in all schools from 2020.'[4]

In 2018, the UK government consulted on these issues. In their response, they state, 'The content of the subjects strikes a balance between prescribing clearly the important core knowledge that all pupils should be taught, whilst allowing flexibility for schools to design a curriculum that is relevant to their pupils. This also enables schools to consider how to teach the subjects, bearing in mind the religious backgrounds of their pupils, and enables schools with a religious character to build on the core content by reflecting the teachings of their faith. All schools must comply with the relevant provisions of the Equality Act 2010.'[5] In their guidance, they urge schools to be sure to comply with the relevant guidance on religion and belief, which are 'protected characteristics'.

You know what else is a protected characteristic?

'It is unlawful for a school to discriminate against a pupil or prospective pupil by treating them less favourably because of their: sex, race, disability, religion or belief, *sexual orientation, gender reassignment,* pregnancy or maternity.'[6]

There is a direct clash here. Already, schools are at times sites of conflict about teaching content when it comes to LGBTQ+ issues, where parents are concerned about this content contradicting their religious or moralistic ideas about what they want their children to know. As I write this, some schools are cancelling their delivery of the *No Outsiders* programme – rated by Ofsted as age-appropriate – in response to parental pressure to do so involving religious beliefs. Many people are angry.

What is it in this (research-based, expert-planned) project that might have sparked such upset?

Here are the aims of the *No Outsiders* project, taken from the Economic and Social Research Council website:

> To add to the understanding of the operation of heteronormativity (the assumption that heterosexuality is normal, so anything else is abnormal) in school contexts.
>
> To create a community of practice within which teachers can develop effective approaches to addressing sexualities equality within the broader context of inclusive education.[7]

Who, exactly, is arguing with this, and why?

According to some press reports, local residents, 'chanting' and 'discussing the sexuality of assistant headteacher Andrew Moffat, who co-authored the *No Outsiders* project.' Andrea Leadsom, Tory MP, also got involved, saying that parents should get to decide when their children 'become exposed to that information',[8] as if knowing about same-sex relationships is a dangerous toxin. What do they suppose is happening in schools where students *don't* learn about LGBT+ relationships? Do they think that the parents, the teachers and the students affected by these issues simply disappear? That they can erase gay people by refusing to name them?

One widely quoted voice in opposition to *No Outsiders* reportedly said, 'Morally we do not accept homosexuality as a valid sexual relationship to have. It's not about being homophobic.'[9] Plenty of voices louder and wittier than mine chimed in to say that, actually, this is pretty much the definition of homophobia.

From the research report on *No Outsiders*:

> Primary pupils from a variety of different geographical, socio-economic, religious and cultural settings engaged successfully with this work, challenging norms and stereotypes relating to sexual orientation and gender expression. However, the fear of adverse media attention and the constraints of the curriculum led teachers to adopt more tentative strategies than they might use in other equalities work.[7]

I can only imagine what 'tentative strategies' means, or what it feels like to teachers. Something like walking a buttered tightrope wearing a backpack full of rocks, I'd imagine.

There are plenty of times when schools stand firm against a minority of parent voices – some parents want to park close to the school and can't; some want to insist that their child can have peanut butter sandwiches when another child has a nut allergy, and so they can't. Some want their child prioritised over others. Some, as in this example, appear to want their views prioritised over the visibility, representation, validity and safety of others. Well, they can't.

Just as in religious education lessons we try to teach balanced and well-informed lessons about 'what others do' and let students explore and decide for themselves, sex and relationships education need be no different. It's that simple.

Bad romance

I'm now in my thirties and, after pursuing routes of therapy, reading widely and having some important discussions with friends and experts, I feel I'm just starting to get a handle on good, healthy relationships. I've had an abusive past and have made some regrettable mistakes. I'm sad about some missed opportunities in my life, but I have had the good fortune to wash up somewhere good, on a calm and sunny shore, and now I am able to consider my own relationship 'scripts' and childhood with an analytical eye.

Have you ever fallen in love? (What about with someone you shouldn't have fallen in love with? Sorry, you'll be singing that all day now.)

How did it feel? What did you do? What did you feel you owed that person, and what did they owe you?

I didn't start to frame these ideas in these terms until well into adulthood. I would meet someone, be attracted to them and perhaps end up 'falling in love' with them. They might feel the same, and we might enter into a relationship – with all the unacknowledged expectations, the not-quite-meeting-at-the-edges of what that might mean. Or, they might not feel the same, or not be in a position to. Films and stories had taught me what happens next. I had to undergo a powerful transformation of some sort – become thinner, or prettier, or amazing at something they liked. Then they would notice me. Then they would owe me a relationship. They would be so forcefully attracted to me that we would fuse together like a newborn cranium and never again be parted.

If they had a current partner, that person became an enemy, a not-person, an obstacle – and their feelings didn't matter. They didn't deserve to keep their partner, they weren't good for them, they weren't what they needed. Easy, right?

That is one of the most dangerous and unhealthy ideas in our culture, and we consistently fail to challenge it.

Ideas about good relationships are actually pretty simple, and I'm angry that no one in my life guided me through this basic stuff sooner. But, rather than place blame (parents, other family members, teachers) it has made me thoughtful about some of the often unspoken rules that we need to make explicit to pupils as they grow. I would characterise them as *feeling feelings, giving and receiving rejection* and *drawing your boundaries*. These constructs come from much reading and reflection (but no specific source except me). They look like this:

Feeling feelings: Much of the strong or hard-to-control emotion we feel is due to unresolved or blocked feelings. It works like this: Something triggers a feeling. Along with that feeling might come shame or guilt, the two worst perpetrators of burying feelings (call them feelings pirates, if you will). We simply do not feel a right to feel what we feel. The desire to hurt someone; the jealous rage when we feel we should own someone; the severe sadness we can't find a cause for; the envy of someone's else 'natural skills' (i.e., hard work); the anguish of a love that isn't returned. So we deny the feeling and lock it up tight. We are likely to have physical symptoms of doing this: tension, tightness, stress that can manifest as pain and illness in our bodies as well as our minds. The adrenalin that pours into our system throbs, uselessly, and we feel terrible – worse than before. But it doesn't have to be this way. Anyone who has been to therapy knows that one of the most healing things you can do is express dark, terrible feelings to someone else and have them listen. They know (and it took me some time to work this out) that accepting someone else's feelings isn't about saying it's ok to act on them, or condoning violence or destruction – it's about hearing them, in the moment. It's about knowing that people have different parts to their selves and that sometimes those parts disagree, that some of these parts go rogue and feel things that we might self-characterise as unspeakable, awful, terrifying. But they are not. They are just feelings. They are not 'us'. They will pass, and if someone is able to hear them and hear us, it really, really helps.

Giving and receiving rejection: Do you remember the first time you told someone you didn't want to be in a relationship with them? What about not wanting to have sex with them? Was it a permanent 'I don't fancy you' or a temporary 'not right now'? How did you deliver it and how did they handle it? It is impossible to have a healthy relationship without dealing with rejection in some way, whether sexual or otherwise. We all have to be able to ask for what we want, to say no and to receive no; otherwise we are simply taking advantage of one another. If one party feels more comfortable doing so (and this is often the case), we end up with a clear asymmetry – and, as society often conditions men to feel more entitled to ask for what they want and to refuse things they don't want to give, then in a heterosexual relationship of some kind, it can often work that way around. If you usually 'give in' to your partner/s because you fear their anger, sadness or manipulation, you are not in an equal partnership/relationship structure. For example, someone very close to me is, as I write, negotiating their first relationship. One of their deepest worries centres on how to say no to the other person; how to negotiate the possibility that they will feel angry at them. Instead of avoiding such a situation by capitulating, I have advised them to think through this scenario – it is not their responsibility to manage their partner's anger at not always getting what they want. Better to draw their own boundaries –and to make them explicit early on in the relationship, so that their partner understands that rejection will happen and can prepare to deal with it. Equally, they cannot be in a relationship where they are so frightened of rejection that they never voices their own needs.

Drawing your own boundaries: I'm going to tell you a secret. There are people in the world, as we speak – maybe your friends and neighbours and family members – who are in relationship structures that are not one-man-one-woman. There are people whose relationships are completely non-sexual, or for whom partner-swapping is a happy part of their social life together. There are people who consider a partner taking a lover to be a welcome and happy part of their life together. There are people who don't have sex with one another at all and are very content with that. If you can imagine it, it's probably happening somewhere – and the biggest mistake we can make is to judge someone else's relationship boundaries as 'wrong' or 'unhealthy' because they wouldn't work for us. (Or maybe we're just jealous, because we think they actually *might* work for us, but we feel afraid to ask for them.) We are all free to set our own boundaries for what we want from our relationships (and this may change over time). We also, therefore, have to be free to not enter into a relationship we are not comfortable with, or to leave a relationship where the boundaries change beyond what we want out of it.

What needs to change

Healthy relationships and attachment aren't just important, they are *the* basis from which all important human activity flows. If a pupil is stuck in a toxic relationship, trapped in a cycle of abuse or frozen in trauma, they are most likely unable to relax their mind and brain into the creative, analytical or open state that is needed for learning. Conversely, we know from research that often, a single supportive relationship is enough for a young person to thrive and learn, even in the most adverse of circumstances. Teachers can be the lighthouse pupils so desperately need.

Equally, plenty of relationships in schools between teachers and other members of staff, across or between hierarchies, are pretty toxic.

Down with love

So often we say 'love' and we mean 'obsession'. Throwing yourself and your identity into another person isn't a healthy thing to do. Checking their Facebook or Instagram or Twitter 50 times a minute won't ever lead to anything good. Hating anyone they speak to or are nice to who isn't you isn't 'loving' them. These behaviours are normalised as proxies for love so often we think that's what it is. Have you ever done those things? Did it end well?

Losing control of your behaviour isn't excused by 'love', or a constituent of it. We just really want an excuse to do it, and society conveniently offers one. We also so often apply the 'we know better' paradigm, and it's disrespectful, if beguiling. 'She says she doesn't love me, but I know she does'. 'He said I was amazing and I know he hates his boyfriend; I'd be so much better for him'. If we start to apply the logic of 'they said *this* but I know *that* is true', we are but one step away from raping someone. Listen to people's words, and respect them. You don't 'know' better. You just wish things were different – a very human condition – but that is nowhere near the same.

The song 'On My Own' from *Les Miserables* elegantly captures this. At the beginning, she walks through the city at night, pretending he's there with her. She romanticises her surroundings; it's all misty lights and silvered trees. By the end of the song, she realises, and we realise with her, that she's 'only been pretending' and that she loves only the *idea* of him; he does not love her. How often have you dreamt and fantasised about someone, only to have them fall from that pedestal in real life because you didn't love who they were, just what you wanted them to be?

We have to listen to people's words, and wishes, and start from who they actually are, and stop overwriting them with fantastical template scripts instead. I was in my thirties before I thought hard about having strong, loving relationships with males that didn't contain any elements of sexual attraction at all. I had pushed relationships into the realms of sexual attraction because I didn't know they could go anywhere else.

I have thought, at various times in my life, that greater intimacy – that loving someone *more* – follows an already-written code which starts with butterflies in the stomach and ends with marriage. I have realised now that this limits our choices and disrespects our feelings. Where's the space for strong professional bonds? Where do I fit a person in my life who parents me but isn't related to me? How do I characterise the love I feel for my ex-partner? Why can't I have a best friend that I would do anything for, but whom I don't have sex with? And why is this person's gender important? So often, it's because we have internalised monoheteronormative scripts that limit powerful expressions of love to sex and, later, marriage.

'Marriage today is the outcome of government imposing its standards on personal relationships, legislating a one-size-fits-all mandate for how people in sexual or domestic relationships ought to run their lives', say Hardy and Easton in their excellent book *The Ethical Slut*.[10] There's a thought.

We need more sizes. We need more relationship scripts, available discourses and language to describe them. We need to value more relationships (and let's start with people like step-parents, please). We need to stop fetishizing marriage and babies like they're the only thing we can celebrate.

'Why is legal recognition of a relationship along with privileges like inheritance and parental rights, restricted to those who are willing to shape their lives to conform to its design'? they continue.[10] It's an excellent point.

We also need to stop thinking sexual attraction is the only valued and valuable type of attraction. Sexual attraction isn't necessarily meaningful to both parties. Me having the hots for Idris Elba doesn't give Idris Elba the responsibility to relieve my sexual frustration, any more than if the same thing happened with Becky whom I work with. In the stories we get on our tellyboxes, it starts with a longing look and, as soon as sexual attraction is established, *it can only end in sex.* If the people deny it, are committed elsewhere or try to ignore it, that only prolongs the agony, and when they do hook up, it makes it even more spectacular. That's not a healthy narrative for real life, and unless we actively combat it, we aren't challenging it.

I noticed this recently in a TV show, where the storyline started with a married woman getting back in touch with an ex-boyfriend. She was away from home for the weekend and went to visit him. He looked good. She looked good. She flirted. So did he.

Then she had a cup of tea and went home, marriage intact, and told her husband all about it.

How often do we see that narrative?

Similarly, we need to consider (and discuss in schools and at home) a wider range of models of healthy sexual relationships, including polyamory, casual hookups, fetishes, the whole LGBTQ+ gamut, and asexuality.

The rules of healthy relationships – consent, honesty and give-and-take – very much apply in good polyamorous relations, just as in good monogamous (two exclusive people) relations. Of course, you can get unhealthy relationships in any kind of structure, but poly relationships are not, by their nature, destructive, deceitful or unequal. Here's an interesting idea about the ethics of polyamory:

> Many monogamous people actually practice "serial monogamy" – jumping from lover to lover to lover – while claiming to be "monogamous" with each one ... Polyamory is more ethical than serial monogamy as it is sometimes practiced; polyamorists do not discard their lovers when the next interesting person walks down the road.[10]

How often do we consider the ethics of relationships in these or any terms?

So often, the basic (mono) heteronormative script is so prevalent that we don't know how to conceptualise love without sex, or a relationship without monogamy. Equally, questions such as the following arise. How could or should a partner deal with a fetish? What could or should be a response to a partner cheating? How can I safely tell my partner I'm attracted to someone else? When is it ok to lie to my partner? All seem to be influenced by a very narrow range of hyper-dramatic responses we see in the media, and live out in tired, repetitive cycles at home, based only on parental retelling or parental rebelling.

What does it mean to be in a loving relationship? What about an ethical one? How do you balance your needs with those of the other person? What have you learned about relationships as you've got older, and how much work have you done on yourself as a result?

Why aren't we teaching ideas like this as part of relationships education?

The strongest counterarguments and why they're wrong

−   'Relationships with pupils make me feel icky and I'm not into that touchy-feely stuff'.

−   'Pupils shouldn't rely on teachers too much or get too attached; it's weird'.

−   'We shouldn't be teaching sexual and relationship deviance − I don't want kids learning about gay or poly people and all that disgusting stuff'.

Relationships are everything there is. Teaching, learning, existing, mediating knowledge, thinking, critiquing − all are based on relationships. The quality of our relationships filters through and into these interactions like conceptual gravy.

Think about some of the most enjoyable and challenging intellectual discussions you have had, and with whom you had them. Did you trust the person? Did you feel basically that you had a solid, kindly relationship, such that when you disagreed, it came from a place that didn't make you feel unsafe? Did you feel that you respected their opinions and thoughts and, therefore, engaged with them better?

This is the dream, for me. Not that we all become yoga-practising meditation experts with expert-level psychology and talk about our feelings constantly – although there's nothing wrong with that – but that we truly understand how important relationships are to everything in schools and everywhere else. And also, that schools are a space where we can put the narrative of relationships under the microscope – the transparent eye itself – and challenge unhealthy ones.

There's a difference between unhealthy attachment and mentoring/ support. No one is suggesting that you need be best mates with the kids you teach. (Well, I'm certainly not). But effective mentoring and support programmes, as well as less formal but equally important supportive relationships, can work absolute wonders. If you don't believe me, look up the video of footballer Ian Wright being reunited with his old schoolteacher,[11] who, in his own words, 'was so supportive all the time; kind of like my special guy'. It's terribly moving; Wright becomes a little boy again, and we see his deep love for the man who believed in him and made him feel like he could do it. We all need those kinds of mentors – those who are invested in our success and want to help us optimise our experiences in some way. Children who have had adverse experiences and disadvantage in other ways really, really need them. Can you think of a time when a teacher made a difference in your life? Were relationships central to the situation?

Are you arguing that there SHOULD be outsiders? Andrew Moffat, the finalist of the Global Teacher Prize who helped devise the *No Outsiders* lessons, is utterly baffled by the fairly recent controversy around the LGBT sections of the programme – some four years after the lessons started being successfully implemented. He explains, '*No Outsiders* is community cohesion. It's about different people in the UK today. It's about Muslim, Christian, Hindu Sikh, black, white, brown-skinned, disabled, gay and lesbian, different families.'[12] The focus on LGBT visibility and 'sex' seems entirely warped if you look at the lesson materials themselves, which I suspect many parents haven't. Who is arguing *against* cohesion, exactly, when it comes down to it?

So much of the disgust surrounding 'LGBT lifestyles', as I have discussed in previous chapters, is related to unexamined and entirely disrespectful cramming of them into the same bucket as 'sexual deviance'. 'This is normal', people say, drawing a careful line around themselves, 'and you are over there, you with your weird ways and doing stuff that

I don't (care to) understand. Go away, you're wrong'. That's the kind of crap we try and kick to the curb in schools, as a rule.

> ## Now/later
>
> Now: Think about your relationships and the patterns they may have followed. What do you value in a relationship and how does this translate into your teaching? How do you give and handle rejection and is it something you explicitly model to pupils?
>
> Later: How do pupils – especially the most needy ones – get the support and mentoring they might need at your school, modelling healthy relationships? Is there a programme, or could you set one up?

Graham says

I am pleased that the DfE (Department for Education) has made the teaching of relationships and health compulsory from 2020, but I do not think that is enough. Already we have seen that things can change overnight, but there is still confusion over what to teach and how to teach it, which might mean that, because of pressure from parents and other groups, not a lot will change. I also think they missed a trick by not making the teaching of all kinds of gender stereotypes compulsory (it was something that I suggested in the consultation period).

My class and I went through quite a learning process from being almost totally unaware of gender stereotypes and their impact to thinking about nothing else. In just a short space of time, my pupils changed their views on so many things, and I feel confident that what they have learned will shape the rest of their lives. There are also so many resources already available – for example, I have a padlet of ideas at https:// padlet.com/grahamandre07/gnresources.

When talking about normal relationships, what is 'normal'? Look at the children in your class(es). There are likely children who have one-parent families or are looked after by grandparents or whose parents are the same sex. We need to make sure that when we talk about families with our children, we cover all possibilities, and not just as an ad-on. We want our children to feel that we fully accept these families as the norm as well.

I was on a flight back to the Isle of Wight after football yesterday, and it was full of people sporting stockings, suspenders, corsets, bras and make up. *The Rocky Horror Picture Show* was being screened locally, and these fans were on their way back home. They all looked amazing: I had no idea who was male, female, bi, trans or cis, but they all seemed so comfortable in the way they looked and felt, also mixing freely and happily with the football fans. It was wonderful to see, and maybe we should all take a lesson from that joy.

Tl;dr

Relationships are so very important that we are teaching them and teaching about them pretty much all the time. We run on some pretty narrow monoheteronormative scripts, and some of them aren't particularly healthy. Not teaching about LGBT 'lifestyles' alongside heteronormative ones isn't solving any problems; it is just erasing and devaluing people.

References

1. Campbell, R., Denford, S., Hutten, R., Johnson, A., Owen, J., Pound, P., Shucksmith, J., Tanton, C. et al. (2017). What is best practice in sex and relationship education? A synthesis of evidence, including stakeholders' views. *BMJOpen,7*(5),e014791.https://doi.org/10.1136/bmjopen-2016-014791
2. Terence Higgins Trust. (2016). *Shh No Talking: LGBT Inclusive SRE in the UK.* Retrieved from https://www.tht.org.uk/sites/default/files/2018-07/Shh%20No%20talking%20LGBT%20inclusive%20SRE%20in%20the%20UK.pdf
3. *Behavioral Risk Factor Surveillance System ACE Data.* Violence Prevention. Injury Center: CDC. (2019, April 9). Retrieved April 22, 2019, from https://www.cdc.gov/violenceprevention/childabuseandneglect/acestudy/ace-brfss.html
4. Curriculum. PSHE Association. (n.d.). Retrieved April 22, 2019, from https://www.pshe-association.org.uk/curriculum-and-resources/curriculum

5. *Relationships education, relationships and sex education, and health education in England government consultation response.* (2019). Retrieved from https://assets.publishing.service.gov.uk/government/uploads/system/uploads/attachment_data/file/780768/Government_Response_to_RSE_Consultation.pdf

6. *The Equality Act 2010 and schools departmental advice for school leaders, school staff, governing bodies and local authorities.* (2014). Retrieved from https://assets.publishing.service.gov.uk/government/uploads/system/uploads/attachment_data/file/315587/Equality_Act_Advice_Final.pdf

7. *No Outsiders: Researching approaches to sexualities equality in primary schools.* ESRC – Economic and Social Research Council. (2009). Retrieved April 22, 2019, from https://www.researchcatalogue.esrc.ac.uk/grants/RES-062-23-0095/read

8. *Andrea Leadsom: Parents should be able to pull children out of LGBTQ+ lessons.* (2019, March 20). Retrieved April 22, 2019, from RightsInfo website: https://rightsinfo.org/andrea-leadsom-lgbt-lessons-parents-classes-children/

9. Kotecha, S. (2019, March 19). *More schools drop LGBT rights classes.* Retrieved from https://www.bbc.com/news/uk-england-birmingham-47613578

10. Easton, D., & Hardy, J. W. (2017). *The Ethical Slut: A Practical Guide to Polyamory, Open Relationships and Other Freedoms in Sex and Love* (3rd edition). California, CA: Ten Speed Press.

11. MITOGEN. (n.d.). *Ian Wright gets a big shock!* Retrieved from https://www.youtube.com/watch?v=omPdemwaNzQ

12. Tes News. (2019). *"I remember being an outsider" – The teacher at the centre of LGBT row.* Retrieved April 22, 2019, from https://www.tes.com/news/i-remember-being-outsider-teacher-centre-lgbt-row

16 Sports and physical education

Autumn-born advantages – 'I used to think women were weak' – humiliated – a theatre in the round of gender – artistic swimming – paying for a chaperone – popping her chest out – performance indicators – phenomenally – real men do not dance – the traditional format – are you a lesbian? – he dictates, she reacts – glitter and a carnival atmosphere – an odd shape – bruise like a peach – not completely resistant – sport is not war – neither the king nor the kingmaker – socially appropriate – a mathematical adjustment – a diaphragm – gendered yoga – swimsuits or leotards – girls can't throw

Stats

Research from the Department for Culture, Media and Sport in the summer found a quarter of girls aged 5 to 10 had not taken part in any sport over in the previous month – a rise of almost 50% in five years.

Separate research by the Women's Sport and Fitness Foundation revealed that just over half of girls – 51% – are put off physical activity by their experiences of school sport and PE lessons.[1]

The issues

Many, many schools still segregate pupils by gender in physical education (PE) or sport in the United Kingdom. It is much more likely in secondary schools but still common in primary too, as far as I can tell (statistics are remarkably hard to find).

How do you feel about that?

You might be thinking, 'But boys are stronger and more aggressive – it's not fair!'

What about autumn-born advantages?[2]

What about height and weight advantages?

What about better fast-twitch muscle capacity or agility advantages?

Where does it end?

There is 'no difference in muscle mass and strength between girls and boys until puberty', says Javid in *No More Boys and Girls*. What are we telling pupils about their bodies by segregating them? I'm wondering. 'Gender-integrating sports might potentially decrease some of the socionegative outcomes attributed to male team sport athletes, possibly including violence against women', explains a research paper called 'I used to think women were weak'.[3]

PE is an important arena for the construction of identity, and not just in terms of gender. Like a Roman gladiator fight, most of this is done in the open, in front of an audience, and that can be intimidating. I have plenty of adult friends who swore off PE at school – finding that it was incompatible with their geeky or creative identities, or that the way it was taught made them uncomfortable or just that they just happened to have been taught sports that they didn't connect well with. Stories of feeling 'humiliated' seem to be particularly frequent. These adults often physically 'find their thing' later in life – running, fencing, dancing, horse riding, yoga – having to do some identity work in the meantime to reconcile their self with doing physical activity and actually enjoying it.

'It is debatable whether many of the traditional sports which dominate school-based physical education lessons are able to meet the needs of a more demanding and consumer-literate younger generation', says Ian Wellard in their book *Rethinking Gender in Youth Sport*. 'The different bodily usages encouraged by secondary school physical education both permit and support the development of particular masculinities and femininities'.[4]

It is difficult to think of an area of school experience where gender seems to intervene, so forcefully, between our pupils and the curriculum. Particular concerns include the encouragement of unbridled aggression and competitiveness of boys, and the disaffection or embarrassment of girls. Dig a little deeper, and many, many pupils seem to find barriers to enjoyment and success in PE, often related to perceived 'flaws' and shame about their own bodies. In PE lessons we see the performance of gender on a grand scale, the insidious stereotypes and clichés popping out of our mouths and decorating our bodies, uncovered as they are from their daily uniforms and newly exposed to the scrutiny of peers. It is a theatre in the round of gender with nowhere to hide. In PE, we undress our bodies and we must face the reactions from others. We expose too, our naked feelings and fears about bodies and what they can or can't do.

Is there a profound asymmetry, a hierarchy within the sexes when it comes to sports?

Name three boys' sports. Now name three girls' sports.

Can you explain why those choices are associated with those genders?

Chaps don't need chaperones

I've just read a news story announcing that mixed-gender events in athletics, swimming, table tennis and triathlon have been approved for the Tokyo 2020 Olympic Games. At the time of writing, every other sporting event in the Olympics is segregated by gender (only men compete against men, and only women against women) except a few mixed-pair categories, and several events are completely different. Women do the heptathlon; men the decathlon. Women do fewer rounds in tennis and boxing, and they are excluded completely from some events in shooting and canoeing (a total of 39 in 2018); men cannot participate in synchronised swimming (now renamed artistic swimming).

'In the early days of the Olympic Games, many [organisations] limited the amount of female competitors they would send because they would incur the cost of paying for a chaperone, which was not necessary for the male athletes'.[5]

I'm tired of the sports I see on my TV being so starkly gendered. I'm tired of the occasional female pundit being 'allowed' as a novelty, so long as her skirts are short enough and her heels are high enough. I'm tired of listening to old men given airtime to thoughtlessly comment on women's hair, makeup and outfits as they prepare for incredible feats of physical skill. I feel physically sick watching my daughter being taught to 'present' herself in gymnastics by flexing her back and popping her chest out, while the boys stick a hand up in the air instead. I'm bored of insisting that women playing tennis, rugby and football are unfairly paid and poorly publicised compared to men, and hearing ill-thought-out arguments like 'But Serena Williams!' in response. (But what? She has had to fight more battles than anyone, you smug idiot.) I'm very, very bored of saying 'or, as I call it, cricket' every time someone says 'women's cricket'.

The long-term solution might seem simple: Stop segregating sport, and focus from the ground up on 'ways in which girls can have access to the same range of activities as boys. However, this can be problematic, as it does not take into consideration one of the main causes of negative experience ... shame and humiliation'.[4]

How has school PE come to this?

'Young people are regarding their bodies as 'performance indicators' of successful (or not) membership of an image-based society', explains Wellard.[4] Bodies as sites of failure, of unfavourable comparison and of hyperinflated value – and the coincidences with gendered ideas are complicated ones, as we all scroll past Insta-images of gym-bodies and plank challenges and before and after shots. What are we aiming for, and how many give up before they begin because it seems so far from where their bodies are now?

The first time I saw the TV advert *This Girl Can*, I cried. In this short film, we see women – older, fatter, less 'able', and more diverse than we are used to seeing them – doing a range of sports, individually and together. They look tough, if not always competent. They wear a range of outfits, from head coverings to swimsuits to baggy sweatshirts. In this advert, which is not perfect (the focus on a woman's jiggling backside made me roll my eyes, for example), we finally get a sense of what it might be like to normalise women doing physical activity for pleasure, for skill development, for camaraderie, in a way that men have had access to for centuries. For most women, taking up physical space – being strong, big, wide – is not permitted alongside being attractive. It's time to change that.

The idea that we could see women doing things with their bodies – training, getting strong, sweating, practising – and that doesn't (have to) translate into 'attractive' is almost unheard of in the media. Women's bodies are for looking at. Sports are a way for the male gaze to penetrate even further, showing women in fewer clothes, covered in sweat, moving their bodies and distracted – perfect.

What about dance?

You may be familiar with the Billy Elliot story (which builds on many similar film narratives before it), in which 'disturbing or disturbed femininity triggers a masculinity crisis which results in dance being set up as the recuperative cinematic space of mainly white male masculinity'.[6]

Have you seen the film or the stage show? What were your reactions? How do you feel about dance as an activity and its relationship to gender?

> These boys and men do not fit into the codes of dance in ways we expect … many of the messages we get tell us 'dance is a feminine space, if men dance, dance is a queer space, and therefore 'real men' (i.e., normal, straight men) do not dance.[6]

Dance is something I think about often. How much (do we believe that) the way someone moves to music says about them? How do we use it as a tool for expression, and how much do we restrict those types of expression to gendered roles?

'In dance and other physical activities, men and women are often thought to move differently due to innate differences in body structure'.[7] Do you agree with this?

I've been watching, like millions of others, *Strictly Come Dancing* on the BBC. In this show, woman/man couples dance together, the expert training the celebrity. It's glamorous and fun. But where is the space for different gender expressions? Many, like me, wondered if Susan Calman's decision to do *Strictly* meant the dawn of a new era, for she is homosexual and publicly out. But this was not the case.

The Reverend Richard Coles, a former contestant, said, 'I used to think the BBC should include same sex couples on *Strictly* but now I've done it I can see why it might choose not to. There's a complementarity when men and women dance together which is different when the couples are same sex … the aesthetic argument'.[8] Susan Calman's decision (if indeed it was hers to make) to dance with a man was both criticised and applauded. Many took to social media to debate this issue.

The 'aesthetic argument'? The 'complementarity'?

I've been a member of the Lindy hop community for some years. This is a partner dance, popular during the 1920s–1940s, in which a leader spontaneously choreographs and a follower responds and completes – or alters – the movement. It can be smooth and silky, jazzy and freeform, or jivey and high-energy. In theory, anyone can dance either role.

As a culture, we are often less-than-comfortable with non-gender conforming ideas. Men following and women leading fall under this bracket. Additionally, it's often assumed that if you don't do the traditional role, you 'must' identify as queer or bi.[9]

It's like the idea of being a lead means 'masculine' and being a follow means 'feminine' … and it is exactly that. There is a TED talk by Trevor Copp and Jeff Fox called *Ballroom dance that breaks gender roles* in which they discuss this issue in some depth, reframing it in a historical context based on the origins of partner dancing: 'You weren't just learning to dance. You were learning to man, and to woman'.[10] Learning to dance might bring with it all sorts of associations about how men and not-men, women and not-women, could and should move.

Have you ever learned to dance in a particular style? How did you feel about it? Did it intersect with your gender identity/ies?

'Even within the … straight couple only paradigm, she can't be taller, he can't be shorter. She can't be bolder, he can't be gentler. He dictates, she reacts. No relationship, gay straight or anything that we would regard as remotely healthy or functional, looks like that', say Copp and Fox.[10]

Let's take apart the 'aesthetic argument'.

'I should add that I have not for a moment felt the slightest twinge of homophobia from a programme which is as LGBT+ friendly as the Sydney Mardi Gras in ruby slippers and on its fourth mojito', says Reverend Coles.[8]

This is terribly lazy, unquestioned reasoning. Glitter and a carnival atmosphere don't make something LGBT+ friendly.

Is it LGBT+ friendly if it never represents same-sex couples?

Is it LGBT+ friendly if it favours heteronormative 'aesthetics' over anything else?

Is it LGBT+ friendly just because it 'allows' LGBT contestants and judges simply to be part of it?

I have participated in enough dance and theatre to know that the heteronormative tall-male-petite-female Platonic ideal is alive and well. I have felt shame and hated my body for not fitting this aesthetic, for not being the perfect half to a complementary male body that somehow fits, that looks right. I have seen directors and choreographers 'match' couples in this way. Is this the only way for two people to dance with one another that we find attractive and aesthetically pleasing? I can't imagine so. Is this another example of giving the people what we think they want, instead of what might creatively break the barriers?

I've just been watching a TV show where a female rugby player demonstrated both her intellectual and her physical prowess. The first thing I thought, as I watched her, was 'That top isn't terribly flattering; she's an odd shape'. I caught myself thinking it. No. The space I have tried to mould her into isn't right; it's an odd expectation. I have drawn a space for her that doesn't fit.

Have you ever tried to exercise to get fitter or to lose weight? How did it feel? How did it relate to your early experiences with exercise?

We all need to love our bodies as they are, even if we are trying to effect change on them. It has to start with love and good mental health. It doesn't work if there's only a tiny narrow range of expectation for 'healthy', 'strong' or 'normal' bodies. It doesn't work if we concentrate on sexualising and gendering movement, on humiliating people for failure and on punishing some more than others for taking risks and being aggressive and ambitious.

What needs to change

I love to consider what the future might hold. I'm imagining, now, a society where splitting sports by gender is considered as eyebrow-raising as doing so by colour of skin or religion. In this society, sport is built on meritocracy. Pupils are taught PE together, and no 'sport' is 'for' one gender or another. Boys play netball with girls without wearing skirts (or with, who cares) or 'accidentally' sexually harassing each other in the changing room. (Everyone gets a cubicle to shower and change in, and they respect each other's space. Done.) Girls play rugby with boys without continually weeping and declaring that they bruise like a peach. There are fervent female cricket pundits as well as male, and everyone puts on clothes to play beach volleyball. People generally get on with running around, throwing things, jumping and catching without stopping for pause about the genital areas of those around them.

(How) would it work? I'm not entirely sure, but I think it's worth considering.

What might be the reasons for separating female and male (and other) bodies for physical exercise? What might be the effects of doing so?

I'm an adult, and I came late to the joys of moving my body purely for my own pleasure and delight. Having felt pushed out of physical pursuits in my school days, I now run, swim, row and dance. I was part of a rugby team for some time. I'm less afraid of my own body, even as I feel its power and agility diminish with age.

What has changed? What has made me feel differently?

For one, I am more resistant to the needs of men to sexualise and humiliate my body (and it is undeniably less sexual to them as I have aged). Not completely resistant. It is still hard to go running in public in the summer or to take a public shower in a swimsuit by the side of a crowded pool. What makes it hard is the internalised messages I have received about my body, as well as the demonstrable responses from men. 'Tits!' one once wittily shouted out of a van as I ran past. Another stopped and smoked on the spot, turning to watch me run from behind. I am not imagining these encounters. But neither am I suggesting that they are unique to being female; we all have body issues, after all. I don't imagine that a body with dwarfism, or a trans body, or a particularly hairy body or an unusually tall body escapes the notice of those determined to humiliate, either.

I also can't escape it easily. If I want to exercise outside, or in public, there are very few gendered spaces for doing so. I also might want to exercise with other people, of all kinds of genders. Segregation makes little sense to me as an adult, and I wonder if less of it as a child would have made a difference to the way I feel about physical activity.

The final difference for me is acceptance – that I will never be an expert, having started late, and with a body with particular challenges (large breasts, childbirth legacy scars running as haphazardly as a spreading ink stain). That my enjoyment, mental health benefits and pushing my own boundaries are my goals, not comparing myself to others, or worrying about how sexy – or idiotic – I look. This is something I would love to have confronted at school.

The gendered ways that people are relating to their own bodies need to go under the microscope, and everyone needs access to a wide range of physical pursuits.

The strongest counterarguments and why they're wrong

- 'If boys and girls play sports together, boys will just take over – they're superior in strength and aggression, and suited to different sports'.
- 'We should separate genders for sports – otherwise boys will be too busy looking at girl's bodies and showing off to them (and maybe vice versa) to concentrate'.

Let's address the real issues. Firstly, the idea that boys 'naturally' play rough and girls need protecting. Ouch. It is true that sports can be dangerous and promote competitiveness, aggressiveness and violence if not handled properly. That is, if rules aren't enforced and players aren't taught to deal with their emotions effectively. This boils down to an argument about how we teach PE in schools, not about whether we need to segregate by gender. Research suggests that parents treat boys and girls differently from birth, for example, with parents consistently overestimating boys' physical abilities and underestimating those of girls, even when babies are younger than 1 year.[11] Once again, our expectations matter. What do we notice, and what do we turn a blind eye to? What is an 'accident', and what is simply malicious behaviour whether it occurs on the field or in the classroom?

Sport is not war. We are not encouraging cruelty or criminality in PE lessons, but a development of skills, teamwork and awareness of one's own body and its limitations and capabilities. If we are worried that boys will hurt girls, what is actually happening here? How 'violent' can and should sports and physical activity be and still be appropriate and healthy ways to exert and express ourselves?

Separating the idea of 'innately' aggressive males and males who learn to be aggressive through cultural and social cues is incredibly difficult to do. Even the idea of testosterone levels as an objective marker of the basic chemical 'difference' between the bodies/brains of males and females is not at all what it appears to be. In Cordelia Fine's *Testosterone Rex*, they draw on a wide range of evidence to show that testosterone is 'neither the king nor the kingmaker – the potent, hormonal essence of competitive, risk-taking masculinity – it is widely perceived to be'[12].

For example, the entire idea that males are more prone to risk-taking behaviour, and that we perceive this as coded masculine, is flawed. Often, this is based on research that has not considered its own assumptions or asked the right questions. (Fine points out that cheerleading and wearing high heels, for example, are quite risky but are often overlooked in such research.) Some activities are demonstrably more risky for women and minorities – they may be less likely to take risks because they simply have more to lose. One study found that women were less likely to take risks when asking for a raise in their salary – not because they were weaker or more afraid to ask, but because they had less expectation of success or support in doing so. The study also suggested non-males may have more to lose from a risky decision being unsuccessful. Fine suggests that (white) males are rewarded much more for risk-taking and potentially aggressive behaviours.

What might happen if we allowed all genders the safety and space to take physical risks and release aggression without hurting anyone in PE lessons? Can or should they do that in the *same* space? What is the message they are receiving if we don't trust them to do that

Another argument is that different sports suit the 'temperaments' of different sexes better. This is an extended version of the first argument, and it presupposes that men and women like or are good at different things – for example, netball versus basketball, which are seen as 'suited' to women and men, respectively. Netball evolved from a specific version of basketball for women:

> [F]rom the start, it was considered socially appropriate for women to play netball; netball's restricted movement appealed to contemporary notions of women's participation in sports, and the sport was distinct from potential rival male sports.[13]

One would hope we now understand that this idea of 'socially appropriate' is nonsense. However, traditions persist. The 2012 Olympics still featured many sports that were completely gendered: synchronised swimming and rhythmic gymnastics for women, boxing, wrestling and baseball for men. 2016 – a full 98 years after women got the vote in the United Kingdom – was be the first year both women and men competed in almost all sports. But separately. And this is the top of the pyramid. Further down, funding, attitudes and ideas will take time to shift. More to the point, this means both men and women have a chance to compete – but crucially, not against each other, because – well what are the reasons?

The most compelling and most commonly advanced reason is that men and women are different, physiologically, and it is unfair to pit them against each other. Should we segregate sports so that women 'have a fair chance', or are we going further down the road of discrimination by doing this? Whether you believe about this tends to reflect whether you think women's bodies are different enough (and by different, in terms of sport, we mean inferior enough) to need a different competition space entirely. There is a truly uncomfortable parallel here with race: There are those who believe that some racial profiles are genetically, inherently better at some sports, and so should compete separately. Like I said, uncomfortable.

If we decide this is nonsense and allow everyone to compete together, then the worry is that women will be knocked out of the top spots altogether and will end up even more under-represented than they are now. Should we allow this to happen – which seems to align with a 'morally fair' argument – or should we do something like a mathematical adjustment taking into account both gender and age? What about height? Weight? Minor injury?

Some say women's bodies are 'catching up', because evolution no longer dictates that they are passive fertility factories, storing fat and resignedly asking men to open jars for them (Hurrah!). Others maintain they will never have the same size hearts, percentage of body fat, muscle mass and endurance capability as men (there is some research to suggest women have the advantage in the latter, however, because they may be more efficient overall at converting glycogen to energy). There is plenty of analysis about the consistency of record-holding by gender, where women seem to stop at approximately 10% lower than men across a variety of fields.[14] It is difficult to predict whether this is a 'diaphragm' (muscular ceiling, I thank you) or something that will change with time, motivation and an injection of money into training and decades of encouraging women to the same level that men have benefitted from.

But this is at an elite level. This is at the highest end of professional sport, and measuring a tiny fraction of practice – and measuring only what can be measured. How much of a bearing should that have on entry-level sport? What might actually change in terms of attitudes towards sports, sexism and one's own body if we completely ditched the gender segregation in PE in schools? It's also worth considering that 'at school age variation within gender is larger than variation between genders, yet there is no tendency to segregate a sports class on the basis of height or strength, only to segregate for gender',[15] which throws the 'protection' argument under the bus somewhat.

However, there is another important dimension to this argument: You may recall that being male/female is not as binary as we think. You may remember the headlines in 2009 when Caster Semanya was subjected to 'gender testing' (and some very nasty personal abuse) after winning gold at the World Championships.[16] Aside from the moral implications, gender testing is neither as easy nor as clear-cut as checking for a chromosome. There are plenty of cases of people developing hormonally as one gender when their chromosomes are the opposite, as well as a variety of people who fit neither specification. As previously discussed, an estimated 1.7% of all people are 'intersex', with another huge number identifying as transsexual, gender-neutral or various other gender concepts that are much more complex than M/F. So where does this leave the 'sports by gender' discussion? How can we respectfully include all genders?

At entry and intermediate levels, one could argue that these differences simply aren't important, especially as ranking pupils isn't or shouldn't be the sole goal of PE. Another compelling argument is the idea that not all physical activity is, or need be, competitive. Do we have gendered yoga? Why not?

If the goal of PE lessons is to develop a pupil's relationship with their own body, enjoying and extending its capabilities, how should or could PE be structured around this?

What gets taught under 'PE' at your school? Do you do dance, Zumba, yoga or pilates? Archery, gymnastics, weight training, hula hooping, horse riding, climbing? Do you feel that any of these are gendered? Why?

There is such a strong message in 'Men are stronger than women; boys are stronger than girls'. Is it true? As a statistician, I know we can prove almost anything with the right data. I also know that the questions we ask really matter. The binary-gender-competition model can be so, so harmful. I don't honestly know the consequences of mixing all genders in when it comes to PE at various levels – and because this is such a complex issue, I wouldn't want to unilaterally advocate for it.

But failing to question the 'Boys and girls are different' message bellowing out from the decision to segregate is something that really worries me.

PE is just the symptom, not the cause

If we assume all boy-girl physical interactions are based on sex, we are suggesting no other discourse is possible. If sexual harassment is happening in PE, it's happening elsewhere too – there's a wider problem.

> At the 2002 [Olympic] Games, men were covered twice as much as women during worldwide primetime slots .... It is interesting to note that all of the sports in which women received the majority of the coverage involved the wearing of swimsuits or leotards.[17]

In the film *Million Dollar Baby*, we see a 'girl' learn to box like a champ. Well, at least like a female champ, which isn't quite as good, but well done anyway for trying, eh? The film is of its time in many ways – predictably sexist (indeed this is the main obstacle in the film), at times racist, full of quirks. One saving grace, however, and something which stands out to me like a neon sign, is that there is *no sex* in the film at all. No attraction. No love storylines. Very few shots of Maggie, the female protagonist, in her underwear; or sweaty skin-montages; or her body slowly getting sexier as she trains. The relief for me (especially as the central relationship, between Maggie and her trainer, is female-male) was enormous, and complete.

Can you think of another film where that is the case?

If we are worried about sexual attraction 'getting in the way' of sports, we have just cause for concern. Dominant media narratives show bodies getting more muscular, thinner or shapelier; physical skills being gained over time (only) as ways to attract others, as if bodies were nothing more than gift-wrapping for oblivion-inducing sexual encounters. Female bodies, so scrutinised anyway, may feel particularly visible under the magnifying lens of lessons in physical development that are often focused on speed, power and strength. Any 'failure' may be met with a need to account for their entire gender: 'See, I told you girls can't throw!' or sexualizing: 'Look at her boobs jiggle when she does that!'

Is segregation the answer to this? Not, I would suggest, in the long term. The problem is the unchecked assumption that relating to one another's bodies follows a script headed 'sexual' or 'humiliation' in big bold letters, that aggressive competition is more important than respectful interaction and that making mistakes in PE, just as in every other subject, needs to be a symbol of our identity rather than a normal part of getting better skills. Separating genders just enforces this message.

Now/later

Now: What kinds of sports do you like and how did you choose them? How do you relate to the limits and capabilities of your body? Does this feel gendered to you? How do you want others to perceive your body and what it can do?

Later: How does your school organise PE lessons and extra-curricular sport, and to what extent are they gendered? What kinds of sports go on at break times and who does them? Can you think of ways to break down these barriers and encourage students to interact with sport in different ways?

Graham says

We need to give our children the opportunity to play different sports regardless of gender and give them the safe space to try these activities, and we need to make sure that children respect each other without regard to their ability. I know many schools do not segregate PE in primary schools, and long may this continue! Mixed PE helps foster a sense of team, of working together, of helping each other that goes across gender boundaries. And most crucially, it helps boys and girls to respect each other more.

A true story: There was once a girls' football team that, despite having plenty of ability and being very keen, could not win a game; they were constantly beaten but enjoyed themselves anyway. Then there was a culture shift in the school, and girls were told they can achieve and do anything they set their minds to, giving them greater confidence and belief in themselves. Two years later and the girls' team were champions, winning both the league and the cup. You could say it was just lucky? A different cohort of girls? Better training methods? Maybe, but maybe it's also about self-belief. We are seeing a whole group of girls now that not only want to play football but play football well and believe they can win. We have also seen a rise in boys wanting to attend dance classes and, generally, children feeling safer trying things that they may not have tried before, because stereotypes told them they couldn't.

As a school we do something called the 'Golden Mile', where classes go out and run for 12 minutes each day, as research shows this helps with concentration and health. We have runners of different abilities, but we all accept and respect this. (I sometimes level out the playing field by asking them to run like different animals.) Because of this, our school has greatly improved the fitness of our children, meaning we are now far more successful at sporting events. Just this year we won several long-distance running festivals, and I'm proud to say our boys and girls did the double, winning both the league and the cup.

Coverage of female sport has improved, but it is still an important area to look at with pupils. Look at newspapers, websites, TV. What do children notice? How much of the coverage is based on male sports? Why do you think this is? Look also at the disparity in wages and prize money, especially in football. Male footballers often earn more in a day than a female footballer earns in a year. Is this fair? Why is there such a difference in prize money? We looked at this as a class and then wrote letters to newspaper, radio and TV stations. We also wrote speeches and created campaigns. The children were passionate about it; it was relevant and important to them.

Just recently the record for attendance of a women's football match was broken; it was a crowd of 60,739 people, there to see Barcelona beat Atletico Madrid. The record before that was 53,000 at Goodison Park to see Dick Kerr's Ladies versus St. Helen's Ladies, and the year was 1920. Coverage of women's sport and the visibility of women as pundits have improved, but TV coverage is still often hidden away on some obscure TV station or at some god-awful time of night. So while things are getting better, we know we have a long way to go.

Tl;dr

Physical education lessons can be the site of identity work for students, and often they are places and spaces where gender is (mis)constructed. Exploring a wide variety of types of activity and reconsidering gender segregation in school sports are important ways to make change, as is questioning the influence of elite professional sports on what happens in schools, where pupils' attitudes to their own bodies and their capabilities are being shaped. We often make assumptions about gender-coded movement. It is time to question those assumptions.

References

1. Paton, G. (2013). *Splitting school PE Lessons by gender 'damages girls.'* Retrieved from https://www.telegraph.co.uk/education/educationnews/10528867/Splitting-school-PE-lessons-by-gender-damages-girls.html
2. Autumn-born children better at sport, says study. Education. *The Guardian*. (2014). Retrieved April 22, 2019, from https://www.theguardian.com/education/2014/jun/22/autumn-born-children-better-sports-study
3. Anderson, E. (2008). 'I used to think women were weak': Orthodox masculinity, gender segregation, and sport. *Sociological Forum*, 23(2), 257–280. https://doi.org/10.1111/j.1573-7861.2008.00058.x
4. Wellard, I. (Ed.). (2007). *Rethinking Gender and Youth Sport*. London, England; New York, NY: Routledge.
5. *Participation of women in the Olympics*. (2019). Wikipedia. Retrieved from https://en.wikipedia.org/w/index.php?title=Participation_of_women_in_the_Olympics&oldid=892265399
6. Weber, C. (2003). *'Oi. Dancing boy!' Masculinity, sexuality, and youth in Billy Elliot*. Retrieved April 22, 2017 from https://www.colorado.edu/gendersarchive1998-2013/2003/01/15/oi-dancing-boy-masculinity-sexuality-and-youth-billy-elliot
7. Oliver, W., & Risner, D. (2017) *An introduction to dance and gender*. Retrieved April 22 from https://d2r6h7ytneza11.cloudfront.net/title/c6712e18-54c1-4bea-8ea7-094e59c26739/oliverrisnerexcerpt.pdf
8. Ward, V. (2018, August 3). *Strictly Come Dancing* will not have same-sex couples this year. *The Telegraph*. Retrieved from https://www.telegraph.co.uk/news/2018/08/03/strictly-come-dancing-will-not-have-same-sex-couples-year/

9. 'Liquid lead dancing': A conversation on fluid lead/follow gender roles. (2016). Retrieved April 22, 2019, from The Dancing Grapevine website: https://www.danceplace.com/grapevine/liquid-lead-dancing-a-conversation-on-fluid-leadfollow-gender-roles/

10. Copp, T. & Fox, J. (2015). *Ballroom dance that breaks gender roles.* Retrieved from https://www.ted.com/talks/trevor_copp_jeff_fox_ballroom_dance_that_breaks_gender_roles

11. Mondschein, E. R., Adolph, K. E., & Tamis-LeMonda, C. S. (2000). Gender bias in mothers' expectations about infant crawling. *Journal of Experimental Child Psychology, 77*(4), 304–316.

12. Fine, C. (2017). *Testosterone rex: unmaking the myths of sex of our gendered minds* (First edition). London: Icon Books Ltd.

13. https://en.wikipedia.org/wiki/Netball

14. Meyer, R. (2012, August 9). *We thought female athletes were catching up to men, but they're not.* Retrieved April 22, 2019, from *The Atlantic* website: https://www.theatlantic.com/technology/archive/2012/08/we-thought-female-athletes-were-catching-up-to-men-but-theyre-not/260927/

15. Hall, E., & Lawson, S. (2014). *Are segregated sports classes scientifically justified?* Conference: 6th IWG World Conference on Women and Sport at Helsinki, Finland. Retrieved from https://www.researchgate.net/publication/282646633_Are_segregated_sports_classes_scientifically_justified

16. Kessel, A. (2009, August 19). Gold medal athlete Caster Semenya told to prove she is a woman. *The Guardian.* Retrieved from https://www.theguardian.com/sport/2009/aug/19/caster-semenya-gender-verification-test

17. Feeney, N. (2014, February 21). *A brief history of sexism in TV coverage of the olympics.* Retrieved April 22, 2019, from *The Atlantic* website: https://www.theatlantic.com/entertainment/archive/2014/02/a-brief-history-of-sexism-in-tv-coverage-of-the-olympics/284003/

Sex, touch and consent

Tentacle porn – the safest place – ornaments – you are mine – a favourite politician's pastime – objects – tethered – a legitimate rape – deep shame – bleeding out of the textbook pages – gone too far – impolite children – tonic immobility – a much larger territory – how binary – the tyranny of hydraulics – insulted by a soft penis – brake and accelerator – sexually successful people – unconscious people don't want tea – a type of punctuation – very, very particular – no when they mean yes – nothing gets done about it

Stats

Seventy-five percent of pupils had not learned about consent during SRE classes.[1]

As of 2006, there were still 53 countries where a husband could not be prosecuted for the rape of his wife. Even in Germany, rape laws were amended only in 1997 to create a legal category of 'marital rape'.[2]

The issues

Picture the scene: You're in your (real or fantasised) lover's (or lovers') arms. (Or not-arms. Human or non-human. Hey, I enjoy tentacle porn. Do whatever you like in your own mind, friend.)

You can feel the warmth of them. They are gently stroking you on the arm. You are safe and comfortable. You have nowhere to be. Your skin feels lightly but electrically charged, a buzzing that goes down a few centimeters deep. You're drowsy but you're not asleep.

How do you feel?

In their book *The Body Keeps the Score*, Dr. Bessel van der Kolk writes. 'Touch makes us feel intact, safe, protected and in charge. Touch is the most elementary tool we have to calm down'.[3]

They interview a touch therapist, who tells them how they work with trauma patients: 'The first place I might touch is the hand or forearm, because that's the safest place to touch anybody – the place where they can touch you back'.

Touch can be an extraordinary expression of love. In the 1980s, researchers realised that the 'minimal touch' rules surrounding preterm babies were holding them back from effective recovery; massaging these little ones gently for a few sessions a day helped them put on weight and thrive much faster – 47% faster – than those who did not receive the touch treatment.[4] Nowadays, we know that giving touch therapy to babies has the effect of 'reduced heart and respiratory rates, enhanced ability to rest, improved coordination in sucking, swallowing, and breathing, and a greater ability to engage with the environment',[5] and infants and children who have missed out on loving touch can suffer a variety of heartbreaking consequences, including malnutrition and even death.[6] Touch saves lives.

The bad touch

All over the world, girls and women are routinely objectified. I don't just mean 'looked at sexually' – I mean treated as objects, things, commodities, trinkets. In the film *Dirty Dancing*, there's a part where Lisa is flirting with Robbie, the sexy-but-no-good waiter, and her parents say that their daughter Baby is going to change the world. 'Lisa's going to decorate it', her mother says smugly, and Robbie responds with the perfect one-liner: 'She already does'.

As a child, this seemed to me the epitome of romance. It's hard not to respond, in the milieu of the film, with anything but a sweet kind of sentiment to that.

But I don't respond that way now.

Women and girls are not scenery or props or wallpaper or ornaments.

We do not exist for the sake of being pretty. We do not owe anyone being pretty. If you identity as female and you are reading this, please tell yourself, if you haven't before, that you don't owe the world something beautiful to look at. You don't. You are not a thing. It is not a duty, to yourself or anyone else, to make the best of yourself or to brighten up the place or to smile, or to display your face or body like a sodding floral vase. You, just you, are enough.

And, unlike a vase, we are not here to be picked up and put down at will.

No one is, right?

What about babies? Infants? Toddlers? Where does it end? This is a continuum problem, and it's related to objectification.

In research literature, objectification is defined as occurring 'when a person's body parts or functions are separated from the person, reduced to the status of instruments, or regarded as capable of representing the entire person'.[7] That's the feeling you get when you see toilet doors separated by gender, and there's an hilarious drawing of boobs on one and a penis on the other. It's also a pretty powerful and scary thing, because if objectification means we see isolated body parts as representing the whole (and, as you'd expect, this effect is way more pronounced on women than on men in our society), and if we continue to live in a world where we casually touch one another without consent, there's a sense of ownership and claiming that goes along with that. I grope your breasts, your breasts *are* you to me, I am touching you and holding you against your will. It's hard not to conclude *You are mine*. Temporarily, when a person is an object to another person, they are less than human, a body part or collection of them, and their power is reduced.

What does this look like in schools?

UK Feminista uses the government's legal definition of 'Unwanted sexual touching': Touching 'wherein the target does not consent to the touching and the perpetrator does not reasonably believe they consent, constitutes sexual assault .... 37% of girls report experiencing sexual harassment, compared to 6% of boys. Female students are also significantly more likely to describe multiple incidents and more severe cases of sexual assault'.[8]

Those reported incidents are likely to be the tip of the iceberg. Grabbing girls by the breast, squeezing their rears and touching their thighs are so frequent as to be commonplace. On Twitter threads, women everywhere are discussing their horribly similar stories. The hashtag #MeToo has been used by millions of women worldwide in the past decade. So has #everyday sexism. Take a moment now, if you can, and search for either one on social media. You might want to sit down. Or you might be unsurprised, if saddened. This isn't just a secondary issue, either; many people, most (but not all) of them women, report being touched in a sexual way at a very young age.

Why do female bodies apparently belong to everyone else?

'Because it's literally enshrined in law. It's a favourite political pastime .... If men, instead of women, had babies, it is reasonable to suspect the right to terminate a pregnancy would not be under constant and aggressive attack across the Western world', writes Laurie Penny for the *New Statesman*.[9]

Women's bodies as vessels for life are often touched, not lovingly, but with fear and hate and intimidation and control, because of the terror that they can make life-or-death decisions; that power has to be wrested away from them, using moral or religious argument, before they have time to grasp it, because otherwise women's bodies would belong to them, instead. Men touch women, but everywhere forbid women from touching themselves: the ultimate contempt for their authority over the female body. The issues of sexuality, pregnancy and abortion pervade the way we think about women's bodies. Women have historically been seen passive vessels, hosts, objects.

At the time of this writing, around a third of the countries in the world have laws forbidding abortion.

How do you feel about abortion? Could you conceive of a time in your life when you were not ready to have children or chose not to do so?

There's a famous philosophical thought experiment that begins with you waking up in a hospital bed.

Terrified, you look around. You are tethered to the bed, and tubes are coming out of your arm. In the bed beside you is a creature unlike anything you have ever seen before, similarly tethered. You notice with horror that the tubes join one another. You are somehow supporting this parasite. The doctor comes in.

'Thank you for your service in an emergency. The Entity was gravely ill and only a brave human like yourself could help. We saw you on the street, seized and tested you, and miraculously you fit the profile we needed. You've been unconscious for a day or so. You are currently sustaining its life. I hope you are not in any pain?'

You are shocked. You give a tiny shake of the head.

'But ... I have a job, and a family! How long will this be for?'

The doctor puts down their folder and smiles at you.

'Oh, less than a year. You have exactly the right blood type and tissue match, and after that time the Entity will be strong enough to be disconnected. We'll bring you everything you need; your family can come and visit'.

Some theories in philosophy suggest that the idea of *moral obligation* or duty does not apply here. It would be a kind and generous thing to sustain the creature for all those months, but morality would not demand that you do. The price is too high, and you didn't ask to be put in the position. All sorts of thing could and should influence your decision – how busy you are, how wealthy, how important your other obligations are – but the crucial thing is that it is your decision to make. No one would blame you for disconnection.

What if you did consent to the original situation, in an emergency? What if you didn't know it might be for such a long time? What if you consented to be tested, knowing the risk that you would be a perfect match was low?

You may be seeing the parallels to pregnancy here. Misconceptions (pun acknowledged) abound. Some people are so misguided about the idea of consent in pregnancy that it has left many policymakers in doubt about whether women can somehow magically control whether sex results in conception or not. Ideas are still rife that women can make a pregnancy disappear if they don't want it, and one that remains must be one they secretly desire. If this sounds utterly bat-shit crazy (and against the rules of biology), have a look at this:

'If it's a legitimate rape, the female body has ways to try to shut that whole thing down', said U.S. Senate candidate Todd Akin in 2012. A 'legitimate rape'?[10]

The same year, presidential candidate Rick Santorum said that rape victims should just 'accept what God has given to you'.[11]

Another American politician, Jody Laubenberg, alleged that rape victims don't need access to legal abortion, because they can just use 'what's called rape kits, where a woman can get cleaned out'[10]

These are some of the people debating and making the laws about women's bodies, their lives and their livelihoods, without even the most basic understanding of the issues.

The other side of this is that women may feel completely unwarranted guilt and shame when they have experienced miscarriage. 'I wish people understood that miscarriages are the flip side of the coin', wrote one woman. 'If you've had a healthy pregnancy that went full term – you won a lottery. Short of obvious substance abuse and bull riding – your healthy baby is not the result of anything you did or didn't do'.[12]

The feelings of guilt, shame and enormous loss from women were prevalent. 'I felt, and feel, literally broken, and betrayed by my body', wrote another woman. 'It's irrational, but there is such a deep shame attached to not being able to carry a baby to term'.[11]

Similarly, people who choose not to have children report all kinds of intrusive questions, comments and value-laden assumptions about them. Let me say this clearly: Procreation is a free choice. Having sex does not mean you have to have children if conception occurs (almost no one thinks this in real life). Contraception, even with the best of intentions, fails. Pregnancy is a particularly powerful and strange co-opting of a woman's body that might bring with it all kinds of feelings, responsibilities and weirdness.

The pupils we are teaching in school will most likely deal with these issues one way or another, if they not done so already. We should be talking about them. Abortion, in particular, suffers from a nasty little backdoor-sinister-room-black-market reputation that makes people hush their voices and widen their eyes when it's brought up, that fosters silence and secrets and strangeness. It's a topic on the religious education curriculum like euthanasia and capital punishment, but unlike those, it is much more likely to be in the here and now, bleeding out of the textbook pages and into the messy and unpredictable domain of breaking news and making appointments and hot-water-bottles in bed. Hormones and abortion and periods and pregnancy-thoughts fill up a great deal of my life and make a heavy dent in all sorts of choices I have made and continue to make. The continued silencing of women on these issues contributes to the needless shame, dread and guilt we feel when we are forced to make these decisions without proper support, discussion or empathy.

In the TV series *BoJack Horseman*, abortion is confronted and explored in a characteristically dark, satirically funny manner. A newsreader asks, 'Has the concept of women having choices gone too far?' And, as is traditional, three old white guys in bow ties 'discuss' the matter around a big table. They conclude that it is indeed wrong for women to have choices about their own bodies. 'I can say that with confidence because I'll never have to make that decision, so I'm unbiased', says one.

This is both funny and painful. Making ridiculous pronouncements, laws and moral judgements about women's bodies and their use by men is so commonplace that we hardly even notice it anymore.

Exploiting women's feelings of guilt, shame and fear about carrying babies is a particularly chilling way to undermine their power. Telling them they shouldn't have sex ever, if they don't want a child, is similarly effective and powerfully gendered. It's a staple of the abortion debate. (Can you imagine telling men that?)

Women have spent many centuries having to work around the fact that if they want to have heterosexual sex, they might get pregnant – and if they get pregnant, everyone will know they've had sex. They have been touched, at times unwillingly, by men, and they have had to deal with life-changing consequences of that, while those same men sail airily by, telling them to feel ashamed and accept the heavy responsibility of dealing with the outcomes of their 'decisions'. Therefore, discussions about pregnancy and abortion cannot take place in a vacuum, and we must necessarily incorporate historical issues of responsibility and fairness. The heavy bias towards men policing women's bodies, and not vice versa, means this is an issue where equality feels difficult to find amid the noise. How might we ensure that all voices are heard and that we have difficult conversations, while still acknowledging the fact that, to a large extent, it is the bodies of women and girls that are being fought over in these political and private debates? And that, despite these issues affecting them disproportionately, their voices have been minimised?

Consentickles

If there's one thing to change about the way we teach our kids at school and at home, it's that we need to add this: Consent is more important than politeness.

It sounds okay when you say it like that, doesn't it?

Reasonable, even. But here's the rub: It is going to cause some arguments and some confrontations and some serious disharmony before things change. This is one of the stickiest ends of equality there is.

Picture this: Your children are at a family party. Uncle Dave comes over and picks one of them up and holds them upside down. They are half-laughing, half-protesting.

Is that ok?

Grandma comes over and starts tickling your nephew. He looks uncomfortable but smiles shyly.

Is that ok?

Your sister takes your screaming toddler from you and tells you to go and have a cup of tea. She rocks her, holding her arms firmly until she calms down.

Is that ok?

Dear me, I've met some impolite children. Kids who grab and stockpile stuff and cram their mouths full of food and never say please and who fail to even notice, never mind appreciate, the effort it takes just to keep them alive and vaguely entertained. I'm a big fan of manners. In the past, I used to tell my classes that I may have been teaching them maths, but first and foremost and always before that, I was teaching them how to be good, polite and considerate humans. But it's only since raising my own children that I've realised a huge truth: When safety is in question, manners don't matter.

We instinctively know this at the extreme end, I think. When a stranger asks for the time, we smile and give it to them; when they ask for our wallet, we aren't worried about their feelings and the social contract anymore; we know only that the situation is a criminal one and we need to protect ourselves. But a few notches down that ladder, there are situations where we are sowing the seeds for a complicated and not altogether helpful relationship with consent, if we are not careful.

In the situations described above, did you think they were okay?

If you did, why?

When we prioritise being polite to Grandma over our bodies being touched without our consent – however well-intended – we tell children that they owe people their touch. That their bodies belong to others. That they cannot say no, sometimes.

You see where I'm going with this?

Touch may have a range of positive benefits for children, but gender differences in touch also have consequences. Mothers tend to touch their daughters more and keep them closer, for example; adolescent boys touch girls more than the other way around. Touch can be a powerful way of controlling others as well as protecting them. Just because someone wants to touch you doesn't mean you have to accept it. The sooner we start to teach children this, the more we help them understand that when touch is unwanted, they are in control of refusing it.

Why is this important?

In England, around 20% of women and 4% of men have experienced some type of sexual assault since the age of 16, equivalent to an estimated 3.4 million female victims and 631,000 male victims.

Five out of six of those crimes go unreported.[13]

When faced with sexual assault, a common response is to freeze – it's called *tonic immobility*. In one study, 70% reported significant tonic immobility, and 48% reported extreme tonic immobility, during the assault. This reaction, as opposed to fighting back or screaming, can cause extreme guilt, stress and posttraumatic stress disorder (PTSD) in victims who are all too aware that they have not done as society 'expects' in the circumstances.[14]

How do we create a consent culture where we understand better what people want (and don't want) regarding their bodies? Where we ask, answer and listen more, routinely, on any issue related to personal touch? And specifically, how do we ensure that when it comes to sex, we talk about consent not as a quick add-on but as central to our understanding of what sexual touch *is*?

What is sex, exactly?

> The parts that most people call sex – the parts that involve lips and nipples and clits and cocks and orgasms. Sex may involve these parts, but we don't think it's about them – the genitals and other erogenous zones are the 'how', not the 'what' …. Sex covers a much larger territory than genital stimulation leading to orgasm.[14]

In the United Kingdom, the legal age of consent for 'any sexual activity' is 16. In practical reality often, there is a spectrum of acceptability where those aged under 16 but near to it are understood to be able to give informed consent depending on maturity. Young people aged 12 and under are not legally able to give consent to any sexual activity.[15]

One of the things that is interesting about sex is how binary we insist it is. 'Did you have sex?' or 'Have you lost your virginity?' feels so much like a yes/no question, doesn't it?

How would you define sex?

Did you think of penetration? Oral or hand stimulation? Did you include masturbation or exclude it? Did you include kissing? Did you include only activities that (for you) lead to orgasm?

Often, as adults, we may tread such well-worn narratives of sexual journeys – beginning with a kiss and ending with a (possibly) mutual orgasm – that we forget there are fascinating stops along the way, not to mention other paths, alleyways and turnings we haven't even explored yet. When an age-appropriate young person starts to explore sexual attraction, we may jump to the (heteronormative) conclusion that this is penetrative male-female sexual intercourse.

At what age do you think it's ok for a young person to kiss someone else? What about touch sexually? Is this affected by their maturity? What If the relationship is with a person of the same sex? What about a person with Down's syndrome or autism or a person who is deaf?

These are not easy questions, and they often feel uncomfortable to consider. 'Who "gets" to have sex?' seems to be an important political and personal question, and it often touches on people's disgust, protection or aggression mechanisms.

To enjoy sex, you have to come to terms with the body you are in. Some people get treated as non-sexual beings, including the elderly, the disabled and those who are not traditionally attractive. 'It is foolish and rude to assume that people with physical disabilities don't enjoy sex'.[14] Likewise, we may feel odd about elderly people's sexual activity or particularly worry about those with special educational needs. Some may respond to this by ignoring the prospect altogether. For parents of pupils with differently abled children, this is something they need to think about carefully, and if you teach such pupils, it is important to consider too. The right to be appropriately sexual when *we* choose is important.

Often, we ourselves are so obsessed with 'performance' and 'expectation' around sex that we forget to enjoy it. Sex raises important questions. Who am I? What's my sexual identity? How do I like to be touched? What does it mean if I say yes or no? What will people say about me? How will my sexual (hi)story unfold, between the sheets and on the streets? Our pupils are grappling with these issues and their precursors in playgrounds and classrooms and lunch halls. They frequently spill into our lessons in all kinds of ways, probably unwanted. How do you deal with it?

I once had a Year 10 maths lesson completely disrupted when it turned out that two of my pupils were in a bitter war over 'attempted' sex the night before. They dissected the episode angrily in front of me and the rest of the students. One thing that seemed obvious is an issue that Easton & Hardy call 'the tyranny of hydraulics'.[16] Sex in films and TV is about soft lighting, enthusiastic kissing and rippling toned bodies aligned in perfect synchrony. Sex in real life is so often about trying to guess the other person's thoughts, accidentally kicking things over, wondering whether to apologise, worrying or surreptitiously picking hair out of your mouth. Without good communication, our expectations may fall painfully short of reality, and we may feel cheated. People may feel insulted by a soft penis or a dry vulva, an aggressive kiss or a misjudged hair-pull. Knees may accidentally poke soft bits, and we may be in pain. Sheets may smell funny. Arguments may erupt over who ends up in the wet bit. Failure to reach orgasm may be blamed on another. Issues may arise over what to do with in-use tampons. Someone may not be as clean as one may have desired. Unexpected things are likely to pop up (or not). All these things require a level of communication and maturity to discuss, if we are to hope for something better and more realistically pleasurable. The discourse around sex needs to be more honest and more commonplace, with consent and listening at the heart of it. 'The historical censorship of sex has left us with another inability: the act of talking about sex, of putting into words what we do in bed, has become difficult and embarrassing'.[14]

In *Come as You Are*, Dr. Emily Nagoski helpfully explains that sexual stimulation may be thought of as a 'brake and accelerator' situation: Not only does a person need to be turned on (accelerator on), but they also need to feel safe, to be in a comfortable environment, to know they can stop, to be able to ask to go slow or to have a backup plan (brake off).[17] Discussion of safe words in schools sounds drastic, but I'm deadly serious. Or gestures. Sometimes we freeze when something hits our reptilian brain. Often, we have internalised the message 'it's not sexy to …' where the thing is really important. In our desire not to break the mood, we break our contract with ourselves to be clear about consent. This is often gendered, where males feel they must 'perform sex' (on, to) females, who must 'receive' it passively. Male in charge, female cannot question. This is heteronormative and unhelpful, and it takes away our sexual independence and freedom. Who initiates sex, controls what happens, asks for things and receives them, moves the action around and on, should be a 'liquid lead' situation (ha ha) – partners take turns being 'in charge', and they share, communicate and listen.

Masturbation

In the 1950s, Masters & Johnson conducted a series of experiments – the first of their kind to be so detailed – and concluded (among other things) that sexually successful (confident and able to communicate their needs) people masturbate.[15]

Knowing what you like and being able to ask for it is crucial (as is ability to read another person, to experiment and to take risks you are comfortable with). 'Your relationship with yourself is what you bring to a relationship with another person; it is what you have to share, personally, emotionally, and sexually'.[14]

If you masturbate, are comfortable with masturbation and are not ashamed, you do not approach another with a desperate need for them to 'fulfil' you. This works beyond sex – it's an emotional thing, too. You don't need another person to 'fix you'. You bring warmth and desire without total dependence. Yet we have gendered expectations about masturbation, too. We expect boys to explore themselves – expect it to the point where it is a funny trope. But we forbid girls from doing so, or think it's odd or shameful. Once again, we appear to be afraid of the power of female sexuality. Why?

What needs to change

As teachers, we are dealing with these issues implicitly and explicitly all the time – from the way we react when we find a tampon on the floor to the way we let very young pupils interact with our pregnant belly. Consent is the most pervasive and important idea, and the way we model it is important. The ideas inherent in it are not confined to sex but express a fundamental truth about bodies and touch – that we consider a person's expressed verbal and non-verbal responses to touch as crucial indicators of whether that touch has been received consensually *and we listen to them*.

Consent: not actually that complicated. The following was initially written as a blog by Emmeline May, and it's worth replicating in full here (with her kind permission).

Imagine instead of initiating sex, you're making them a cup of tea. You say 'hey, would you like a cup of tea?' and they go 'omg fuck yes, I would fucking LOVE a cup of tea! Thank you!' then you know they want a cup of tea.

If you say 'hey, would you like a cup of tea?' and they um and ahh and say, 'I'm not really sure ...' then you can make them a cup of tea or not, but be aware that they might not drink it, and if they don't drink it then – this is the important bit – don't make them drink it. You can't blame them for you going to the effort of making the tea on the off-chance they wanted it; you just have to deal with them not drinking it. Just because you made it doesn't mean you are entitled to watch them drink it.

If they say 'No thank you' then don't make them tea. At all. Don't make them tea, don't make them drink tea, don't get annoyed at them for not wanting tea. They just don't want tea, ok?

They might say 'Yes please, that's kind of you' and then when the tea arrives they actually don't want the tea at all. Sure, that's kind of annoying as you've gone to the effort of making the tea, but they remain under no obligation to drink the tea. They did want tea, now they don't. Sometimes people change their mind in the time it takes to boil that kettle, brew the tea and add the milk. And it's ok for people to change their mind, and you are still not entitled to watch them drink it even though you went to the trouble of making it.

If they are unconscious, don't make them tea. Unconscious people don't want tea and can't answer the question 'do you want tea?' because they are unconscious.

Ok, maybe they were conscious when you asked them if they wanted tea, and they said yes, but in the time it took you to boil that kettle, brew the tea and add the milk they are now unconscious. You should just put the tea down, make sure the unconscious person is safe, and – this is the important bit – don't make them drink the tea. They said yes then, sure, but unconscious people don't want tea.

If someone said yes to tea, started drinking it, and then passed out before they'd finished it, don't keep on pouring it down their throat. Take the tea away and make sure they are safe. Because unconscious people don't want tea. Trust me on this.

If someone said 'yes' to tea around your house last Saturday, that doesn't mean that they want you to make them tea all the time. They don't want you to come around unexpectedly to their place and make them tea and force them to drink it going 'BUT YOU WANTED TEA LAST WEEK', or to wake up to find you pouring tea down their throat going 'BUT YOU WANTED TEA LAST NIGHT'.

Do you think this is a stupid analogy? Yes, you all know this already – of course you wouldn't force feed someone tea because they said yes to a cup last week. Of COURSE you wouldn't pour tea down the throat of an unconscious person because they said yes to tea 5 minutes ago when they were conscious. But if you can understand how completely ludicrous it is to force people to have tea when they don't want tea, and you are able to understand when people don't want tea, then how hard is it to understand when it comes to sex?

Whether it's tea or sex, Consent Is Everything.[18]

As well as considering touch in general, this makes me reflect that we desperately need a new model for sexy stuff. That model has to include things like changing your mind, being able to say no to someone you've previously had sex with, taking rejection calmly and with understanding, being able to 'just' kiss someone and understanding that sleeping in a bed with someone is not, on its own, an invitation to sex.

This is a problem for many people – wrongly – because they've been brought up on a diet of shameful legacy ideas about women's enigmatic powerful sexiness and men's inability to control themselves in the face of its being unleashed. Let's think about that.

Do you think that I, as a pansexual woman, should be able to get changed next to other naked women?

Do you think their nakedness might, could, should, must arouse me?

Do you think these women are teasing me by getting naked?

Do you think they are safe around me?

Do you think I have the right to look at them and/or find them attractive?

Do you think that I, once aroused, I have the right to have sex with any, some or all of those who have 'provoked' that arousal?

'In the world around us, the sexualised female form features so often in almost every medium that it's essentially a type of punctuation'.[19] If you must, think of it as a full stop. Take a breath and pause.

People, you do not owe anyone else sex. Not after they've paid for drinks; not after they've bought you dinner; not after they've kissed you or got you a cab or walked you to your door. It's a complex social etiquette that works on sinister underground 'implications'. Breaking it will require some (re)education.

The strongest counterarguments and why they're wrong

'Pregnancy and particularly abortion are sensitive and political issues that we shouldn't discuss with pupils'.

'It shouldn't be left to us to teach consent in schools'.

'Kids shouldn't be having sex until at least 16; let's not talk to them about it until then'.

If they're (thinking about) having sex, we need to talk about pregnancy and abortion. The median age for first heterosexual intercourse in the United Kingdom is 16, but a third of respondents had sex before then.[20] If we consider sexual activity as a continuum rather than a binary, students begin to feel attraction and want to touch each other at a wide range of ages (and of course some not at all). If we wait to consider the possibility of pregnancy, conception, contraception and abortion until they are 16 or older, we are failing to include these really significant issues in the way our pupils think about and around sex. Properly thinking about abortion for the first time, not in the abstract but in the very, very particular, when you have just found out you might be pregnant and are probably terrified, when you may be emotional or anxious or off-guard, is not the way. A relatively small proportion of under-16s get pregnant in the United Kingdom (around 1 per 1000),[21] but the younger they are, the more likely they are to get an abortion – there are 12-year-olds out there, right now, having to face these issues.

> The various sexual offences laws in force in the UK do not affect the ability of professionals to provide confidential sexual health advice, information or treatment. Each specifically states that it is not an offence to provide information, advice and/or treatment if it is in order to protect the young person's sexual health, physical safety or emotional wellbeing.[22]

Yes, these issues can be both sensitive and political. Yes, there are possible clashes with religion and parents, and these may present real challenges. But we are talking about real bodies, real lives, real decisions and real young people who need help. I've seen up close what happens when a 13-year-old gets pregnant and doesn't have anyone to turn to, doesn't know what her choices are and what support is available and doesn't think her life is worth anything.

Consent issues are happening in schools; we can ignore them or deal with them. Research shows that schools are sites of unwanted touching. Young people are telling us this, too, in their own voices. What can or should we do in schools?

First, we think about the overt communication: the language – both spoken and non-verbal.

When was the last time you had sex with another person? If you wouldn't mind, think about how it was initiated. Was it a kiss? A touch? Did you speak?

Do you have 'patterns' of initiation with a partner you have known for a while where certain actions indicate sexytime?

Do you find it more difficult to know whether those you don't know as well want to have sex? Or easier, because it's more up front and out there?

The media models we have for sex tend to be twofold: almost completely silent (film and TV) or constant talking/groaning without actually saying much (porn). It's not surprising that people are weird about sexual communication. Talking about sex can be pretty tough. But you'll probably be surprised to hear that it may well be one of the most important things we can do to foster a good and healthy culture around consent.

You might find it odd and unsexy to hear someone say, 'May I kiss you?'

You might wince if someone said, 'Would it be ok if we had sex now?'

You might feel weird if someone asked as they touched you, 'Is this ok?'

You might feel it breaks the mood if, during sex, someone says, 'How are you doing?'

But the good news is this stuff can change. What is or can be sexy to folks is a source of never-ending wonder for me. If you have developed patterns of initiation in the past, especially non-verbal ones, then you can develop new ones that work in a similarly Pavlovian fashion. Sex is one of the arenas where weird becomes normal pretty quickly, in my experience.

Not only is it important to ask those questions (in whatever ways you feel comfortable doing so), it is also crucial that we be able to answer honestly. We can say no without rejecting the other person/ people. And that's a really, really hard thing to do.

But the alternative is paradigms of 'token resistance', such as this, taken from a real research paper written in my lifetime, looking at 'the common belief that many women say no to sex even when they mean yes and that their protests are not to be taken seriously'.[23] You might recognise this concept from a variety of song lyrics. It hasn't gone away. It's insidious in our culture.

But how, you may be asking, will this change my classroom? Are you asking me to change my sex life, actually? How on earth will one affect the other?

Of course, I can't guarantee it. But changing your behaviours and beliefs around consent, considering ideas about entitlement to touch and valid responses to touch, will likely change the way you respond to pupils who are dealing with – or not dealing with – these issues. It's so easy to say 'But curriculum!' 'But tradition!' or 'But parents!' We need to take the lead here.

> Expectations around asking for and receiving affirmative consent in intimate relationships have changed, and that is a very positive development for society. But just as we wouldn't expect students to learn the rules of algebra on their own, students deserve clarity – delivered sensitively – when it comes to consent.[24]

The alternative? *What we have right now.*

'Boys touch girls inappropriately in corridors and at lunch/break times. They all seem to find this normal'.

'The boys also slap the girls butts and touch their breasts without any consent'.

'In class boys talk about girls' bodies and what they "would do to them"'.

'A boy touched my bum and tried to touch my boob. I felt uncomfortable and I didn't tell him because I was scared but I tried to ignore him'.

'Boys often lift skirts up and whistle and treat girls in a sexual manner and nothing gets done about it'.[25]

Would you send your child to this school?

> ## Now/later
>
> **Now: Think about the way you model consensual touch in your school. How are pupils lifted, restrained, stopped, confronted or rewarded? How does this work in PE? Do pupils ever hold hands, and if so, how is this managed? Do pupils ever 'have' to touch anyone?**
>
> **Later: Can you discuss consent explicitly with pupils – in an assembly, in a PSHE lesson or as a response to an incident? Do they know and understand the word, and is it written into school policies?**

Graham says

We are lucky in our school because our headteacher understands the importance of a hug, and we have space to do this with our pupils (after asking permission first). This means that if our children of any gender are distressed, we can help to calm and soothe them. Do you find yourself treating boys and girls differently? Are you more caring and tactile with girls, and are you a bit rougher with boys? Don't be embarrassed; I am sure there are many people up and down the country who treat boys and girls differently, but we really need to reconsider these ideas.

We talk to our children about personal space, about having our own bubble and about not encroaching into anyone's safe space without permission. We talk about consent and what it means. This topic is not discussed in a sexual context with younger children. Rather, it means that if someone is doing something you don't agree with (such as if a sibling is annoying you), you have the power and the right to say stop. It is about teaching children about boundaries, and letting them know that if they feel uncomfortable about something, often these boundaries have been crossed. Lucy talks about family members kissing children, hugging them, turning them upside down and tickling, and often children are coerced by their parents into doing this. The familiar comedy trope might be 'Oh go on, give your granny a kiss' – but if our children don't feel comfortable with it (I often didn't), we should respect children's right to say 'NO'.

Tl;dr

The important, positive implications of sex and touch mean we have to consider the difficulties of issues that come along with them, like pregnancy, abortion and consent. The asymmetry of law and expectation surrounding female bodies is important to consider as part of these issues. Early discussion and reflection on these ideas – before pupils may have to confront them in their lives – is crucial.

References

1. Terence Higgins Trust. (2016). *Shh no talking: LGBT inclusive SRE in the UK*. Retrieved from https://www.tht.org.uk/sites/default/files/2018-07/Shh%20No%20talking%20LGBT%20inclusive%20SRE%20in%20the%20UK.pdf

2. Harari, Y. N. (2015). *Sapiens: A Brief History of Humankind* (J. Purcell & H. Watzman, Trans.). London: Vintage Books.

3. Van der Kolk, B. A. (2015). *The Body Keeps the Score: Brain, Mind and Body in the Healing of Trauma*. New York, NY: Penguin Books.

4. Goleman, D. (1988). The experience of touch: Research points to a critical role. *The New York Times*. Retrieved from https://www.nytimes.com/1988/02/02/science/the-experience-of-touch-research-points-to-a-critical-role.html

5. Hanley, M. A. (2008). Therapeutic touch with preterm infants: Composing a treatment. *Explore* (New York, NY), 4(4), 249–258. https://doi.org/10.1016/j.explore.2008.04.003

6. Szalavitz, M. (2010). *Touching empathy*. Retrieved April 22, 2019, from *Psychology Today* website: http://www.psychologytoday.com/blog/born-love/201003/touching-empathy

7. Gervais, S. J., Vescio, T. K., Förster, J., Maass, A., & Suitner, C. (2012). Seeing women as objects: The sexual body part recognition bias: Seeing women as objects. *European Journal of Social Psychology*, 42(6), 743–753. https://doi.org/10.1002/ejsp.1890

8. *Sexism in schools*. (2015). Retrieved April 13, 2019, from NEU website: https://neu.org.uk/advice/sexism-schools

9. Penny, L. (2015). *If men got pregnant, abortion would be legal everywhere.* Retrieved April 22, 2019, from https://www.newstatesman.com/politics/feminism/2015/12/if-men-got-pregnant-abortion-would-be-legal-everywhere

10. *Todd Akin still doesn't get what's wrong with saying "legitimate rape."* (n.d.). Retrieved April 22, 2019, from *Time* website: http://time.com/3001785/todd-akin-legitimate-rape-msnbc-child-of-rape/

11. *FACT CHECK: Did Republicans actually say these things about rape?* (n.d.). Retrieved April 22, 2019, from https://www.snopes.com/factcheck/personal-foul/

12. *People have misconceptions about miscarriage, and that can hurt.* (n.d.). Retrieved April 22, 2019, from https://www.mprnews.org/story/2015/05/08/npr-miscarriage

13. *Sexual offences in England and Wales.* Office for National Statistics. (n.d.). Retrieved April 22, 2019, from https://www.ons.gov.uk/peoplepopulationandcommunity/crimeandjustice/articles/sexualoffencesinenglandandwales/yearendingmarch2017

14. Möller, A., Söndergaard, H. P., & Helström, L. (2017). Tonic immobility during sexual assault – A common reaction predicting post-traumatic stress disorder and severe depression. *Acta Obstetricia et Gynecologica Scandinavica, 96*(8), 932–938. https://doi.org/10.1111/aogs.13174

15. *11 findings that revolutionized our understanding of sex – business insider.* (n.d.). Retrieved April 22, 2019, from https://www.businessinsider.com/11-findings-that-revolutionized-our-understanding-of-sex-2013-10?r=US&IR=T

16. Easton, D., & Hardy, J. W. (2017). *The Ethical Slut: A Practical Guide to Polyamory, Open Relationships and Other Freedoms in Sex and Love* (3rd edition). California, CA: Ten Speed Press.

17. Nagoski, E. (2015). *Come as You Are: The Surprising New Science That Will Transform Your Sex Life.* Scribe UK.

18. May, E. (2015). *Consent: Not actually that complicated.* Retrieved April 22, 2019, from http://rockstardinosaurpirateprincess.com/2015/03/02/consent-not-actually-that-complicated/

19. Burnett, D. (2018). How "provocative clothes" affect the brain – and why it's no excuse for assault. *The Guardian.* Retrieved from https://www.theguardian.com/science/brain-flapping/2018/jan/25/how-provocative-clothes-affect-the-brain-and-why-its-no-excuse-for-assault

20. *Sexual behaviour factsheet.* (2013). Retrieved April 22, 2019, from FPA website: https://www.fpa.org.uk/factsheets/sexual-behaviour

21. *Births in England and Wales.* Office for National Statistics. (2017). Retrieved April 22, 2019, from https://www.ons.gov.uk/peoplepopulationandcommunity/birthsdeathsandmarriages/livebirths/bulletins/birthsummarytablesenglandandwales/2017

22. *The law on sex.* (2013). Retrieved April 22, 2019, from FPA website: https://www.fpa.org.uk/factsheets/law-on-sex

23. Sprecher, S., Hatfield, E., Cortese, A., Potapova, E., & Levitskaya, A. (1994). Token resistance to sexual intercourse and consent to unwanted sexual intercourse: College students' dating experiences in three countries. *The Journal of Sex Research, 31*(2), 125–132.

24. *To empower young people, schools should teach students about consent.* (2018). Retrieved April 22, 2019, from https://www.forbes.com/sites/catherinebrown/2018/10/12/to-empower-young-people-schools-should-teach-students-about-consent/#1c90b570b6c8

25. *Sexism in schools.* (2017). Retrieved April 13, 2019, from NEU website: https://neu.org.uk/advice/sexism-schools

18 | Books, games and literature

Yum – seven pints of coke – better face cream – origamied – immersion therapy – a story about llamas – dainty and light – hardest to budge rocks – a big cat wrangler – an absent partner – a huge red F – segregated bookshelves – on a throne of dead babies – forced to play as men – spiteful little princes – YES! That's ME! – cultivation theory – a screaming racist misogynist alcoholic

Stats

A study by Florida State University of 6000 children's books found that only 31% had a central female character[1].

In 150 video games analysed in a large-scale content analysis, male characters were found to represent 85% of all video game characters, with only 15% of characters representing female identities; these researchers also found that 41% of the games surveyed did not include any female characters at all.[2]

The issues

I've just come back from a holiday, where I gluttonously feasted on seven whole books. Yum. In fact, I devoured them so fast that I had to ask to borrow two more from my mother-in-law. She asked what sort of thing I would like.

I thought to myself. If I gave her no guidance, what might she give me? How could I short-hand the types of book I liked to read versus the types I felt were wasting my time?

Now, I'm no book snob. I'll read light literature as well as heavy; I enjoy young adult fiction as well as research tomes. But some books are … well, toxic. Some books seem to serve the same function for the soul as seven pints of coke (liquid or powder, you decide) for the body: so easy and selfish and pleasure-giving that you forget about the distasteful aftermath. And after a while, so very boring.

Have you ever read a Jack Reacher book?

Cupcakes and shoes

So what did I tell my mother-in-law?

'Not too girly-looking', I messaged her. The reasoning being that while men get thrillers and noirs and sci-fi and crime novels and space operas (however light), and women seem to get … the leftovers. The worst end of the pink-cupcakes-and-shoes books, the ones where gender stereotypes might as well be straitjackets and all the men are 'hunky' and all the women are in need of a makeover and some gin with their girlfriends and there is almost never any kind of plot except a woman is having a hard time and she simply needs to 'find herself'. Which means to get drunk or buy better face cream.

I've now read seven Jack Reacher books. I fold over the corners of the pages when I read something I consider problematic; they're all pretty dog-eared and origamied by this point, which is how I imagine I'd end up if I tried to confront Jack Reacher about his internalised misogyny and toxic masculinity. (Maybe Reacher doesn't hit women as a rule, but I'm not exactly female, so it might be an interesting confrontation.) Why am I reading them if they're so sexist?

A friend described them to me, and I was intrigued. His words were something like 'I think … they're probably really sexist?' but with that lift at the end, like – can you tell me what you think? (Don't look so surprised: some men in some circumstances can be taught quite successfully to defer to the opinion of a more expert woman.)

So I read one. And another. And another. I'm so very intrigued by Lee Child's Jack Reacher books that I'm not even sure how to describe them. The writing is gratingly, achingly terrible, but you can get used to anything. Ditto the sexism. And I have got used to it, in the sense that the jarring isn't so absolute, so painful now as it was. Reading

Reacher books has been an exercise in immersion therapy, which has made me reflect extremely hard on what a person can indeed get used to and accept as 'normal'.

When you read a book, do you notice characters behaving in discriminatory ways? Does it bother you? Would you ever stop reading a book on that basis alone?

One of the main problems we all have – those of us who aren't incredible visionaries and boundary-breakers – is that we are largely confined to what we know. We tell the same stories. We adapt and extend the narrative, but we use the template, the model, the format. We can only use available discourses. Here's the beginning of a story for you:

> 'I'm going to tell you a story about llamas. It will be like every other story you've ever heard about llamas: how they're covered in fine scales; how they eat their young if not raised properly; and how at the end of their lives they hurl themselves – lemming-like – over cliffs to drown in the surging sea. They are, at heart, sea creatures, birthed from the sea, married to it like the fishing people who make their livelihood there.
>
> Every story you hear about llamas is the same. You see it in books: the poor doomed baby llama getting chomped up by its intemperate parent. On television: the massive tide of scaly llamas falling in a great majestic herd into the sea below. In the movies: badass llamas smoking cigars and painting their scales in jungle camouflage. Because you've seen this story so many times, because you already know the nature and history of llamas, it sometimes shocks you of course to see a llama outside of these media spaces. The llamas you see don't have scales. So you doubt what you see, and you joke with your friends about "those scaly llamas" and they laugh and say "Yes, llamas sure are scaly!" and you forget your actual experience'.[3]

If the available discourses about boys and girls are similarly twisted, confining and at odds with what we observe in experience, what might be the consequence of that?

'Women are dainty and light; men are large and strong'.

I've seen countless teachers ask for boys to carry equipment around the school. I've seen members of my family turn to male relatives to deal with heavy, messy or distasteful tasks. I've encountered expectations that I will dance a following role as a female-presenting person. I've seen my daughters patronised for taking part in strength training. I've been told I 'couldn't' carry things that I knew darn well I could.

Here's some problems with that narrative:

Up until about sometime around puberty, there is simply no clear difference in the physical strength of boys and girls. After that, the picture changes, with different rates of strength often (but not entirely) explained by variations in body size and composition and the puberty process affecting boys and girls differently. Girls seem to come out overall higher on other physical measures, such as flexibility and balance, and boys develop higher strength overall as they enter their teens. But the idea we keep returning to here is one of restriction. The variation *within* the category of male or female is *huge*. Although it may well be perfectly true to state that 'men are overall stronger than women', using this narrative to uniformly *classify* men and women as 'strong' and 'weak' is both restrictive and unhelpful. There are very strong women and very weak men. There are middling people of both genders. There are both boys and girls and others in our classrooms who don't know who they want to be yet, and the boring and binary message that boys are strong and girls are weak has huge implications for them.

Because we know that girls can be strong, in our experience (my youngest daughter at the time of this writing is a fearsome gymnast who can easily perform pull-ups and bench-press several kilograms and has a notably high pain threshold). But we don't make room for it in the discourse. We act surprised or disconcerted, or we simply don't allow them to show or develop strength or be interested in it or do activities that promote it. We keep on insisting that those llamas are scaly.

Which books do you remember reading and re-reading from your childhood? What kind of discourses did they present that might be problematic? Do you feel like you have internalised any of them?

What about textbooks?

Textbooks are often seen as objective organisers of knowledge, mere collections of reified curriculum content. In fact, as history has shown, teaching materials (including printed and commercially available textbooks) can be biased, discriminatory or just plain wrong. A UNESCO Policy paper on this issue:

> Textbooks convey not only knowledge but also social values and political identities, and an understanding of history and the world. Teachers and students trust textbooks as authoritative and objective sources of information, assuming that they are accurate, balanced and based on the latest scientific findings and pedagogical practice.[4] Gender bias in textbooks is one of the best camouflaged and hardest to budge rocks in the road to gender equality in education.[5]

This is a worldwide problem on a grand scale.

In the same global study, we see extensive evidence of 'the invisibility of women in teaching and learning materials and how this perpetuates women's marginal status in society. In many textbooks, stories, images or examples in textbooks either do not include women or depict them in submissive, traditional roles, such as housework and serving men'.[4]

How might you feel to see yourself continually painted in this light? That phrase is somewhat apt. Like a pre-Raphaelite model, you might feel someone has made you into someone you are not, all feminine and breasty and floaty and passive and sandwich-making, when you're actually a pretty deft motorbike mechanic or a fearless big cat wrangler or a scientist about to cure cancer, thank you very much.

'Studies of gender and language have found that gender bias and gender stereotypes in written text and pictures have deleterious effects for female students .... These effects include feelings of exclusion, devaluation, alienation and lowered expectations'.[6]

Women, as well as people of colour, disabled people and LGBTQ+ people are often invisible in our curriculum. If they're present, they may be represented in a way that minimises their contribution, or stereotypes them.

'When children do not see girls and women in the pages of textbooks and teachers do not point out or confront the omissions, our daughters and sons learn that to be female is to be an absent partner'.[7]

How often do you design your own classroom resources? Do you ever consider the gender balance, possible stereotypes or creeping biases that might be present in them?

Not only can there be small, implicit stereotypes in our lesson materials; sometimes there are great big gaping ones as well.

A parent tells a story in the book *Still Failing at Fairness* of her daughter coming home from school with a worksheet with the smiling faces of a man and woman at the top, and objects such as a nail, a sewing needle and thread, a screwdriver and a broom at the bottom. The students were supposed to connect the person with the tool that 'belongs' to them. 'In my house my husband does the cooking and I do the repair work, so you can imagine what the lines on my daughter's paper looked like. There was a huge red F in the middle of her worksheet'.

The parent contacted the teacher, who apologised and said the F would not count. Except ...

'This year my son is in her class. Guess what he brought home last week. Same worksheet – same F. Nothing had changed at all'.[7]

Let's not be that teacher who gets that feedback and doesn't listen to it.

Explicitly gendered

And these are just the insides of the books. Have you ever seen books titled *The Great Big Boy's Book of Adventures* or *Tiny Tales for Princess Tots with Tiaras* or something similar? Have you seen libraries or bookshops segregated by pink and blue, princesses and dinosaurs, glitter and adventure?

In Graham's documentary, we see his classroom bookshelves segregated by gender. 'Up and down the country', says the voiceover, 'there are segregated bookshelves like this'.

We see a shot of the 'passive princesses and aggressive heroes' on the fronts of the books. Javid says, 'It only takes a few books to change the children's minds, to offer them alternatives to macho men and passive women'.

What needs to change

The very understandable lag in time between new textbooks being produced and schools purchasing them, coupled with funding issues and budget cuts, may mean that schools are working with textbooks that may be 10, 20 or 30 years old. Add to this the ideas about quality that might prevail (such as that a good textbook will 'stand the test of time') and the cyclical nature of educational discourse, and it may be relatively common for textbooks that were written some time ago to be used in contemporary classrooms. While the idea, explanations and exercises might still be of good quality, elements of culture and zeitgeist that influence perception of gender and/or sexuality may then creep in 'under the radar'. Marie Curie might be standing behind her husband at the microscope; the pronoun 'he' might be used exclusively; only white male discourses might prevail; ideas about women's and LGBTQ+ rights might be completely missing. We've got to notice and challenge this stuff at multiple levels.

I'm a big board game fan. In 2016, a game called *One Deck Dungeon* was launched on Kickstarter.

Here are a few of the 1-star Amazon reviews:

- 'Why are all five characters female? ... [S]eeing a woman that huge and beefed up is very abnormal but a natural choice for a male. This is very sexist, and shouldn't be tolerated'.

- 'Unfortunately, it was only after getting this discrimination-laden game that I decided to check out the reviews – something I should have done before buying'.

- 'My boys and I (and my wife) have no interest in playing female characters that have thematic disparity and I have no interest in supporting companies that have no intelligent reason to have gender disparity in games'.

- 'Only women characters. I guess they don't want me to play. Don't think I'll be buying this after all. Misandry noted. If they make a version for men, or for both sexes, I may buy that'.

- 'This gets a single star because of the agenda it pushes. No male heroes for those of us who don't want to be forced to play as women'.

- 'Sexist game by excluding males'.

Its crime, as you may have guessed, is to have an all-female-presenting suite of characters. Such exclusivity has been something of a staple of video games, board games, films and books since, um, forever – except the other way around, with men. Note the language here. These men are experiencing the feeling of being 'forced' to be represented by something they don't identify with, and they're angry about it. They're irritated. They feel excluded and invisible. They feel pushed out and unheard.

Smarts, doesn't it?

One study [of board games] found that only five percent of games analyzed featured only women on the cover, 5.8 percent featured a group of people made up of primarily women and 62.6% had a cover that featured only men.[8]

In our world, so many have been 'forced to play as men' for so long, you might forgive their lack of sympathy. (Studies show that women engage in 'gender masking' online to protect themselves from harassment and confrontation.[9]) So many have been 'forced to play as white' or 'forced to play as straight' – and fighting for some kind of representation has been billed as 'bringing politics into gaming'. Ha. Like it wasn't there before. Like the unthinking orator who swears they 'don't have an accent', our games, our stories and our narratives have been chock-full of politics, always – it's just that some of you just didn't see it because it represented you so well. It didn't jar because it chimed, instead. The deep, self-satisfied note of resonance is the background to your life, the white (male) noise that lulls you sweetly to sleep. You only notice it when it isn't there anymore, and then you wake up and start squalling.

Our stories need diversifying, desperately.

This is not just about women and men. It encompasses so many of our other intersectional identities, too.

> Across the world, people with disabilities are underrepresented in textbooks, perpetuating their invisibility and disadvantage .... In the English primary school textbooks, only seven images out of 867 (0.8%) showed people with a disability.[4]

Some people are invisible, and some are depicted negatively and harmfully. Discussing harmful messaging – and that which is invisible, erased, the never-quite-made-it-to-publication ghosts of our textbooks – with students is absolutely vital, not only to counteract such messages but to explore the idea that textbooks, story books and both printed and digital materials are as fallible as the humans that make them.

The strongest counterarguments and why they're wrong

- 'We can't make every category of person a protagonist in a story – it's artificial'.

- 'Books are just stories, just fun, just entertainment – take your politics elsewhere'.
- 'We can't just replace all the textbooks – there's no budget, and anyway, they're all biased'.

My kingdom for some representation. There are so many people on this planet that seem to get angry if a female, disabled, queer or trans person gets to be the hero, without that unusual characteristic being their 'character flaw'. Being queer is not a character flaw. It is not the only important thing about a person. One sweet, sweet day we won't even need to comment on this stuff anymore – but right now, it seems to piss people off so royally that they act like spiteful little princes who've been asked to share a single toy from a heap of thousands.

Judging by our English curriculum in 2019, you might be forgiven for thinking that people with disabilities, women or LGBTQ+ people simply don't exist. What we have *right now* is artificial, and it's contributing to the nasty little sense of entitlement some men are growing up with, convinced that the world revolves around them, their needs and their stories, and that everyone else is a bit-player in their storyline. Exactly how much representation is the right amount, and who gets to be represented and how, are complex and messy issues, and people's feelings will no doubt get hurt. But the alternative – a diet of books and games and stories so vanilla, so blessedly bland and blindingly boring that we don't, each of us, now and then get to jump up and yell 'YES! That's ME!' when we identify strongly with a character – *that's* a world we should have left behind 50 years ago with routinely smoking ourselves to death in the name of glamour.

Just not so stories. We can only use available discourses. Stories, books, narratives, tropes – all contribute to the way we act, react and interact with one another. Stories carry power.

> Cultivation theory posits that, over time, exposure to media that selectively limits or presents stereotypical depictions of certain demographic segments can shift social perception and drive real-world decision making.[8]

'Children's books reinforce, legitimate and reproduce a patriarchal gender system'.[10] We still have a real absence of central characters in children's and young adult fiction who are non-male, who are non-heteronormative and whose difference is not the pivotal plot point of the story. A few recommendations from the hundreds that exist: the *Circle of Magic* series by Tamora Pierce; *The Other Side of Truth* by Beverly Naidoo; *Rosie Revere, Engineer* by Andrea Beaty; the *Pippi Longstocking* series by Astrid Lindgren; *Infinity and Me* by Kate Hosford. You don't need me to decide for you: Order or borrow a few new books that look at gender or nonconformity in new ways, and share them with your pupils.

A discriminating eye. Of course, we can't just replace everything problematic (and we would probably get things that are also problematic, in different ways). The solution has to also include teaching pupils and staff to look at things with a discriminating eye, to encourage them to notice, to critique and to rewrite bits of 'accepted' texts so they understand these are not mystical and received, semi-religious and perfect, but human and fallible and written by Dave a few miles away who was on a deadline and wanted to get to the pub, or Henry 50 years ago who was a screaming racist misogynist alcoholic. Texts are just people's ideas written down; published texts are just the same with a bit of (usually capitalist) weight behind them. That weight might have all kinds of agendas that don't include equality, fairness or representation. (Why should it, unless we demand it?) Thinking more medium and long term, then, it's about factoring in gender biases when making decisions about what to buy or design and putting pressure on publishers to care about this stuff too.

Now/later

Now: Look at the textbooks you use in your classroom. Who has written them and how old are they? Have you come across any explicit or implicit bias in them? Do you feel able to share these thoughts with your pupils?

Later: How often do reading or library books in your school get updated, and who does the updating? What are the criteria for choosing them? Can you suggest some criteria that explicitly address gender or other stereotyping?

Graham says

One of the things that I didn't expect when the documentary was being filmed was for Dr. Javid to scrutinise my book corner. Looking back now, it makes perfect sense – my books were pretty gendered. As a teacher we want to foster a love of reading in our children, so I went to book stores and bought books that I thought would interest my children, such as the 'Beast Quest' books for the boys and 'Fairy Flower' stories for the girls. Of course, these show male protagonists having adventures and battling evil, and female protagonists worrying about friendships and flying around. What I failed to realise is that I needed to provide different stories for the children that went across gender – stories that showed brave, bold, strong female characters and boys who cared and showed emotion. Then, and only then, could we improve our emotional literacy by talking about how the characters in the story behaved.

There are so many brilliant gender stereotype-busting books now available, and there are new examples being released almost daily, but here are a few I would recommend:

- *This Is Not a Bedtime Story* by Will Mabbit. Dad wants to read Sophie a bedtime story, but she doesn't want one filled with kittens and pink fluffy bunnies – she wants monsters and action!
- *William's Doll* by Charlotte Zolotow. William wants a doll – to hug, to feed, to tuck in and kiss goodnight. 'Don't be a creep', says his brother. 'Sissy, sissy', chants the boy next door. His father buys him trains and a basketball – but not the doll that William really wants. Then one day, someone comes along who understands why William should have his doll.
- *Pearl Power* series by Mel Elliott. Pearl is a feisty 5-year-old who believes in equality and wants the world to believe in it too.
- *10,000 Dresses* by Marcus Ewart. In her dreams, Bailey is a young girl. Every night she dreams about magical dresses. Unfortunately, when Bailey wakes up, nobody wants to hear about her beautiful dreams, because Bailey is a boy and shouldn't be thinking about dresses at all. Then Bailey meets an older girl who is touched and inspired by Bailey's dreams and courage. Eventually they start making dresses together that represent Bailey's dreams coming to life.

- *Dogs Don't Do Ballet* by Anna Kemp. Biff is not like ordinary dogs. He doesn't do dog stuff like peeing on lampposts, scratching his fleas or drinking out of toilets. Biff likes moonlight and music and walking on his tiptoes. You see, Biff doesn't think he's a dog, Biff thinks he's a ballerina, which is all very well .... But dogs don't do ballet – do they?

- *The Paper Bag Princess* by Robert Munsch. Princess Elizabeth is to marry Prince Ronald when a dragon attacks the castle and kidnaps Ronald. In resourceful and humorous fashion, Elizabeth finds the dragon, outsmarts him and rescues Ronald – who is less than pleased at her un-princess-like appearance.

How about rewriting a classic fairy story with your class, where, say, Red Riding Hood saves herself and her grandma without the need for a woodcutter, or Cinderella gets fed up with her life of drudgery and decides to become a high-powered lawyer and sues her sisters for compensation for years of low-paid work?

Finally, as a school, make sure that equality is part of your curriculum. Before we teach a new topic, we get together and share ideas about what we are going to teach. We do this for all curriculum areas with a focus on gender equality, so we make sure we are looking at a range of male and female role models and explicitly updating and revising what we present to pupils.

Tl;dr

We use all kinds of texts in (and out of) schools, and so many of them carry both explicit and implicit biases. Research suggests that women and other minority groups are underrepresented - and often, when they appear at all, are presented in passive ways – in textbooks, literature and games. We can't replace everything that feels problematic, but we can highlight and explore these issues explicitly with pupils, try to raise visibility in other ways and attempt to consider stereotyping when purchasing or designing new materials.

References

1. *No More Boys and Girls* (2017). Outline Productions/British Broadcasting Corporation. Broadcast August 2017, BBC 2.
2. Pobuda, T. (n.d.). *Analog game studies.* Retrieved April 22, 2019, from Analog Game Studies website: http://analoggamestudies.org/
3. Hurley, K. (2016). *The Geek Feminist Revolution* (1st edition). New York, NY: Tor.
4. *Textbooks pave the way to sustainable development.* UNESCO Digital Library. (2016) Retrieved April 22, 2019, from https://unesdoc.unesco.org/ark:/48223/pf0000246777
5. Blumberg, R. L. (2008). The invisible obstacle to educational quality: Gender bias in textbooks. *Prospects*, 38(3), 345–361.
6. Gharbavi, A., & Mousavi, S. A. (2012). A content analysis of textbooks: Investigating gender bias as a social prominence in Iranian high school English textbooks. *English Linguistics Research*, 1(1). Retrieved from https://www.academia.edu/1646173/A_Content_Analysis_of_Textbooks_Investigating_Gender_Bias_as_a_Social_Prominence_in_Iranian_High_School_English_Textbooks
7. Sadker, D. M., Zittleman, K. R., & Sadker, M. (2009). *Still Failing at Fairness: How Gender Bias Cheats Girls and Boys in School and What We Can Do about It* (Rev. and updated ed). New York, NY: Scribner.
8. Pobuda, T. (2018, December 2). *Assessing gender and racial representation in the board game industry.* Retrieved April 22, 2019, from Analog Game Studies website: http://analoggamestudies.org/2018/12/assessing-gender-and-racial-representation-in-top-rated-boardgamegeek-games/
9. Ferganchick-Neufang, J. K. (1998). Virtual harassment: Women and online education. *First Monday*, 3(2). https://doi.org/10.5210/fm.v3i2.575
10. Mccabe, J., Fairchild, E., Grauerholz, L., Pescosolido, B. A., & Tope, D. (2011). Gender in twentieth-century children's books: Patterns of disparity in titles and central characters. *Gender and Society*, 25(2), 197–226. Retrieved from JSTOR.

Expert view: gender in classroom texts

Roussel De Carvalho

Gender representation matters. Gender representation in schools and in the classroom matters a great deal – and gender representation in teaching resources matters just as much. To be able to see yourself represented in books, textbooks, films, stories, assemblies, careers advice posters, well-being posters and other resources in the school environment is incredibly meaningful to young people. Personally, as a cisgender, heterosexual, atheist, white male, I appreciate that I am over-represented in all aspects of our society, and I have gone through a great deal of personal transformation in the past 16 years: as a human being, as a teacher, as a teacher educator and as an academic. Having been born in a deeply religious country (Brazil) with a conservative and normative outlook towards gender norms and identities, I have learned to observe, to listen and to respect others. As Koch (2013) argues, 'an awareness of the role of gender in learning and behaviour can help educators to avoid the trap of limiting children's growth by making and acting upon stereotypic assumptions about individual students' abilities and development'.[1]

Therefore, Koch asks us to acknowledge that within schools and classrooms, there are a series of complex and dynamic interactions which operate within a wider sociocultural setting. We all have embedded beliefs about gender that we have 'accumulated' over our lives, and challenging these assumptions requires educators to recognise such biases, as well as their own knowledge and behaviours, in order to design interventions which would tackle inequity in the classroom. So yes, gender representation matters. It matters especially when one examines the intersection among gender identity, sexual orientation, ethnic background, religious affiliation, nationality, legal status, disability and work/class status. Although it is impossible to disassociate gender from all the other intersectional aspects in our society, this text focuses on gender in schools and the associated texts/resources we use as teachers.

As teachers, we must understand that students spend a large amount of their time in school negotiating meanings of themselves as humans, through their friendship/relationship groups, their relationships with teachers and the local community which the school serves, the clothes they wear, the music they listen to and so on. Students (and their parents and teachers) also make meaning from the TV programmes and ads they watch, the books they read, the newspapers they skim through and the social media outlets they consume. They are constantly bombarded by multimodal stimuli that convey a particular set of ideas and of ideals about gender and its visibility. Current research-based documentaries and books on gender (*The Ascent of Women* by Dr. Amanda Foreman, *No More Boys and Girls* by Dr. Javid Abdelmoneim, *Queer Britain* by Riyadh Khalaf and many others) have exposed the fallacies of the patriarchal and heteronormative world we all live in and the importance of gender identity within our societies. If you can't acknowledge it, it is either because (a) you choose to ignore it, or (b) your belief system and the sociocultural sphere you have grown up in does/did not allow you to see/recognise it in the first place. That is worth really thinking about deeply.

When using books or other texts in the school classroom, teachers and students are always engaging with gender issues – even if they aren't aware of it. This is happens through their own socioeconomic and cultural lens, often interacting with the text register and their related images mediated by the official school curriculum. As a teacher and as a teacher educator, I have always found it important to question my own and other teachers' choices of texts, books, and images in slides, worksheets and other resources. From a science lesson on motion consisting only of images of male sports personalities (or male-only scientists), through to the white male hero of a children's book and simple body diagrams/images that are clearly male-centric. Similarly, from documentaries which contain only white male 'experts' to textbooks that contain a diagram of a hand with nail polish ironing a shirt – all these contain messages about gender and gender identity. We could let them pass by unremarked upon, or we can actively engage with them. For example, back to the nail polish example:

If your mind just visualised a woman, don't blame yourself. That is years of male-centric and heteronormative bias that have been ingrained in you by your culture and media. There are other options, of course:

- **A man can wear nail polish and still identify as cisgender and heterosexual.**
- **The hand may be of a trans woman or of a non-binary person.**
- **Anyone can iron clothes, although I wonder why anyone still does. (It's a waste of electrical energy, time and money. I haven't ironed anything in 15 years).**

Ultimately, the role that school texts, textbooks and other educational resources play in the classroom means they are directly involved in the learning experiences, and thus potentially influencing the discourse related to sexual orientation, gender identity, cultural identity, nationality, legal status, disability and ethnicity. Pictures of people within textbooks and the captions that accompany them also must not be seen as 'neutral' knowledge,[2] since information in textbooks leads to complex power relations between textbook producers and school-based users through identifiable representations such as class, race, gender and the like.[3]

Therefore, the impact of stereotypical in-text representations of gender and other intersectional issues continue to leave a lasting biased legacy within our cultural framework.[4,5] As teachers, we must consider our own bias as well as the prejudice (or tokenistic approach) that may be embedded in textbooks and other texts used in the classroom., because they are often seen as offering legitimate knowledge[6] and as reflecting a normative rather than a subjective interpretation of the world.[7] School books, resources and textbooks have been shown to reproduce traditional sex roles and other heteronormative stereotypes.[8]

So we have a problem: Textbooks and other printed resources are central to learners' education and are often the main curricular resource for teachers to use in school classrooms. My suggestion: The texts and featured images that teachers and students engage with in the classroom, as well as the role of the textbook within classrooms, have to be engaged with in a critical manner. They must be questioned by authors, readers, teachers and students. Not only do we need further research and understanding about the issue of texts that are used in the classroom, we also must develop a critical understanding of the role they play in the overall curriculum development within schools.[9]

Even more important, representing real people in textbooks[10] can support learners' feelings of being excluded from a 'grown-up world of truth and truth telling' often represented in writing.[11] This continues to be a critical issue in the sciences and other professions where there is still a disparity in the numbers and visibility of women, as well as of non-binary, trans men and trans women.

Central to this critical understanding of gender in texts in the classroom is the development of a robust framework to analyse the representations of gender (and any other intersectional label) within textbooks (and any other texts or resource that teachers decide to use in the classroom). In order to achieve this, teachers, students and parents must develop a better understanding of the portrayal of gender across the varying modes of information they engage with. Teachers, students and parents can also do a themed analysis[12] of any given resource. Here are some ideas of areas to explore:

–   The *placing of the item*, which addresses the physical locations, ordering, sizes and links between images and its textual representations in the resources which help to create meaning.

–   *Content knowledge*, which aims to address the links between texts and images to specific subject knowledge within the text/resources by considering its structure as well as the pronouns, choice of adjectives and other vocabulary used.

–   *Pedagogical outlook*, focused on critiquing how specific texts and associated images are used during teaching within the classroom to reproduce gender norms; the teaching of broader content and skills (that is, gender norms in physical education), and the readability of texts and images depending on the schools' context.

–   *Design*, exploring the explicit connection between texts and illustrations, the use of technical vocabulary and the idiosyncrasies of classroom texts/resources' visual design and their reproduction of gender (examples include the cover of a book and other choices of illustrations).

Many textbooks are starting to show more women and ethnic minorities, although this can often happen in a stereotypical fashion (a woman as a housewife or a nurse, rather than as a businessperson or doctor, and a tokenistic approach to represent ethnic minorities as named characters in exercises/questions). A different point to note is that many images within textbooks/classroom resources do not appear to be an integral part of the learning experience, but rather often appear isolated and mostly illustrative with a short subtitle. This also demonstrates a lack of rationale for using images within textbooks or even on slides and other resources, which may highlight the lack of understanding of the impact they can have on recipients and users.

But it is important to say that other gender identities are often not represented at all.[13] When Zittleman and Sadker[14] conducted a content analysis of teacher education texts on gender and education, they found that 'Despite decades of research documenting gender bias in education, and the creation of resources to respond to such bias, these twenty-three teacher education texts devote only about three percent of their space to gender. In some texts, gender is not even on the radar screen'.

In summary, in all the multimodal classroom resource we might use – our speech/language, books, worksheets, textbooks, slides, posters, videos and so on, we must actively encourage a thoughtful scrutiny of these resources, as well as engage with *how* they may be used as tools to help teachers, students and parents to engage with gender issues (and all other intersectional narratives) in a forward-thinking way.

References

1. Koch in Weiner, I. B. (Ed.). (2013). *Handbook of Psychology* (2nd edition). Hoboken, NJ: Wiley.
2. Apple, M. (2000). *Official Knowledge: Democratic Education in a Conservative Age.* (2nd edition). London, England: Routledge.
3. Marsden, W. E. (2001). *The School Textbook. Geography, History and Social Studies.* London, England: Woburn Press.
4. Walford, G. (1983). Science textbook images and the reproduction of sexual divisions in society. *Research in Science and Technological Education, 1*(1), 65–72.
5. Ullah, H., & Skelton, C. (2013). Gender representation in the public sector schools textbooks of Pakistan. *Educational Studies, 39*(2), 183–194.
6. Apple, M. (2013). *Ideology and Curriculum* (3rd edition). London, England: Routledge.
7. Sleeter, C. E., & Grant, C. A. (1999). *Making Choices for Multicultural Education: Five Approaches to Race, Class, Gender* (3rd edition). New York: John Wiley and Sons.

8. Blumberg, R. (2007). The invisible obstacle to educational equality: Gender bias in textbooks. *Prospects*, 38, 345–361.
9. Lambert, D., & Widdowson, J. (2006). Using geography textbooks. In D. Balderstone (Ed.), *Secondary Geography Handbook*. (pp. 146–159): Geographical Association
10. Gilbert, J., Hipkins, R., & Cooper, G. (2005). Faction or fiction: Using narrative pedagogy in school science education. *Redesigning Pedagogy: Research, Policy, Practice Conference*. Singapore: Nanyang University Institute of Education.
11. Montgomery, S. L. (1996). *The Scientific Voice*. New York, NY: Guilford Press.
12. Gough, D., Oliver, S., & Thomas, J. (2012). *An Introduction to Systematic Reviews*. London, England: SAGE Publications.
13. Bazzul, J., & Sykes, H. (2011). The secret identity of a biology textbook: Straight and naturally sexed. *Cultural Studies of Science Education*, 6, 265–286.
14. Zittleman, K., & Sadker, D. (December 2002/January 2003). Teacher education and gender equity: The unfinished revolution. *Educational Leadership*, 60(4), 59–62.

20 | Conclusion

So now what?

I hope by now you've realised that I'm not about making any conclusions on anyone else's behalf. I hope you've enjoyed reading this book, but I acknowledge that you may not have, and that's ok; maybe some of the most interesting or thought-provoking bits might have been the most uncomfortable. I really, really hope that it's made you think, but precisely *what* you've thought is exactly your own business.

This conclusion belongs to you now. It is yours to draw – not once, but multiple times, recursively, iteratively, maybe collaboratively, through thoughts and conversations and feelings and words and deeds. It need never be final. I hope you can keep returning to ideas and prompts that started here and branched off into tiny gleaming lightning-bolts of power and innovation and ended up somewhere, I hope, extraordinary.

I leave you with one thing only, and that (because I am an atheist) is a prayer:

> *Deep peace of a joyful identity to you.*
> *Sweet quiet of a true acceptance to you.*
> *Sunshine of finding out who you are, pour its warmth upon you.*
> *Rain of finding out you can be someone else, wash away your tears.*
> *May your inner child be loved and comforted, always.*
> *May you give the small ones around you what you never had and yet always wished for.*
> *May your soaring rainbows be as muted or as blinking-bright as you wish them.*
> *And may your body be a safe and beautiful place you want to inhabit that truly belongs to you.*

I wish you the strength to say no, and to receive no.
May you question until you are weary.
And then rest until you are whole again.
May you know when you are empty, and find replenishment.
May you know when you are full, and give generously.
May you be surrounded with those who love and challenge you in just the right ratio.
And may you pass this on
To whoever passes through your classroom, your house, your life, your heart.

Lucy Rycroft-Smith, 2019

Index

Abdelmoneim, Javid 150–1,
    229, 271
abortion 214, 248–51, 259
Acaster, James 18, 152
Adverse Childhood Experiences
    (ACE) 214
agency of children 27–8, 53–4
aggression 16, 30, 43, 81, 89–90,
    236–7
Alderman, Naomi 16
Amstell, Simon 21
Apprentice, The 155
artwork *see* displays
asexuality 22, 198, 201–2
assault, sexual 106, 205, 247, 259
attraction 136, 194–5,
    201–2, 222

ballet 105, 124–5, 277
Beard, Mary, 142
Bechdel Test, the 153
bias, 4–5, 70, 283, 279–81;
    unconscious 57, 76
bisexual 191–3, 194, 198
Billy Elliot 232
biological determinism 72
Bloom, Lisa 119
BMI 40
bodies; discourses about 35, 46–9,
    234, 268 diversity of 46;
    sexualising of 240–1

BoJack Horseman 250
books; gendered 96, 98, 273–7;
    about gender diversity 57–8
boy *see* language
brain difference by gender 33–4,
    42, 236
breasts 68, 119, 135, 179, 247
Buzzing from the Bathroom, the 196

caring 36, 39, 65–6, 72, 77, 94,
    98–9, 104, 124, 164
Carnage see Amstell, Simon
Carson, Deanne 53–5
catcalling 110–11, 107, 118–20
changing rooms 175–6, 181–2
child-centred approaches 54
cisgender 170–1, 213, 279, 281
clitoris 36, 43, 48, 206
clothing: gendered 130–1, 140,
    143–5; non-gendered 28–9,
    57; pockets 132; shoes 143; skirts
    128, 132, 146
Collaborating with Men 115
compliance 38, 42, 63, 82, 85,
    89, 129
compliments 107, 110, 118–20, 146
confidence 67–8, 71, 106, 242
Conjunction Fallacy, the 194
consent 195, 205, 209, 249,
    251–2, 255–7; cultures of
    53–5

control 20, 21, 130, 161, 192, 248–9, 252, 255, 258; loss of 63, 220
Copp and Fox 233
Couples Come Dine with Me 64
Craig, Daniel 65
Crazy Ex-Girlfriend 203; *see also Buzzing from the Bathroom*
creativity 20, 42, 45, 82–3, 92, 220, 229
Creed: Rise to Glory 90
Crenshaw, Kimberlé 4
cultural safety 183
culture *see* nature vs
curriculum 23, 54, 84–5, 197, 200–1, 214–16

Daddy babysitting 65
dance 85, 105, 181, 232–4
deviance 3, 55, 105, 129–30, 169, 193–4, 199, 202–3, 223–5
Devlin, Kate 152
dinosaurs 82, 97, 88–9, 145–6, 271
Dirty Dancing, 246
discrimination; *see* gender
displays 50, 55, 143
Don Draper 66, 140; *see also Mad Men*

eating 39; disorders 41, 46, 214
education 114, 154, 175; early years 24, 27–30, 188–91; lack of 116; point of 71, 139
Emerson, Ralph Waldo 120
emotional 16, 256; literacy 24, 276; pain 64; wellbeing 259; work 40, 42, 66
emotional labour *see* emotional work
enby *see* non-binary
equalities audit 55, 190
expectations 209, 217, 234, 236; gendered 29, 61–3, 94, 204–5, 237; of sex 254–5

Facebook 13, 220
fashion 23, 86 128–30, 143–4

fat 5, 35, 39–40, 238
fathers 24, 56, 65–6, 180, 276
femininity/ies; discourses of 35, 42, 57, 64, 81, 98, 104, 130, 146, 170, 183, 229, 232–3, 270
feminism 16, 27, 29, 45, 47, 53–4, 57, 74–5, 83, 113, 122, 152, 153, 203
film 165, 240; industry 154
Fine, Cordelia 34, 236
fractal 289

gay 191–2 207, 214; perceptions of those who are 198–9
gender: audit *see* equalities audit; binary 135, 170–1, 173; coding 144–5; data gap 70; discrimination 90, 121–3, 151; historical view of 28; in job role 28; neutrality 92, 100, 127, 134–6, 141, 147, 169, 175–7,185, 239; non-conforming 171, 184, 188
Gender Diary 190
generic masculine 152
Gould, Stephen Jay 70
greeting cards 13–14
Groundhog Sexism 114
guilt; *see* shame

Harari, Yuval Noah 14, 200
Hardy and Easton 221–2, 225
heteronormative 22, 131, 196; aesthetics 233–4; love stories 9; relationships 215–16; scripts 204, 221–3; segregation 177, 182
homophobia 153, 161, 199, 207, 216, 233
homosexuality *see* sexualities; gay; lesbian

identity/ies 178, 194–5; freedom of 28, 45; gender 171, 233, 279–80; restriction of queer 198; sexual 254; work 193, 229
independence 27, 47, 76–7, 88 113; sexual 255

intersectionality 4, 6, 273, 279–83
intersex 31, 34–5, 135, 169, 239
invisibility 35, 37, 270–4
ironing boards 81–2, 86–8
It's Always Sunny in Philadelphia 35

jobs 82, 95, 105, 124, 152–3

Kolk, van der, Bessel 7, 246
knitting 64, 86

leadership 35, 68–9, 115
language: gendered 18, 64, 76
    160–3; for genitalia 42; for job
    roles 152–3; infantilising
    155–7; reclamation of 159; use of
    boy and girl 155–7
Lees, Paris 178
Lego 85, 92, 95, 99
lesbian 46, 131, 193, 198, 224;
    perception of relationships 194, 198
Let Clothes be Clothes 145–7
Let Toys be Toys 92, 95–7, 101
Letterbox Library 58
LGBTQ+ 137; as character quirk
    154; invisibility 274; rights 272;
    labels 172; in sex education
    214–16; stereotypes 199;
    teachers 214
love 217–21, 223, 224

Mad Men 48, 66, 184
male gaze 46, 131–4, 231
masculinities: discourses of 14–17,
    42, 98, 164, 229, 232, 236, 267
masturbation 183, 206, 208, 253, 258
mathematics 23, 44, 74, 54
May, Emmeline, 256–7
McKnight, Lucinda 104
Men Behaving Badly 15
men in early years education 56, 124
Mendick, Heather 154
midwifery 73, 104–5
Million Dollar Baby 240
minority stress 199

miscarriages 249–50
misogyny 99, 267
Moran, Caitlin 39
Morgan, Piers 65, 134–5

Nagoski, Emily 8, 206, 255
Naked Attraction. 176
nappy changing 53–6
natural 33–4, 42, 44, 138;
    vs cultural 28, 200
needlework *see* sewing
neuroplasticity 32, 43
neurosexism 34
No More Boys and Girls 2, 10, 11, 17,
    43, 76, 87, 89, 91, 97, 105, 121,
    134, 141, 150–1, 229, 280
No Outsiders 216, 224
non-binary 9, 56, 105, 110, 159,
    163, 168, 182, 281, 282
normal and norms 9–10, 19, 22, 24,
    28, 55, 99–100, 171, 199, 224–5
nudity 175–6, 181, 203

objectification 132, 246–47
obligation: moral 249; sexual 258
OECD 54
Olympic Games 230, 237, 240
Orbach, Susie 39
orgasm 48, 196, 253–5

pansexual 136, 155, 192, 198,
    199, 258
parenting 28, 54, 56, 65, 66, 89,
    180, 208; gendered 97; gender-
    neutral 100; homosexual 194;
    trans child 171–2
PE (physical education) 228–30
Peep Show 205
penis 36, 47,120, 135, 147, 180,
    181 195, 204, 205, 209, 247,
    255; fencing 14
Penny, Laurie 248
Perez, Caroline Criado 175
periods 35–8, 41, 47, 64, 135, 170,
    174, 175, 177, 179, 209

Perry, Grayson 146
pink 28, 87, 88, 89, 90; and blue 82, 145, 271
play/playful behaviour 55, 84; importance of free choice in 96–7
polyamory 9, 194, 219, 222
porn 206, 260
power 134, 151; of words 159
princesses 94, 98, 140, 144, 161, 165, 271, 277
privilege 21, 74, 170, 179, 183–4
Project Runway 130
pronouns 23, 158, 162–3, 177–8, 272, 282
PSHE *see* SRE
puberty 31, 48, 68, 107, 176, 177, 229, 269

queer 2, 131,177, 194, 199, 274
queering 22

race 4–6, 155–7
rape 205, 245, 249; culture 42
Reacher, Jack 267
red sneaker effect 129
rejection 195, 213, 218–19, 258, 261
relationships 193, 201–2, 217–19
relevance of gender 18, 152
religion 16, 215, 259
Rippon, Gina 45, 49, 70, 87
risk-taking 236–7
Rocky Horror Picture Show, The 226
Role models/modelling 27, 49, 165, 193
Rubin, Gayle 19
RuPaul's Drag Race 15, 85
Russ, Joanna 67

school uniform 130; sexualisation of 108, 133–4, gender neutral 146
schools; design of 175
Section 28 200
Semanya, Caster 239

sewing 64, 86
sex 202, 205–6, 253–5, 260; thinking about 204; with snakes 197
sex and gender 31, 135, 139, 169, 173
sexism 75, 98–9, 124; benevolent 81, 105; insidiousness of 116–17
sexual harassment 103, 106–8, 112–14, 247–8
sexual violence 48
sexuality/ies 131, 154, 159, 189, 192–5; assumptions inherent in 192, 198, 204
shame 196, 205–6, 208, 218, 230, 233, 249–51
She-Ra 49
silencing 161, 250
spatial awareness 85, 87, 92, 97
sports 228–31; segregation of 238–9
SRE (sex and relationships education) 213–16
steelmen 8
STEM 82, 145
stereotype threat 158
stereotyping 48 56–7, 98 145, 146, 165, 190, 279
strength 16, 229, 231, 234, 239, 268, 269, 276
suicide 98, 137, 146, 163, 168, 170
swing music 155–6

teenage pregnancy 48
textbooks 269–71, 280–82
theatre 155
This Girl Can, 231
Titles 160
toilets 173–5, 179–82
token resistance 261
tonic immobility 253
touch 53–4, 104, 106–7, 118, 198, 202, 204, 205, 246–7
toys 2, 28, 55, 80–8; marketing of 92, 95
tradition 44

trans people 158, 163, 168–74;
  definition of 169; healthcare for 168
transphobic behaviour 178
trauma 2,7, 196, 213, 220, 246, 253
Twitter 124–5, 140, 163, 207, 247

UNESCO 45
uniform *see* school uniform
upskirt images 108–9

vagina 42–3, 132, 170, 205, 206, 209
veganism 21
victim blaming 111, 175
vulva 43

wage gap 72
Webb, Robert 146, 164
Wellard, Ian 229
Williams, Joanna 74
Wimbledon 133
Women 16, 29, 35, 36; of colour
  4–6, 157; in leadership 74;
  ownership of 117; rights 156; role
  of 45
women's issues 39, 45,115
Wright, Ian 224

Yacht Club Swing 155–6

Zuckerburg, Mark 129